Family of Faith Library

W9-AOC-893

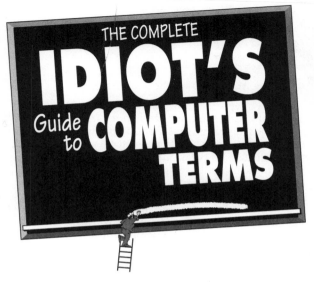

THE COMPLETE IDIOT'S Guide to COMPUTER TERMS

Joe Kraynak
and Mary-Terese Cagnina

Property of
FAMILY OF FAITH
LIBRARY

alpha books

A Division of Prentice Hall Computer Publishing
11711 North College Avenue, Carmel, Indiana 46032 USA

To my parents, John and Adeline Kraynak, for knowing when to hold on and when to let go.

To Ger and Phyl, for the same reasons.

©1993 by Alpha Books

All rights reserved. No part of this book shall be reproduced, stored in a retrieval system, or transmitted by any means, electronic, mechanical, photocopying, recording, or otherwise, without written permission from the publisher. No patent liability is assumed with respect to the use of the information contained herein. While every precaution has been taken in the preparation of this book, the publisher and authors assume no responsibility for errors or omissions. Neither is any liability assumed for damages resulting from the use of the information contained herein. For more information, write to Alpha Books, 11711 North College Avenue, Carmel, Indiana 46032.

International Standard Book Number: 1-56761-266-0
Library of Congress Catalog Card Number: 93-71525

96 95 94 93   8 7 6 5 4 3 2 1

Interpretation of the printing code: the rightmost double-digit number is the year of the book's printing; the rightmost single-digit number is the number of the book's printing. For example, a printing code of 93-1 shows that the first printing of the book was in 1993.

Screen reproductions in this book were created by means of the program Collage Plus from Inner Media, Inc., Hollis, NH.

Special thanks to Michael R. Hanks for ensuring the technical accuracy of this book.

Printed in the United States of America

Publisher

Marie Butler-Knight

Associate Publisher

Lisa A. Bucki

Managing Editor

Elizabeth Keaffaber

Development Editor

Mary Cole Rack

Production Editor

Linda Hawkins
Michelle Shaw

Copy Editor

Audra Gable

Designer

Roger Morgan

Production Team

Diana Bigham, Katy Bodenmiller, Tim Cox, Meshell Dinn, Mark Enochs, Linda Koopman, Tom Loveman, Beth Rago, Carrie Roth, Greg Simsic

Introduction

Another computer dictionary? That's exactly what we thought when we were asked to write this book. We went down to the local bookstore and saw at least seven different computer dictionaries staring us in the face and asking the same question. Not till we started reading them did we realize why the computer world needed another dictionary. We read definitions like this:

> **nesting**   In programming, the positioning of a loop within a loop. The number of loops that can be nested may be limited by the programming language. See *loop*.

> **RAM disk**   An area of electronic memory configured by a software program to emulate a disk drive.

> **real time**   The immediate processing of input, such as a point-of-sale transaction or a measurement performed by an analog laboratory device.

Don't get us wrong. We're not knocking these dictionaries. They cover a lot of terms, and most of the definitions they give are very complete and accurate. The problem is that the definitions are not directed at regular-type people. Instead, these dictionaries focus on presenting the exact meaning of a word without worrying about whether a real human person can understand it.

This dictionary is different. It defines computer terms using plain English, plenty of examples and comparisons, and lots of pictures. We wrote the dictionary as if we were sitting down with someone and trying to explain the various terms. When our explanation didn't seem to work, we tried to imagine a real-life example that would help. And if that didn't work, we drew a picture. In other words, we did whatever we could to help our imaginary person understand the term.

Then, real people went through the book and tested each entry, making sure they could understand the definitions, the examples, and the pictures. The result is a collection of plain English definitions for the computer terms you will most commonly encounter.

How to Use This Book

Since we didn't really follow any rules when writing this book (except for listing the terms in alphabetical order), we can't really prescribe any one way to use it. However, we can give you a few ideas:

- Flip through the book and look at all the pictures. Read the entries for the pictures that catch your eye.

- Read the book from cover to cover, skipping around when needed. It's a relatively short book, and parts of it are funny. So enjoy and learn at the same time. It's got lots of stuff in it you won't see on TV.

- Keep the book on your desk as a reference. Whenever you come across a term whose meaning you don't know, look it up. This is the most common way to use a dictionary, but you might miss some good stuff.

Whatever you do, don't try to learn everything at once. The computer world is chock-full of information, and if you try to know it all at once, your head is liable to burst. Or you might even give up trying, which is worse than bursting your head. So learn a little bit at a time, try what you learn on the computer, and keep buying more books.

Acknowledgments

We owe thanks to two people at Alpha Books who helped kick-start this book. First, thanks to Barry Childs-Helton for coming up with the idea for this book and for quietly inspiring us to always do our best. Thanks also to Marie Butler-Knight for creating an environment in which all ideas are welcome, for accepting Barry's idea, and for asking us to write the book.

Special thanks also to the editorial staff at Alpha Books for fine-tuning the book.

Thanks also to the wonderful, unheralded production department at Prentice Hall Computer Publishing for transforming a stack of pages into an attractive bound book.

Did you know that every archive has an attribute? That all functions have arguments? And that orders can ascend? Read on.

* A wild-card symbol used in many programs, including DOS, to stand in for one or more characters when you're searching for a file or an entry but you're not sure of its name. See also *wild card*.

? In many programs, this serves as a wild-card symbol that can stand in for a single character when you're searching for a file or an entry. See also *wild card*.

3.5" disk A magnetic record used to record the facts and figures you type and save. Just as you can store sounds on a cassette tape, you can store data on a diskette and later play back the data on your computer. 3.5" diskettes are enclosed in a hard plastic case that is 3.5 inches wide. A metal piece covers an opening to the disk to prevent damage by fingerprints and dirt. When you insert the disk into the drive, the metal piece is slid back to expose the disk so the computer can read it. See also *floppy disk* and *disk drive*.

5.25" disk A magnetic record used to record the facts and figures you type and save. Just as you can store sounds on a cassette tape, you can store computer data on a diskette and later play back the data on your computer. 5.25"

diskettes are enclosed in a flexible plastic case that is 5.25 inches wide. Parts of the disk are exposed so the computer can read the disk. The exposed areas can be damaged by fingerprints and dirt, so be careful when handling the disk. See also *floppy disk* and *disk drive*.

8-bit computer   Every computer has a *central processing unit*, or brain. An 8-bit computer is the least brainy of all personal computers because it can take in only one character (eight bits) at a time. See also *bit*.

16-bit computer   This computer is twice as smart as an 8-bit computer. It can take in two characters at one time. See also *bit*.

32-bit computer   This computer is four times as smart as an 8-bit computer. It can process four characters at one time. See also *bit*.

286, 386, 386SX, 486, 486SX, 486DX, 8086, 8088, 68000, 68020, 68030   See *microprocessor*.

A drive   Your computer might have more than one removable disk drive (the slot where a disk goes when you want to get data off it or record data on it). Each drive is known by a different letter so that the computer can keep track of each. If you only have one drive, it's known as the A drive. If you have more than one, the drive on top or to the left is usually the A drive. You can also boot from this drive if there is a system disk in it. See also *boot* and *system disk*.

abort   To stop an activity in progress. In many DOS programs, you can abort by pressing the Esc key or by holding down the Ctrl key and pressing the Break key.

absolute cell reference   In a spreadsheet program, rows and columns intersect to form cells. Each cell has an address consisting of the column letter and the row number. For example, the address of the cell in the upper left corner of the spreadsheet is A1. You can use these cell addresses along with mathematical operators to create formulas. For example, you can insert the formula +A1+B1 in cell C1 to have the program add the values in cells A1 and B1 and insert the total in cell C1.

If you copy the formula in cell C1 into cell C2, the addresses in the formula change; the formula in C2 will be +A2+B2 rather than +A1+B1, because these are relative cell references, the default. Sometimes, however, you may not want the addresses to change. If you mark a cell as an absolute reference, it will not change no matter where you move or copy the formula to in the worksheet. See also *relative cell reference*, *spreadsheet*, *cell address*, and *formula*.

accelerator board   A fiberglass card with electrical parts that plugs into the guts of your computer and makes it work faster (sort of like a turbocharger on a car engine). Because other elements in your computer may limit its speed, installing an accelerator board is not always the best solution. For example, installing a faster hard drive may give better results. See also *expansion slot*.

access   The freedom to use a program or get information. For example, if you try to get into the government's secret files, you will probably get the message "Access Denied." Also used as a verb to describe the process of getting data; for example, you might need to *access* a file.

access time   The time it takes your computer to get and deliver requested data. If you retrieve a file from a hard disk, the time it takes the disk drive to get that information from the disk is the access time. Access time is typically measured in milliseconds (thousandths of a second). Although a thousandth of a second might not seem that long, milliseconds add up quickly when you're talking about transferring a lot of information. A computer with a hard disk that has an access time of 10 milliseconds will work noticeably faster than one with an access time of 30 milliseconds.

accounting package   A specialized program that performs the accounting services for a business. Many such programs allow you to keep track of inventory, payments, and receipts; create purchase orders and invoices; do payroll; keep track of fixed assets; and determine job costs.

Integrated accounting packages offer a general ledger that keeps track of all transactions and integrates the various accounting tasks. Whenever you enter a transaction, related information is automatically updated. For example, if you enter an invoice or a purchase order, the inventory figures are automatically updated.

Popular accounting packages for IBM and compatible computers include Quicken, DacEasy, and Peachtree Complete.

active cell   In a spreadsheet program, the active cell is the one you selected. When a cell is active, you can type data into the cell; edit the cell's data; or enhance the cell by drawing lines around it, shading it, or changing the size or style of text. See also *cell*.

active file   To work with a file you've created, such as a letter or memo, you must first open or retrieve the file in the program you used to create it. When the file is displayed on-screen and the cursor appears in the text (so you can type or edit), the file is active.

active program   The program you are currently running and using to perform a task.

active window   Some programs, including Microsoft Windows, allow you to have more than one window on-screen at the same time. However, only one window is active at a time. To work in a window, you must switch to it and make it active.

activity light   On the front of many computers, near each disk drive, is a light that shows when the computer is reading or writing information to the disk in that drive. Before you insert or remove a disk, make sure the activity light is off.

Ada   A programming language developed by the U.S. Department of Defense so it would have one standardized language for all Defense Department systems and applications. The language was developed in the 1970s and named after Augusta Ada Byron, Countess of Lovelace and Lord Byron's daughter, who is known as the first programmer because of her work in the mid-1800s with computer visionary Charles Babbage.

adapter   A plastic or fiberglass card with electronic components that plugs into the guts of a computer and allows other devices to be connected to the computer. For instance, a Video Graphics Adapter allows a special type of monitor (video screen) to be connected to the computer.

add-in   In many programs, you can use subprograms from other software companies to add features to the main program. For example, in a spreadsheet program called Lotus 1-2-3, you can use a spreadsheet publishing add-in that gives you more control over the layout, design, and printing of the spreadsheets you create.

add-on   Any device that's connected to the computer to make it do more work faster.

address   See *memory address* and *cell address*.

Adobe Illustrator   This drawing program from Adobe Systems, Inc., originally won fame as a Macintosh product but now is also popular in the Windows environment. Illustrator contains sophisticated features that include controlled shading, Bézier curves, color coding for professional printing, and PostScript output. See also *illustration program/drawing program*.

Adobe Photoshop A popular image processing program from Adobe Systems, Inc., used to enhance and manipulate scanned images or photographs, or graphics created in illustration programs, such as Adobe Illustrator. See also *image processing program*.

Adobe Type Manager A utility program that converts bitmapped fonts into outline fonts so they smooth out the jaggies (those jagged edges that distort the curves of a font when you display or print it in a size that's not loaded into the computer) and take up less RAM.

adventure game A type of entertainment software that places you in a challenging situation, with lost treasure to find, a new world to create, or an impossible journey to complete, and pits you against a cast of on-screen foes. You can often replay the situation at greater degrees of difficulty, and keep score to compare your performance with other adventure gamers.

Aldus PageMaker A page layout program from Aldus Corporation for Macintosh, DOS, and Windows. See also *desktop publishing*, the term that was invented by the president of Aldus when they introduced PageMaker in 1985. Today's PageMaker devotees range from absolute computer beginners to design professionals, who use it to lay out ads, brochures, newsletters, and books (including this one).

aliasing See *jaggies*.

alignment See *justification*.

alignment, read/write head See *read/write head*.

alphanumeric characters   Characters are classified as alphabetic (A–Z), numeric (0–9), special (other characters you can type, such as symbols), and control (codes that control printing and other operations). In general, alphanumeric characters are any characters you can type: letters, numbers, punctuation marks, and symbols on the keyboard.

Alt key   In most programs, you use the Alt key in combination with other keys (such as the function keys: F1, F2, and so on) to enter commands. For example, in Word 5.0, if you press the F1 function key by itself, you switch windows. If you hold down the Alt key and press F1, you can set a tab.

Ami Pro   A word processing program with advanced page layout capabilities that is marketed by Lotus Development Corporation. This was the first commercial word processing program to be developed especially for the Microsoft Windows environment, and its heritage is obvious because of its graphical environment filled with point-and-click desktop publishing tools. See also *word processing*.

Amiga   A unique series of personal computers from Commodore International. While not the most popular personal computer platform around, the Amiga's superior color graphics and sound capabilities give it a definite edge over comparably priced Macs and PCs—especially for playing adventure games and composing music. Later models of the Amiga, including the Amiga 2000, have optional IBM PC compatibility, making the Amiga a more reasonable option for game aficionados who also have to bring work home from the office.

anchor   In most programs, you can move a cursor to highlight individual characters. To do this, you must *anchor* the cursor in its current location and then use the arrow keys or the mouse to *stretch* the cursor over additional characters. In a spreadsheet program, you can anchor the selector in a cell and extend the selection over additional cells; the selection is then called a *cell block* or a *range*.

animation development program   You can create your own cartoons with an animation program. It works by recording images you create or import as if they were "frames" in a conventional film animation. After you create enough of them, you edit them into the desired order and then play the series back quickly enough that the eye perceives realistic motion, as it does with a conventional film cartoon. These files can be saved and replayed on computer, or they can be exported to a videotape if you have the necessary special hardware.

answer mode   Two computers can communicate over the phone using modems. Just as with any phone call, the call doesn't go through unless the modem on the other line answers. For your computer to answer the call of another computer, your computer must be in answer mode. You can set up your computer to answer on the first ring, the second ring, and so on. See also *modem*.

ANSI   Stands for American National Standards Institute. This group develops standard versions of programming languages and encourages their use by programmers in order to standardize programming efforts in American industry. ANSI C, for example, is the version of C developed and endorsed by these folks.

anti-aliasing   Counteracting the unsightly effects of aliasing, or the jaggies, by smoothing the stair-stepped edges of distorted characters and images into the curving lines that were intended. One common anti-aliasing technique is dithering, which fills in colored and gray pixels around the edges to reduce the jagged effect.

antivirus program   A program that prevents a computer virus from attacking a computer or provides early detection of a computer virus so you can prevent it from destroying information. These programs usually function in two ways: by identifying known viruses and by looking for the effects of viruses (damaged files). Although no known viruses damage hardware (they usually damage only data), they can make a computer useless if they wipe out information the computer uses to get up and running. See also *virus*, *Trojan Horse*, and *vaccine*.

append   To add text or other data to the end of a file. In many programs, you can cut or copy information to a temporary holding area and then paste the information somewhere else. However, when you cut or copy information, it usually replaces the existing information in the holding area. If, instead, you append the information, it is added to the existing information without changing it. See also *clipboard* and *scrapbook*.

Apple Computer   Founded in 1976 by Steve Jobs and Steve Wozniak, this microcomputer manufacturer pioneered the way for personal computers first with the Apple II family of computers, and in 1984, with the introduction of the Macintosh. See also *Macintosh*.

application   A computer program that lets you use the computer to perform a specific task, such as writing a letter, balancing your budget, or playing a game.

application control menu   In Windows, or any Windows application, every window has a control menu (indicated by a little box in the upper left-hand corner of the window). By opening the menu, you can control the size and shape of the application window, or switch to other applications.

application icon   In Microsoft Windows, you can shrink a program window down to the size of a symbol that represents the program. This symbol is called an *application icon*. If the program is not running, its icon is called a *program-item icon*.

archive   To store copies of program files or data files for protection (also referred to as *backing up files*). If the original files get damaged in any way, you can then restore the archived files to get back some or all of your data. The amount of data you can recover using archived copies depends on how recently you archived the files. If you entered a lot of changes since the last time you archived, your archive copies will differ a great deal from the original files.

Although you can create backups by copying files from one disk to another, it is easiest and fastest to use a backup program, such as Central Point Backup (which comes with PC Tools) or Fastback Plus. See also *back up*.

archive attribute   When you archive files using a backup program, the program marks each file as backed up by turning its archive attribute off. The next time you back up files, you can have the backup program skip any files whose archive attribute is off (files that have already been backed up). If you edit a file, the archive attribute is automatically switched on. This tells the backup program that the file has changed since the last backup and needs to be backed up fresh. See also *file attribute*.

area graph   A graph used in business presentation graphics and in spreadsheet programs to illustrate the difference between one set of data points and another.

argument   A statement that follows a function or command and tells the function or command specifically what to do. For example, you can use the following function/argument combination in a spreadsheet to determine the average of 15 values:

@AVG(A1..A15)

The function would then determine the average of the 15 values in cells A1 to A15 in the spreadsheet.

arithmetic operator   A symbol that tells a program which mathematical operation to perform. For instance, a + means to add. Table A.1 shows examples of several mathematical operators commonly used in spreadsheets. See also *formula*.

Table A.1   Mathematical operators.

Operator	Performs	Sample Formula	Result
^	Exponentiation	+A1^3	Enters the result of raising the value in cell A1 to the third power.
+	Addition	+A1+A2	Enters the total of the values in cells A1 and A2.
−	Subtraction	+A1–A2	Subtracts the value in cell A2 from the value in cell A1.
*	Multiplication	+A2*3	Multiplies the value in cell A2 by 3.
/	Division	+A1/50	Divides the value in cell A1 by 50.

arrow keys   The keys on the keyboard that are used to move the cursor or insertion point left, right, up, or down on the computer screen.

artificial intelligence (AI)   The area of computer science dedicated to making computers and computer programs that mimic human thought processes so they can do more of our work for us. The main challenge is that computers are so darned logical, and human beings are so darned illogical. Whereas computers reach conclusions based on recorded input and a solid set of rules governing how to act on that input, humans fly by the seat of their pants when they haven't the foggiest idea how to solve a problem, and never seem to structure a sentence (much less an argument) the same way twice. Consequently, AI specialists are devoting their lives to instilling computers with ambiguity and fuzzy logic— qualities that earned us C's and D's in school.

ascender   The part of a tall lowercase letter that rises above a short lowercase letter. For example, with *fe*, the part of the *f* that rises above the *e* is the ascender. Think of the ascender as being a head above the rest of the characters.

ascending order   You can use a database to store and manage information, such as phone lists and parts lists. Once you enter information into your database, you can sort the information in any number of ways. For example, you can sort alphabetically by last name. You can also select the order in which to sort: ascending order (A, B, C . . . or 1, 2, 3 . . .) or descending order (Z, Y, X . . . or 10, 9, 8 . . .).

ASCII, American Standard Code for Information Interchange   Pronounced ASK-key. Whenever you create a document, such as a letter, the program adds special formatting codes, such as codes to set the margins and codes to make bold text bold. If you try to open the file in another program, the program may tell you that the file is in an *incompatible format*. That is, the formatting codes used by the other program are unknown to this program. Many programs allow you to save a file as an ASCII file, which strips out any special codes and saves only text. You can then open and use the file in various programs. However, this plain-vanilla file will contain only text; you will lose any special formatting you used in the file.

aspect ratio   Used in computer graphics to refer to the relationship of the width of an image or display to its height. When resizing (or scaling) a graphic image, you must keep the aspect ratio the same to avoid distortion; otherwise, you may turn a roomful of giraffes into a roomful of zebras.

assembler   You use a programming language to write a program. This language provides commands that you can understand (through some study). However, computers understand a different language, called *machine language*, which consists of ones and zeros (and really represents on and off states). An *assembler* translates programs written in assembly language (a low-level programming language) into machine language. If you write a program in a high-level language (such as BASIC, Pascal, or C), you must use a compiler to translate the program into machine language.

   Don't associate *low-level* with *simple* and *high-level* with *complex*. The high-level language is further removed from machine language, so it is a language that is actually easier for you to understand. Low-level languages are closer to machine language. See also *compiler*.

asterisk (*)   A character used to stand in for a group of characters. For example, in a program that offers a search feature, you can use wild-card characters to broaden a search. To have the program search for the words *bookstore*, *bookkeeper*, and *bookish*, you could enter book*. A commonly used wild-card character for single letters is the question mark (?).

The asterisk is commonly used to specify a group of files when you are copying or deleting files from a disk. For example, the entry *.BAK specifies all files with the extension .BAK. *.* (pronounced star-dot-star) is used to select all files.

The asterisk is also commonly used in mathematical formulas to indicate multiplication.

AT keyboard   AT stands for Advanced Technology. It is one of three keyboards commonly used with IBM and compatible computers. The PC-style keyboard was first, followed by the AT, followed by the Enhanced. See also *PC keyboard* and *Enhanced keyboard.*

attribute, character   See *character attribute.*

attribute, file   See *file attribute.*

audit trail   Many accounting programs offer a feature that keeps track of your transactions, providing an audit trail. If you later find that your figures don't stack up, you can then follow the audit trail back to the error.

Other programs may also keep audit trails or audit logs that allow you to keep track of any changes you made using the program. For example, if you correct disk problems using The Norton Utilities, the program provides a log of the fixes it made.

authoring language   A tool you can use to create your own computer-assisted instruction programs and tutorials. These tutorials are often used in the training departments of large corporations to help orient new employees or teach current employees how to use new technology.

auto-dial   Two computers can talk over the phone using modems. One modem dials the phone number of the other modem. Although you can type the number manually to have it dialed, many communications programs (the programs that control the transfer of data through a modem) offer an auto-dial feature that can dial the number for you.

AUTOEXEC.BAT A DOS file that runs a series of commands whenever you start your computer. Its name explains its function; it AUTOmatically EXECutes a BATch of commands. See also *DOS*.

Turns echo off so subsequent commands are not echoed to the screen.

Tells DOS to display the prompt in the form C:\directory>.

Displays the DOS version number.

Runs WordPerfect when you start your computer.

Makes it so you can run WordPerfect from any directory.

automatic backup A handy feature of many software programs. It automatically saves the file you're working on under a special name every five minutes (or at whatever interval you choose), so that if the power goes out or your PC crashes, you'll have the last automatically saved version of the backup file, thus reducing your losses. Note that most automatic backup programs do not save the file under the name of your file, so after your PC recovers you have to look for it under a name with a .BAK extension, or in whatever format the feature uses.

automatic font downloading Every printer comes with one installed font (a family of type that has the same design and size). The printer may also have internal memory that is separate from the memory in your computer. You can purchase soft fonts (font software) for your computer that provide additional fonts. Before you can use a soft font, however, you must *download* the fonts to the printer; that is, you must send the information for the fonts you want to use from your computer to your printer. Some programs automatically download fonts to your printer as needed.

autorepeat key   Also known as *typematic*. A key that repeats a character, symbol, or space as long as you hold down the key. Many programs allow you to increase the rate at which the character is repeated (the key repeat speed) and the delay time (the amount of time you must hold the key down before it starts repeating).

Autosave   As you work on a file, any changes you make are stored only in your computer's electronic memory (RAM). This memory and anything stored in it relies on electricity to keep it going. A flicker of the lights, and everything you type can disappear. To prevent the changes from being lost in the event of a power outage or some other mishap, you should regularly save the work to disk (a permanent storage location). Many programs offer an *autosave* feature, which automatically saves your work to disk on a regular basis. If the power goes off, you lose only those changes you made since the last time the file was saved.

auxiliary equipment   A fancy name for the supplemental equipment that makes working with your computer and peripherals easier. This would include equipment like disk storage cases, glare filters, and mouse pads, but not peripherals such as the printer, monitor, and mouse. See also peripheral.

auxiliary storage   See *secondary storage*.

You are about to enter a clandestine world of background operations, baudy communications, base fonts, and bombs. You'll even learn about Bézier curves.

B drive   If you have more than one floppy disk drive in your PC, the one on top or to the left is usually called the A drive, and the one on the bottom or to the right is usually called the B drive. The computer distinguishes them in this way so it knows which one you're referring to when you want to get information from or send it to one of these drives.

back up   To copy files, usually from a hard disk, to some other storage unit, such as a floppy disk or a backup tape. If the original files become damaged, you can then use the backups to help restore the files to their previous condition.

background color   In many programs, you can control the colors of the display or printout by setting the background color, the foreground color, and the foreground pattern. The background color is the color over which everything else is printed or displayed. If you were coloring on a piece of paper, the background color would be the color of the paper.

background operations   Many programs allow you to continue working while the program carries out some time-consuming task, such as printing a document or performing a series of complex calculations. In such programs, the computer is said to be working in the *background*.

backlit screen   Most laptop computers have an LCD (Liquid Crystal Display). If you've ever seen a digital watch, you know what an LCD display looks like. Because LCDs do not emit light, you may have trouble reading the screen in a poorly lit room. To help, some laptop computers offer a backlit screen, which lights the area behind the text. This makes the text contrast more sharply against the background. However, backlit screens generally drain the computer's batteries more quickly. See also *plasma display*.

backspace   A key on the keyboard that moves the on-screen cursor to the left, erasing any character to the left of the cursor. If you want to move the cursor left without deleting a character, use the left-arrow key.

backup utility   A program that takes the hassle out of backing up all the files on your computer. After asking a few questions about your preferences, it manages the whole process, stopping only to ask you to insert another disk when it needs one. If you are using a tape drive, it can probably handle the whole backup with one tape cartridge. This type of utility is often sold as part of a larger package of utilities, though you can also purchase one (such as the Norton Backup) separately.

backward compatible   A new release of a software program whose files can be recognized by earlier versions of the program is said to be backward compatible. For example, I can open and revise a spreadsheet in Excel 4 that I created in Excel 3, because Excel 4 is backward compatible with Excel 3. A computer is backward compatible if it can run the same software as the previous version of the computer did. A Mac II, for example, is backward compatible with a Mac Plus. This feature is also called *downward compatibility*.

backward search   Many programs offer a search feature that allows you to search for a word or phrase in a file. Normally, the program searches for the specified word or phrase from the current position to the end of the file. If you want to search from the current position to the beginning of the file, you must perform a *backward search*.

bad disk   A disk that is unusable. A disk stores information magnetically. If the surface of a disk is damaged (usually by fingerprints or mishandling), it cannot reliably store data. If you try to use a bad disk, you will get an error message telling you that the disk is bad. You may be able to fix the disk using a utility program, such as PC Tools DiskFix. Such a program will fix the disk (if possible), salvage any data on disk, and mark any unusable portions on the disk so the computer will not try to store information there in the future.

Bad sector

bad sector   Each disk is divided into sectors (the smallest unit), clusters, and tracks. If a sector is damaged, that sector will not reliably store data. If you save a file, and part of the file is stored on the damaged sector, you will not be able to open or use the file. You may be able to recover the file using a utility program, such as PC Tools DiskFix.

bar graph   A graph used in presentation graphics and spreadsheet programs that presents each data point as a bar. Bar graphs are generally used to compare data at one point in time.

base font   The default font in a given program. Any time you create a new document in that program, it will appear in the base font unless you change it.

base memory   See *conventional memory*. When you purchase a computer, it comes with a certain amount of RAM (Random-Access Memory). This is your computer's electronic memory—the place where information is temporarily stored while you and your computer are working on it. The base memory is the portion of RAM that your computer and operating system can directly use. On an IBM running DOS, the base memory is the first 640 kilobytes of RAM that programs can use. You can add RAM in the form of extended or expanded memory, but this additional memory can be used only by programs specifically designed to use it.

BASIC   Short for Beginner's All-Purpose Symbolic Instruction Code. This is a programming language that is usually included with MS-DOS. BASIC is considered by many to be easier to learn than other languages.

basic input-output system (BIOS)   A set of instructions that is permanently stored in your computer. These instructions tell the computer how to control traffic between the various elements that make up the computer, including disk drives, the printer, the communications ports, and the display. These instructions are stored in the computer's ROM (read-only memory); the computer can read the instructions but cannot change them in any way. When you turn on your computer, it first reads the BIOS to determine what to do next.

batch file   A file with the extension .BAT that contains a series (a *batch*) of DOS commands. For example, you can create a batch file called W.BAT that automatically changes to the WINDOWS directory and enters the command needed to run Windows:

CD\WINDOWS

WIN

To run the batch file, you would type W and press Enter at the DOS prompt.

baud rate Pronounced like the first syllable in "bawdy." *Baud rate* is the maximum number of changes per second in the electrical signal. To understand what that means, let's look at modems. Modems allow two computers to communicate over the phone lines. Modems transfer information at different speeds, commonly measured as baud rates. The higher the baud rate, the faster the modem can transfer data. However, when you connect computers via modem, the slower of the two modems determines the maximum baud rate.

   Baud rate is commonly confused with *bits per second* (*bps*). Bits per second refers to the number of bits of information transferred per second. During high-speed data transfers, a modem may send more than one bit of information for each change in the electrical signal. For example, a modem operating at 300 baud may be transferring at 1200 bps. See also *bits per second.*

BBS Short for Bulletin Board System. A BBS enables a computer to automatically answer the phone when other computers call. The BBS allows the calling computer to copy files to it (*upload* files) and copy files from it (*download* files). Although you can purchase a BBS program to set up your own BBS, most users work with BBSs set up by computer companies and professional associations. A BBS set up by a software company may offer help with common problems, ideas for using the software, and a list of products.

bells and whistles Desirable but nonessential features of a program that make it especially irresistible. At one time, 3-D charting was among the bells and whistles of the hottest new spreadsheet program. Now that all the major products have this capability, it's considered standard. This phrase is never used singly, as in "That's a nice whistle on that program," but always in the plural, as in, "Yessir, this here product has all the latest bells and whistles."

benchmark test   A measure of a computer's performance. Not all computer equipment is created equal. A benchmark test runs the computer (or one of its components) through a series of exercises and measures its performance. For example, a benchmark test may read and write information to a hard disk to determine the speed in milliseconds at which the disk operates. Many benchmark tests compare the performance of the tested unit against that of comparable equipment. See also *throughput*.

Bernoulli box   Pronounced ber-NOO-lee. Equipment that can store large amounts of data on a single, removable cartridge. Bernoulli boxes are often used to store backup copies of files.

beta   An early version of a program that is not sold to the public. When software companies create new or improved software, they release a beta version to a limited group of people. These testers use the software under realistic conditions and tell developers of any problems (bugs) in the program. The software company then makes the necessary corrections before releasing its product commercially.

Bézier curve   Pronounced BEZ-ee-ay. In a drawing program, a curve that you can change and blend with other curves to form smooth lines in drawings. A French mathematician, Bézier, theorized that you could define any curve by specifying two launch points and two control handles. The launch points refer to the ends of the curved line. The control handles refer to the vectors that determine the angle of the curve and how strong the curve will be. Is that clear? If not, think about shooting a cannonball straight up into the air. Now, reload and shoot it at a slight angle. Notice the difference in the path that the cannonball travels? Try shooting the cannonball using more or less gunpowder. Notice the difference? Notice your neighbors' frowns?

The same thing occurs with Bézier curves. You control the vector forces (the power and angle) at which the curve is shot. Lengthening a vector is like using more gunpowder. Lowering the angle of the vector is like shooting the cannonball lower.

bidirectional printing   The capability of a printer to print from right to left as well as from left to right. A bidirectional printer works faster than one in which the carriage has to return to the left every time it prints one line before it can print the next. A bidirectional printer prints one line from right to left, then the next line from left to right, so there's no wasted motion.

Big Blue   Nickname for IBM, the computer manufacturer who uses a distinctive shade of blue in their corporate logo. See also *IBM*.

binary   A binary numbering system uses 0 and 1 only. Because computers are electronic devices that understand only two states—on and off (high current or low current)—the binary numbering system is used to tell the computer what to do.

To understand how binary numbers interact with the computer, you must understand a little about *bits* and *bytes*. A bit stores a single binary value—0 for off or 1 for on. Eight bits make up one byte of information. For example, 01000001 is a byte that represents the letter A. Whenever you type A on your keyboard, that byte is sent to your computer. A binary file is usually a program file consisting of a complex collection of bytes that tell the computer how to run the program.

BIOS   See *basic input-output system*.

bit Short for BInary digiT. To understand a bit, it may be better to first look at a *byte*. A byte is a group of eight bits and usually represents a character or a number from 0 to 9. For example, the byte 01000001 represents the letter A. Each 0 or 1 in the byte is a bit representing one of two states: 0 for off or 1 for on. The various combinations of eight 0s and 1s represents all the data in a computer.

You will rarely hear anybody talk about bits; instead, you will hear people talk about *bytes*. Or thousands of bytes—*kilobytes*. Or millions of bytes—*megabytes*. Or even billions of bytes—*gigabytes!* But it all starts with the lowly bit—0 or 1.

bit map A computer screen consists of thousands of small dots of light called *pixels*. In programs you use to paint images on-screen, you turn the pixels on or off or change their shading or color to create an image. A bit of information tells whether the pixel is on (bit=1) or off (bit=0). A bit map is a file that tells the computer how to display or print the pattern of dots.

bit-mapped font A way to handle typed characters that treats each character as a collection of bits (dots). Bit-mapped fonts differ from scalable fonts, which treat each character as an outline. With bit-mapped fonts, the program needs a dot pattern for each character you use. For example, the program uses one dot pattern to print a character in Courier 10-point type and a separate pattern to print in Courier 11-point type. This takes up room in your computer's memory and takes a lot more time to display and print the text.

With scalable fonts, the program can adjust the size of the font's outline—it doesn't need a separate outline for each font. See also *outline font*.

bit-mapped graphics Images created and stored as a pattern of dots, with each dot in a specific position

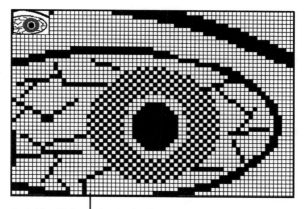

Each bit of information in the file turns one pixel on or off.

on the screen and with its attributes (color, intensity, etc.) described independently from the dot next to it. Compare to *object-oriented graphics*.

bits per second (bps)   When computers communicate over the phone lines, they transfer information at different speeds, commonly measured in bits per second. A bit is the smallest unit of information the computer can process.

Bits per second is commonly confused with baud rate. Bits per second refers to the number of bits of information transferred per second. During high-speed data transfers, a modem may send more than one bit of information for each change in the electrical signal. For example, a modem operating at 300 baud may be transferring at 1200 bps. See also *baud rate*.

bleed   Refers to one of two undesirable occurrences: On paper, it's the excess ink that fuzzes up the outline of your characters or graphics when the paper isn't heavy enough to absorb the ink neatly. On-screen, it's the fuzzy effect that can occur when two lines intersect each other and cause a halo effect.

block   A selected section of text that you can work on as a single unit. You will often select a block of text (in a word processing program) or a block of cells (in a spreadsheet program) to copy, cut, or move the text or cells to another location.

block operation   A set of operations you can perform on a selected area of text. Common block operations include cutting, pasting, and moving a block; changing the type style of a block; and changing the margins for the block.

block protection   In word processing and desktop publishing programs, you can mark a block (section of text) to prevent it from being split by a page break. This ensures that the protected block will remain on a single page.

boilerplate   A fancy word for *template*. Text you use over and over again, such as the headings for a memo.

boldface   Displaying or printing selected text darker than surrounding text.

bomb   Failure of a system or program. You know your system has bombed when the display or keyboard locks up.

boot   To start your computer with the operating system in place. The word *boot* comes from the phrase "to pull yourself up by your bootstraps." When you turn on your computer, it automatically reads the instructions that it requires to get up and running. If you have a hard drive, the files your computer requires to get started are probably on the hard drive. If your computer has only floppy drives, you have to insert a startup disk into the drive before turning on your computer.

boot record   The first sector (section) of a disk contains the system information required to boot your computer. If this sector is damaged, you will not be able to use the disk to boot your computer.

bps   See *bits per second*.

break   To stop an operation in progress either temporarily or permanently. In DOS, you can stop a program by holding down the Ctrl key and pressing the Break key.

brownout   A brownout is sort of like a blackout. With a blackout, the power goes out—the lights go off, the TV goes blank, and your computer stops running. With a brownout, the lights flicker—you miss the *Jeopardy!* question, and your computer may run erratically. Brownouts commonly occur when the demand for electricity in the area increases dramatically, as when suburbanites are all cooking dinner.

   Because electrical fluctuations of any kind are not good for a computer, it's a good idea to install a surge protector or a UPS (Uninterruptible Power Supply).

buffer   A temporary holding area for data. The purpose of a buffer is to make up for the different speeds between two components. One of the most obvious buffers is the *printer buffer*. Whenever you start printing a document, the program sends the information required for printing to your printer's memory (its buffer). Your printer reads this information as needed. If you cancel the printing, you'll notice that the printer continues printing for a short time. Even though you cancelled the printing, there is some leftover information in the print buffer that your printer continues to process. You can clear the print buffer by pressing the printer's reset button (if it has one) or by turning its power off, waiting a few seconds, and turning it back on.

bug   This term comes from the 1940s, when computers used tubes instead of integrated circuits. Bugs,
which were attracted to the brightly lit tubes, would
fly into the computers and cause short-circuits,
disabling the computers. The term *bug* is now more
commonly used to refer to problems in programs
that cause the program or computer system to behave erratically or crash.

built-in font   Every printer comes equipped with at
least one font (a family of type that has the same type
design and size). This font is referred to as the built-
in font. You can add fonts in the following ways:

> *Font cartridges*   Many laser and inkjet
> printers have plug-in cartridges that contain
> memory chips that store selected fonts.

> *Soft fonts*   Many printers contain additional
> memory that can temporarily store informa-
> tion about other fonts. You can purchase
> fonts on disk (*soft fonts*) that you load into
> this storage area whenever you want to use
> a particular font. This is called *downloading*
> the font.

built-in function   In spreadsheet programs, this is a
premade formula or macro that performs many
types of complex or time-consuming calculations
for you. One of the built-in functions in Excel, for
example, is the AVERAGE function. Say you want to
find the average value of the numbers in cells A1
through A10 and show it in cell A11. You could
either type in a formula at A11 like
"=(A1+A2+A3+A4+A5+A6+A7+A8+A9+A10)/10," or
simply paste in the AVERAGE function and highlight the desired cells, and A11 would contain the
formula "=AVERAGE(A1:A10)." Depending on the
program, there are built-in functions to calculate the
rate of return on an investment, trim extra spaces in

a string of characters, date-stamp your worksheet, and perform many other timesaving operations.

bulletin board system   See *BBS*.

bundled software   Several software programs that are packaged together and sold for a single price. Many computer companies now bundle software with their computers.

burn-in   A period of time, usually 48 hours, when the computer is operated continuously to test its circuits. Dealers put computers through a burn-in period to make sure the computers work. The theory is that if the computer can be operated for 48 hours nonstop without suffering damage, its circuits are reliable.

bus   A superhighway that carries information electronically from one part of the computer to another. There are three such highways:

> *Data bus*   Lets data travel back and forth between memory and the microprocessor.

> *Address bus*   Carries information about the locations (addresses) of specific information.

> *Control bus*   Carries control signals to make sure traffic flows smoothly, without confusion.

bus architecture   The bus architecture of your computer has a big effect on how powerful and upgradable your PC is. It tells the overall structure of a data bus system in a particular type of computer system—whether the computer uses an eight-lane highway to move data around, a 16-lane highway, or a 32-lane highway. As you can imagine, the 32-lane highway moves things along the fastest. If you're shopping for a PC, you'll see three types of bus architecture:

Industry Standard Architecture (ISA), a 16-bit bus structure that is downward compatible with 8-bit adapters; Enhanced Industry Standard Architecture (EISA), a 32-bit bus that is downward compatible with ISA adapters; and Micro Channel Architecture (MCA), IBM's 32-bit bus architecture that is found exclusively in IBM PS/2 computers.

business presentation graphics   Special graphics programs designed to help create graphics presentations in a business environment. These programs assume that businesses require only a few graphic elements (often referred to as charts): graph charts, text charts, organizational charts, and flow charts. With business presentation graphics, you supply the facts and figures and specify how you want this

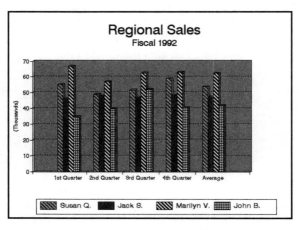

information displayed. The graphics program takes care of the rest, drawing the specified chart. You can then modify the chart for your own use. With many presentation graphics programs, you can send your files on disk to a special service bureau to have them made into slides that you can show using a slide projector.

With the advent of multimedia personal computers, many business presentation programs are starting to let users add sound and motion to their presentations. The current technology in this area is making great strides.

button   In any graphical user interface program, this is a simulated on-screen button that represents a choice or command. It's called a button because, like a car radio button, you can "push" it by selecting it with the cursor and pressing the Enter key or by clicking your mouse.

byte   A group of eight bits that usually represents a character or a number from 0 to 9. For example, the byte 01000001 represents the letter A. Each 0 or 1 in the byte is a bit representing one of two states: 0 for off or 1 for on. The various combinations of eight 0s and 1s represent all the data in a computer.

Lay down your cache, pick up your chips, and play your cards right. Otherwise, you might end up getting a cold boot.

C An extremely powerful structured programming language. Developed at Bell Laboratories in the early 70s, it is widely taught in schools and used by professionals to write commercial software programs. Its popularity is greatly due to its flexibility in application building and portability to almost every computer platform. See also *programming* and *structured programming language.*

C++ The object-oriented version of C. Bell Laboratories' programmer Bjorne Stroustrup brought object-oriented capabilities to the C language and gave it a name that in the C language means "much more than C." See also *object-oriented programming.*

cache Pronounced cash. A reserved portion of a computer's electronic memory—Random-Access Memory (RAM). Frequently used information is stored in the cache so that your computer can get the information more quickly.

CAD Short for Computer-Aided Design. Today's engineers and designers rely on CAD programs to help create a pattern for a structure or part. With CAD, designs are created in three dimensions with various levels of detail.

With computer-aided design, engineers can design and test a part to determine any faults or weaknesses—before they even make the part! Some programs can test the stress that a machine will place on a human being to determine if the machine is safe.

When the manufacturer finally decides to manufacture the part or the machine, the programmers can write a program that uses the dimensions in the drawing to instruct a special computer-operated machine how to cut or drill the part. Such machines are called *Computer-Numerical-Controlled (CNC)* devices. They follow the instructions in the program to move a tool (such as a drill) to cut the part to the specified dimensions. This is called *Computer-Aided Manufacturing (CAM)*.

CAI Short for Computer-Aided Instruction. Education programs are set up to run on a computer; they may consist of a tutorial, a drill, or a question-and-answer session that helps you learn a task or topic. You can learn nearly anything—from playing poker to understanding particle physics—on your computer with CAI.

calculated field In a database program, you create records, each containing one or more field entries. Each record contains information for a single person, place, or thing. Each field contains a single piece of information about the person, place, or thing—for example, a street address or a phone number. A calculated field contains the results of calculations performed using other fields. For instance, age might be calculated from birthdate, or quarterly sales might be calculated by adding entries over three months.

```
ORDER NO: 100002  DATE:     March 28, 1991   SOLD BY: 104    SHIP VIA: Ground

                                    CUST. NO. 00002
SuperService Supply Co.             Jack Pollack
1990 Avian Way                      Action Designs
Bldg. 4                             Production Dept.
Palomar, CA 90006                   3220 Umbrian Way
(619) 905-5000
(800) 040-2143                      Seaside, CA 93732
                                    PHONE: (400)555-6721
Item no. Quant         Description              Unit price    Total

CS-10211  10    5 1/4" DSDD Diskettes Premium (10)     10.50     105.00
CS-10217  10    3 1/2" DSHD Diskettes Premium (10)     17.90     179.00
PP-79863   5    Roller Pens Fine Red                     .89       4.45
PP-79865   3    Roller Pens Fine Green                   .89       2.67
ST-21919   1    Fine folders 1/3 cut letter gross      21.99      21.99
ST-23122  12    Mailing envelopes tyvec 10x12 (12)      6.59      79.08

                                              Subtotal:    392.99
                                              Sales Tax:    25.54
                                              TOTAL:       418.53
```

Formula in selected field determines subtotal.

calculator Many programs include a calculator that
   you can use to perform calculations. The calculator
   works just like a hand-held calculator, except you
   use the keyboard or mouse to press the buttons.

cancel To stop an operation. In DOS, you can often
   cancel an operation by pressing the Esc key or by
   holding down the Ctrl key and pressing the Break
   key.

capacity The amount of information a unit can store
   or the number of operations a unit can perform in a
   given amount of time. Capacity is commonly used
   to represent how much data a disk can store. For
   example, a 5.25" high-density floppy disk can be
   formatted to store 1.2 megabytes; this is the disk's
   storage capacity.

Caps Lock key An optional key that locks the keyboard so you can enter all uppercase characters
   without holding down the Shift key. This key acts as
   a toggle switch; that is, pressing the key once turns
   Caps Lock on, and pressing the key again turns it off.
   Most keyboards have a Caps Lock light that lights up
   when Caps Lock is on.

card A printed circuit board that plugs into the inside of a computer. It contains one or more ports (receptacles) that allow other devices to be connected to the computer. For example, a Video Graphics card allows a special type of monitor (video screen) to be plugged into the computer.

carpel-tunnel syndrome A type of repetitive stress injury that affects the wrist. Repeated and prolonged typing—especially without proper ergonomic behavior (like positioning the keyboard near lap level and using a wrist pad)—can cause this serious disorder. Pain and/or numbness in the wrist and hand can eventually lead to loss of muscle control in these areas if it goes untreated. Don't underestimate its dangers. Insist on the right equipment to suit your height and posture, and take frequent breaks. Tell your boss you're saving the company money through greater productivity and fewer insurance claims.

carriage return On older typewriters, you commonly press the carriage return to start a new line. With most word processing programs, the program usually starts a new line when needed (see *word wrap*). To start a new paragraph, you press the Enter key or the Return key. These keys act as replacements for the carriage return.

cartridge Removable units used to store data. Each cartridge contains disks, magnetic tape, or memory chips that can store data.

You can use cartridges with many inkjet and laser printers to add fonts (different type designs and sizes) to the printer. You buy a cartridge with the fonts you want to use and plug it into a receptacle on the printer. Many data storage systems also use cartridges that contain tape or disks for storing data. Such cartridges are commonly used for storing backup copies of files. See also *Bernoulli box.*

cascading windows   Some programs, such as Microsoft Windows, allow you to work with more than one program and/or file at a time. Each program or file is displayed in its own window. You can usually arrange the windows in either of two ways: tiled or cascading. Tiled windows are arranged side-by-side without overlapping. Cascading windows overlap, so only a portion of each window is visible.

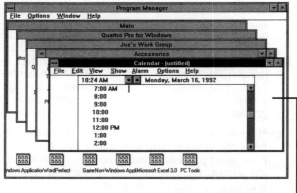

Selecting a window moves it to the front.

case-sensitive   A program's ability to tell the difference between uppercase characters (A, B, or C) and lowercase characters (a, b, or c). Many programs offer a Search feature that allows you to search for a word or phrase. If the Search feature is case-sensitive, it will distinguish between uppercase and mixed case versions of a word, such as *bill* and *Bill*.

cathode ray tube (CRT)   Also known as *VDT* (*Video Display Terminal*) and *VDU* (*Video Display Unit*). The tube in a computer monitor. Often used to refer to the screen.

CD-ROM   Short for Compact Disk Read-Only Memory; pronounced seedy rahm. A storage technology that uses the same kind of disks you play in an audio CD player. The disks are made of hard plastic and measure about 4 ½ inches in diameter. Instead of music, CD-ROM disks store computer files and programs. A single disk can store over 500 megabytes of information, which is almost equivalent to a complete set of encyclopedias.

In fact, CD-ROM disks are commonly used for storing encyclopedias and books, complete with text, full-color photos and illustrations, and sounds. Just think of that bookcase full of encyclopedias you just bought for Junior—all on a single disk! And, with the proper equipment, the encyclopedia can even talk. Look up *Lion* and you may hear a lion roar; turn to *India* and you may hear a native Indian speak.

As the term CD-ROM implies, you can only read information from the disk into your computer. Currently, you cannot save programs or files to the CD-ROM disk.

cell   A spreadsheet consists of a series of alphabetized columns and numbered rows. (Columns run down, and rows run across.) The columns and rows intersect to form rectangles called *cells*. Think of a spreadsheet in terms of your checkbook register. A box in the register, say the one for debits, is equivalent to a cell.

To create a spreadsheet application, you enter text, numbers, formulas, and functions into the various cells. The spreadsheet then performs all required calculations for you. See also *spreadsheet*.

cell address   A spreadsheet consists of a series of alphabetized columns and numbered rows. (Columns run down, and rows run across.) The columns and rows intersect to form rectangles called cells. Each cell has an address that indicates the column and row the cell is in; for example, the cell in the upper left corner of the spreadsheet is cell A1. To the right is cell B1, and below A1 is cell A2.

cell animation   A type of animation program in which you manipulate the object you want to "animate" against a background that stays constant. This way, you don't have to draw an entirely new picture for every frame. This is the way Disney animation works. To show Mickey Mouse walking down the street, there's one drawing of a street, and a series of cells (paintings on clear plastic or celluloid. Cell is short for celluloid) of Mickey moving from right to left. Each cell of Mickey is laid on the background, photographed, and picked up and replaced with the next. The final effect looks like Mickey is strolling along the street. Computerized animation programs use this same principle. One such program is MacroMind Director, for the Apple Macintosh.

central processing unit (CPU)   The computer's brain. The CPU in a personal computer is contained in a single microprocessor chip.

CGA   Short for Color Graphics Adapter. The first video adapter for the IBM that displayed colors and graphics. CGA can display four colors at the same time with a resolution of 200 by 320 pixels (dots of light on the screen), or one color with a resolution of 640 by 200. Compare with EGA (Enhanced Graphics Adapter), which can display 16 colors with a resolution of 640 by 350 pixels, and with VGA (Video Graphics Array), which displays 256 colors with a resolution of 640 by 480 pixels.

A typical color TV screen displays 1000 by 1000 pixels, which is why you can see a lot more detail on your TV than on your computer screen.

character   Any letter, number, or symbol you can type.

character attribute   In word processing programs, you can choose a font in which you want the text to appear. The font is defined by the typeface (for example, Helvetica) and the type size. You can add attributes, such as bold and italic, to a font to enhance its appearance.

character-based program   A program that can display only a fixed set of characters. In character-based programs, all text is displayed in the same size and style on-screen no matter how the text will print. In contrast, *graphics-based programs* display text as it will appear in print by forming a graphic image of each character. Character-based (or text-based) programs typically run faster than graphics-based programs, because generating graphics takes more time.

characters per inch (cpi)   The number of letters that occupy one inch on a line. Common measurements are 10 cpi and 12 cpi. Do not confuse characters per inch with points (another unit commonly used to measure type size). Points are used to measure the height of the text; there are 72 points in an inch. The greater the point size, the larger the type. With characters per inch, however, the larger the cpi, the smaller the type. With 24 cpi, you have 24 characters crammed into every inch of text, which makes for mighty small type.

10 characters per inch

12 characters per inch

14 characters per inch

16 characters per inch

characters per second (cps)   The speed at which a device (usually a printer) processes text. Typical printers have speeds ranging from 50 cps to 800 cps. A good speed for printers is about 120 cps when printing in high-quality mode, and 240 cps in draft mode. If you go much slower than this, you'll be doing a lot of waiting.

change directory   In DOS, you can create directories on a disk in order to organize your files. Whenever you want to work with a file in a given directory (to copy, delete, or move the file), you must change to that directory, using the command

> **cd***directory*

where cd\\ is the command to Change Directories, and *directory* is the name of the directory to which you want to change. md*directory* is the command for making directories, and rd*directory* removes them. A directory must be emptied before it can be removed.

change drive   IBM-compatible computers have one or more disk drives. Each drive can read information from a disk so that your computer can process the information and you can work with it. Before you can run a program on a disk or open a file that's on the disk, you must change to the drive where the disk is located. (You may have to change directories as explained above.) In DOS, you change drives by typing the following command and pressing Enter:

> **d:**

where d is the letter of the drive (it must be followed by a colon). The letter A stands for the first floppy disk drive (the top or far left drive). B stands for the second floppy drive (if your computer has two floppy drives). And C stands for the first hard drive. You can have additional hard drives D, E, F, and so on. See also *path*.

check box   In many programs, you will encounter dialog boxes, which display messages and ask you to provide additional information. The dialog box may contain a series of check-box options and/or radio-button options. With radio-button options, you can select only one option in a group; if you select a different option, the currently selected option is deselected. With check-box options, you can select more than one option in the group. When you select an option, an X or check mark appears in the box, indicating that the option is on. To turn the option off, you select it again.

checksum An error-detection technique (often used in modem communications) that compares the data sent with the data received in order to determine if the data was damaged in the exchange. The sending computer totals the number of bits in a unit of data and stores the sum in a checksum—an extra word of data. When the receiving computer receives the data, it totals the number of bits in the unit of data and compares it against the checksum. If the actual sum does not match the checksum, the receiving computer requests that the data be re-sent. See also *parity bit* and *stop bit.*

child Commonly used to refer to a subdirectory on a disk. The main directory is sometimes called the *parent* directory, and the subdirectory is called the *child.* Unlike real life, in this case a child learns only from the parent and does exactly as told!

chip Another name for an integrated circuit. A chip is a silicon crystal or other material that is designed and manufactured to perform the same operations as hundreds, thousands, or millions of electronic components (transistors, resistors, and so on). A large chip may be the size of your fingernail. Because chips are so small and powerful, computer manufacturers are now capable of producing powerful computers that can fit on a desk or in a briefcase.

circular reference Have you ever felt like your boss is talking in circles? Now imagine how your computer feels when you do the same. In a spreadsheet, if you want to total the values in cells A1, A2, and A3, and insert the result in cell A4, you would type A1+A2+A3 in cell A4. If the formula uses its own cell address in the calculation, it contains a circular reference. For example, if you typed A1+A2+A3+A4 in cell A4, you would have created a circular reference. When the spreadsheet calculates the result, it will indicate an error.

In some spreadsheet programs, you can use circular references intentionally—for example, to determine an incremental increase over time. If you do so, you need to specify the number of times you want the formula calculated (the number of iterations). If you don't, the spreadsheet may continue calculating the formula forever.

circuit board   A flat, plastic or fiberglass card on which electrical components are connected. Because the circuit board is a unit, you can install the board quickly without having to install each separate component.

clear   To remove a document from your computer's memory (random-access memory) or to remove displayed information from the screen (sort of like erasing a blackboard). This gives you a clean workspace on which to begin a new project.

click   To move the mouse pointer over an object and press and release a mouse button once without moving the mouse. In general, you click on a character, object, or command to select it. You can double-click on a command (press and release the mouse button twice quickly) to execute a command.

client   In a network, computers can play either of two roles: client or server. The client is the computer on which you work. The server is the central computer (usually with a huge disk drive) that provides information to the client. Whenever the user enters a command requesting information, the server supplies that information.

clip art Ready-made pieces of art. If you are not qual-
ified or motivated to draw your own pictures, you
can purchase clip-art packages that contain collections of art drawn by professionals. You can often
buy specific clip-art packages, such as sports, business, or education-related clip art.

clipboard A temporary storage area for text and graphics. You can cut or copy a section of text or a picture
to the clipboard. The text or picture is stored there
until you cut or copy something else to the clipboard, replacing its original contents. Whenever
something is on the clipboard, you can paste it
somewhere else in the current document or into
another document.

In Microsoft Windows, the Windows Clipboard
is available to all Windows programs, so you can use
the Clipboard to share data between programs. For
example, you can copy a picture created in Paintbrush to the Windows Clipboard and then paste that
picture into a document in WordPerfect for Windows.

clock speed The speed at which a computer performs
calculations and operations, often measured in megahertz (MHz)—one million cycles per second. The
system clock emits a steady stream of electrical
pulses that synchronize all operations in the computer.

Table C.1 shows some typical clock speeds and
how they translate into the actual time a computer
spends calculating numbers.

Table C.1 Time needed to add 10,000 numbers.

Microprocessor	Speed	Time Needed
8088	4.77 MHz	128 seconds
80286	12 MHz	32 seconds
80386	20 MHz	8 seconds

clone A computer, a component, or a program that mimics the original. The term *clone* is most commonly used to refer to a less expensive computer that uses the same parts and runs the same programs as its more expensive counterpart. Sometimes, clones are superior products. See also *compatibility*.

close To remove a file or program from your computer's memory, or to remove a window from the screen.

cluster Every disk used to store data is divided into sectors. The sectors are grouped in clusters—two to eight sectors per cluster. When the computer stores data on disk, the smallest unit of disk it uses is a cluster. That is, when you store a file on disk, no matter how small, it will take up at least one cluster. For example, if you store a 350-byte file on a disk that contains 1-kilobyte clusters, the file will consume 1 kilobyte of disk space. See also *sector* and *track*.

CMOS Short for Complementary Metal-Oxide Semiconductor; pronounced SEA-moss. An electronic device (usually battery operated) that stores information about your computer. Information stored in CMOS includes the current date and time (if your computer is equipped with a clock) and the number and type of disk drives your computer has. If the information in CMOS is damaged by battery failure or a system glitch, you may not be able to use the hard drive, and information may mysteriously disappear from your disk. Some utility programs, such as PC Tools, provide a way to restore the lost or damaged CMOS information and allow you to test the CMOS battery.

cold boot   To turn on your computer with the operating system in place. The word *boot* comes from the phrase "to pull yourself up by the bootstraps." When you turn on your computer, it automatically reads the instructions it requires to get up and running.

   A warm boot (reboot) differs from a cold boot in that when you perform a warm boot (typically by pressing Ctrl+Alt+Del), you boot a computer that is already running. With a warm boot, the computer simply clears its mind and rereads the instructions it needs to get back on track. A cold boot requires you to turn on the power to your computer.

Color Graphics Adapter   See *CGA*.

color monitor   A display screen that is capable of displaying colors. Contrast this with a monochrome monitor, which can display only two colors: commonly white-on-black or green or amber-on-black.

color separation   In computing, the process of preparing a color graphic for professional printing. This feature in an image processing, page layout, or illustration package will save each color in the graphic as a separate document. The Printer then processes each document and combines them to achieve the full-color final product.

column   In spreadsheet programs, each spreadsheet is comprised of alphabetized columns and numbered rows. The columns (running up and down) and rows (running across) intersect to form cells, the basic unit of the spreadsheet.

   In word processing programs, *columns* refer to narrow strips of text. Most word processing programs distinguish between *parallel columns* and *newspaper columns.* Newspaper columns snake from the bottom of one column to the top of the next. Parallel columns align the text in one column with its corresponding entries in the other columns.

COM port Short for COMmunications port. A receptacle, usually at the back of the computer, into which you can plug a serial device, such as a modem, mouse, or serial printer. If your computer has more than one COM port, the ports are numbered COM1, COM2, and so on.

comma-delimited file In database programs, this is a way to save a file with all the information organized as simple text with a comma separating each unit of information (for example, Joe, Smith, 375 Main Street, Chicago, Illinois). Saving a file this way often enables you to import it to an incompatible program. The only downside is that you then have to go into the new program and reformat your file the way you want it.

command An order that tells the computer what to do. In command-driven programs, you have to press a specific key or type the command to execute it. With menu-driven programs, you select the command from a menu.

COMMAND.COM In DOS, COMMAND.COM is a file that must be present to boot your computer. It displays the on-screen prompts, interprets the commands you type, and executes required operations.

command-driven program A program that requires you to memorize the keystrokes you must press to execute commands. Although command-driven programs are slightly more difficult to learn than are menu-driven programs, once you memorize the required keystrokes, you can enter commands much more quickly. However, most newer menu-driven programs offer keyboard shortcuts for common tasks.

command language A type of programming language designed to work within an application for use by average folks—not programmers—to communicate with the computer. For example, when you enter a command at the DOS prompt, such as "CD\WP51," you are using a command language to tell the computer you want to access the WordPerfect 5.1 directory.

communications program A set of instructions that allows a computer (equipped with the necessary hardware, such as a modem) to communicate with other computers through the telephone. Many modems come with the communications software that you need to use the modem. If the modem does not come with software, you must purchase a separate communications program.

Most communications programs allow you to store the phone numbers you dial most often and can automatically dial these numbers for you. Advanced communications programs allow you to set up files that can call other computers in the middle of the night (when phone rates are low), perform the necessary operations automatically, and hang up when they're done.

communications protocol A set of rules that controls the transfer of data between two computers. If you connect your computer to another computer or to an on-line service, such as Prodigy, you must make sure both computers are using the same communications settings. Otherwise, errors may result during data transfer. For example, if one modem is talking at 2400 baud and the other is listening at 300 baud, it is likely that some information will be lost. Common communications settings include the following:

> *Baud rate.* The speed at which the two modems transfer data. The transfer can only be as fast as the slower of the two modems allows.

Parity. Tests the integrity of the data sent and received. A common setting is *none* or *no parity.*

Data bits. Indicates the number of bits in each transmitted character. A common setting is *8.*

Stop bits. Indicates the number of bits used to signal the end of a character. A common setting is *1.*

Duplex. Tells the computer whether to send and receive data at the same time (full), or send data or receive data but not both at the same time (half). A common setting is *full.*

compact disc   See *CD-ROM.*

Compaq Computer Corp   A leading manufacturer of IBM-compatible computers. They were the first to develop and sell an IBM-compatible personal computer, the first to offer a 386-powered computer, and among the first supporters of an industry standard for 32-bit bus architecture, which makes it easier for consumers to compare PCs from different manufacturers.

compatibility   With computers and computer equipment, the term *compatible* is used to describe the ability of one component to function error-free with another component. For example, if you have an IBM computer, you should purchase a printer that's IBM compatible. Compatible is also used to describe a computer that mimics the standard computer. For example, an IBM-compatible computer can run programs designed for the IBM computer, even though it isn't a true-blue IBM computer. These wanna-be computers are often referred to as *clones.*

Software programs also offer compatibility with competing programs in two ways: *command compatibility* and *file compatibility*. With file compatibility, the files created in another program can be opened and edited in this program. With command compatibility, the program offers commands that are similar to those used in the other program; for example, you can press F10 to open a file in either program.

compiler Most users run commercial programs on their computers and rarely, if ever, venture into creating their own programs. If you write your own programs, however, you need to use a programming language. This language provides commands that you can understand (through some study). You enter the commands in the order in which you want them carried out.

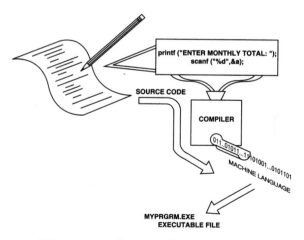

```
printf ("ENTER MONTHLY TOTAL: ");
   scanf ("%d",&a);
```

SOURCE CODE

COMPILER

011..01011...1?101001...0101101
MACHINE LANGUAGE

MYPRGRM.EXE
EXECUTABLE FILE

When you are done, you have a program written in a programming language. However, computers understand a different language, called *machine language*, which consists of ones and zeros. When you are done writing a program in a high-level language, such as Pascal, you must compile it (using a compiler); this translates the program into machine language. Low-level assembler languages (which are often complicated to work in, but have certain programming advantages) are *assembled* into machine language, rather than compiled.

Machine language is a language that your computer can understand, but that most people cannot understand. It consists of codes made up of 1s and 0s. In the good old days, however, our moms and dads were forced to work in machine language, and they liked it.

Complementary Metal-Oxide Semiconductor See *CMOS*.

compression The compacting of files so that they take up less space. You can purchase separate programs, such as PKZip, that compress and decompress files. Users commonly compress rarely used files so the files consume less disk space. You can also compress files before sending them over the phone lines (using modems) to another computer. Because the file is smaller, it takes less time to send, and you save money. However, whoever receives the file must have the necessary program to decompress the file after receiving it.

CompuServe A commercial on-line information service. If you have a modem, you can connect your computer to any of several on-line information services, including CompuServe, Prodigy, and America OnLine. These on-line bureaus allow you to access news, sports scores, travel and entertainment services, stock market information, various publications, on-line encyclopedias, and other sources of information. They also provide free or inexpensive programs and allow you to make financial transactions, enter conferences with people having similar interests, and send and receive electronic mail. The costs for these services vary.

computer   In general, any machine that accepts input (from a user), processes the input, and produces output in some form.

Think of a computer as a general-purpose machine, sort of like a human being. A person is capable of doing any number of things, such as performing brain surgery, fixing cars, or preserving bodies for burial. Likewise, a computer can perform any number of tasks, including balancing your checkbook, printing your resumé, or letting you talk to another computer.

In order for a person or computer to perform a given task, however, it needs instructions telling it what to do. Once given these instructions, the person or computer becomes a specific-purpose machine. In other words, it has a marketable skill.

computer-aided design   See *CAD*.

computer-based training   Training that uses interactive computer programs to teach new skills or information. A well-designed interactive program is like the most patient teacher in the world: it organizes information in a step-by-step format; provides practice sessions and tests that stop you when you make a wrong move and politely remind you of the correct way to do it; and enables you to seek further information on topics you're having trouble with. A CBT package, as they're called, might include an interactive program plus supplemental materials, like a book or video, for use away from the computer. In this way, it offers a multifaceted learning experience with which you can learn at your own speed.

computer graphics   Any graphic created by or displayed on a computer. Computer-generated images or effects that are displayed on hard copy or on-screen, or are transferred to video or film, are computer graphics (as are the icons and other graphics that appear on-screen in a computer program). The term is usually used to refer to the practice of generating and manipulating images using a computer, whether it's creating an illustration for a magazine or a multi-dimensional logo for broadcasting in a television show.

computer literacy   The ability to use a computer productively.

There are levels of computer literacy just as there are levels of reading skills in school: novice users understand computing well enough to navigate an operating system, and use a program to create, print, and save their work; intermediate users use more advanced features of a program and operating system to work more efficiently; power users actively seek out complex and undocumented program features, write involved macros, and dabble in light programming to optimize their work and get a kick out of the experience; programmers understand computers enough to write the programs everyone else uses; and computer scientists traffic in the very principles of computing to devise new languages and new machines that move the very technology further ahead.

Unlike reading skills, you don't have to proceed to the next level of computer literacy unless the current level isn't serving your needs. However, just as basic literacy is essential for getting along in the civilized world, computer literacy is fast becoming indispensable in today's business and education arenas.

computing power   The measurement of a computer's ability to process data and give results. It's usually measured by the speed of the processor in MIPS (Million Instructions Per Second). A powerful mainframe may have a MIPS rate of 10 (meaning it can process ten million instructions per second), whereas a personal computer might have a MIPS rate of .05, or 50,000 instructions per second. MIPS is only one factor in the actual performance of any computer. See also *bus architecture*, *RAM*, and *ROM*, for other factors you should consider when judging the relative power of a computer.

concatenation Pronounced con-CAT-un-NAY-shun. Combining two items to make one. Commonly used in word processing programs to refer to the process of adding one document to the end of another document. You can also concatenate fields in a database (for example, combining the first and last name fields).

concordance file In a word processing program, a concordance file contains a list of all the words you want included in the index. In most word processing programs, you must mark each occurrence of each word you want to include in the index. Besides being tedious, this method results in a lot of missed words. Advanced word processing programs allow you to create a single list of all the words you want included in the index. When you enter the command to index the document, each word listed is included in the index with its corresponding page numbers.

condensed type A style of type in which the characters are reduced in width and set closer together.

conditional statement In programming and in spreadsheet programs, you can use conditional statements to determine which operation to perform next. For example, in a spreadsheet program, you can use a conditional statement with the @IF function to determine whether to charge sales tax to a given customer. The statement might read as follows:

@IF(C6=IN,.05*D15,0)

That is, if the entry in C6 is IN (Indiana), multiply sales tax percent (.05) times the total in cell D15; otherwise, enter zero (0).

configuration   A specific combination of hardware and software that is set up in a particular manner. When you configure your computer, you are customizing it to work most efficiently with the hardware and software you are using. Think of it as redesigning your kitchen so you can cook more efficiently.

configuration file   A file that contains information about how a particular system or program is set up. For example, in many programs, you can customize the screen colors and other options to suit your needs and preferences. When you exit the program, these settings are usually saved in a configuration file. The next time you start the program, it looks to the configuration file in order to determine how to run.

constant   A fixed value. In spreadsheet programs, you use constants and variables in formulas. Variables tell the formula to insert a value from a particular cell that contains a calculated value. Because the value is calculated, it can vary depending on other values and calculations. Constants are fixed values that do not change as the spreadsheet is calculated.

context-sensitive help   Most programs offer a help system that provides information about commands, keystrokes, and tasks related to the program. You can usually get help through a help index—a list of topics or procedures about which you can get help. With context-sensitive help, you don't have to search through an index to find the appropriate topic. The program displays information for the operation you are currently performing.

contiguous   Next to one another. For example, in a spreadsheet program, you may be able to select a group of contiguous or noncontiguous cells. Noncontiguous cells can be scattered throughout the spreadsheet.

continuous form paper A type of paper used in most impact printers. It's actually one long strip of paper, perforated horizontally at every page break (every 8 1/2 inches if it's letter-sized) and perforated vertically along either side to allow the hole-punched edges to run along a tractor feed and keep the paper on track. Once you print on the paper, you can tear off the perfs, and you end up with a standard size letter. The name comes from the fact that preprinted forms are usually printed in this continuous format for use in a tractor feed printer.

Control (Ctrl) key The Ctrl key is commonly used with other keys to enter commands. For example, in Microsoft Word 5.0, you can switch from one document to another by pressing the F1 key by itself. If you hold down the Ctrl key and press the F1 key, you expand the window of the current document to take up the entire screen. Whenever you're instructed to press Ctrl plus another key, press and hold the Ctrl key and then press the other key.

control panel In Microsoft Windows and the Apple Macintosh, this is a window where you can make choices about the look and feel of your computing environment, such as on-screen colors, repeat key speed, how fast you want the cursor to blink, and so on. The host of choices differs between Windows and the Mac.

conventional memory When you purchase a computer, it comes with a certain amount of RAM (Random-Access Memory). This is your computer's electronic memory—the place where information is stored while you and your computer are working on it. Conventional memory is the portion of RAM that your computer and operating system can directly use. On an IBM running DOS, conventional memory is the first 640 kilobytes of RAM that programs can use. You can add RAM in the form of extended or expanded memory, but this additional memory can be used only by programs specifically designed to use it.

conversion   Whenever you create a file (such as a letter) in a program, that file is saved with codes that tell the program how to display, print, and process the file. Usually, if you want to open the file in another program, you must first convert the file into a format that the other program understands. Some programs are able to automatically convert files because they contain features that allow you to convert various file formats. However, you may have to use a special program, such as Software Bridge, to convert a file before you can open it in another program.

coprocessor   A microprocessor that supports the main CPU (Central Processing Unit). The most common coprocessor is the math coprocessor, which is designed to perform mathematical calculations much more quickly than the main CPU. Users who create complex spreadsheets often add math coprocessors to their computers to speed up calculations.

copy   To create an exact duplicate without changing the original. The COPY command is commonly used in DOS to create duplicate copies of a file. You can copy the file to a different disk or directory or to the same disk and directory under a different name.

Most programs allow you to copy selected text or graphics to a temporary holding area. You can then paste the material into another location in the same document or into a different document.

copy protection   Many programs sold commercially (especially games and educational programs) copy-protect their disks to prevent software piracy (using the program without paying for it). The program may prevent you from copying the disk, or it may require you to insert the original disk in the disk drive before running the program. (Both of these methods are referred to as *on-disk* copy protection.) Other programs may require you to enter a password that is included in the program's documentation. (This is called *off-disk* copy protection.) However, whether or not a program is copy protected, you are still legally bound to pay for any programs you use (except for public domain programs). See *public domain programs*.

CorelDRAW!   A high-end illustration package for Windows from Corel Systems Corporation. Its popularity with designers stems from its integration of illustration tools with computer-aided design program features. See also *illustration program* and *CAD*.

corrupted file   A file whose contents have been unintentionally altered or destroyed.

Files get messed up in any number of ways. A power fluctuation can alter the magnetic storage on a disk, erasing parts of a file or erasing the map that tells the computer where the parts of the file are located. You may turn off your computer without quitting the program you were working in, creating a situation in which part of the file is lost. Or the computer can simply lose track of your data for no apparent reason.

Whatever the cause, you may be able to fix the file using a utility program, such as PC Tools or The Norton Utilities.

cpi   See *characters per inch*.

cps   See *characters per second*.

CPU   See *central processing unit*.

crash   Failure of a system or program. Usually, you will realize that your system crashed when the display or keyboard locks up. The term *crash* is also used to refer to a disk crash or head crash. A disk crash occurs when the read/write head in the disk drive falls on the disk. This would be like dropping a phonograph needle on a record. A disk crash can destroy any data stored where the read/write head fell on the disk.

cropping   Most graphics programs allow you to trim a picture to electronically cut away any undesired portions of an image. This trimming operation is called *cropping*.

cross hair   In many graphics and desktop publishing programs, the mouse pointer that appears on-screen can take on several different forms. Usually, it appears as an arrow, which allows you to point at and select objects. Other times, it appears as a cross hair pointer, which looks like the cross hair on a rifle's sight. When the cross hair pointer appears, you can usually use the mouse to draw an object on-screen.

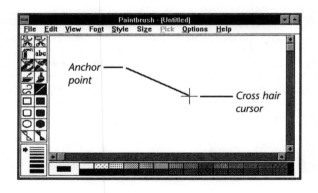

cross-hatching   A pattern that is created by crossing lines. Cross-hatching is commonly used in graphs to distinguish one set of data from another.

Ctrl-Alt-Del   A key combination that is used to perform a warm boot on IBM and compatible computers. A warm boot restarts the system without turning the power off and without running it through its internal checks. To use the key combination, hold down both the Ctrl key and the Alt key while pressing the Del key.

Warm boot only when your system locks up. Booting can cause you to lose any work stored in RAM, so you should first try to exit any program you are working in. If you cannot exit the program, you may have to perform a warm boot. Because this keystroke is used so often when a user does not know what else to do, it is commonly referred to as the *three-key salute.*

current cell   Spreadsheets are made up of columns and rows that intersect to form cells. When you select a cell, it becomes the current cell. You can then enter text or a number into the cell or edit the contents of the cell.

current directory   In DOS, you can organize a disk using directories. You can then store related files in separate directories. To work with a file in a directory, you must first activate the drive that contains the directory. Then you must change to the desired directory in order to make it the current (or active) directory.

current drive   IBM and compatible computers have one or more disk drives. Each drive can read information from a disk so that your computer can process the information and you can work with it. Before you can run a program on a disk or open a file thats on the disk, you must change to the drive where the file or program is located. When you change to a drive, it becomes the current (or active) drive. You also need to change to the directory where the file is located, as explained above.

cursor   An on-screen marker that shows where keystrokes will appear. In most programs, the cursor appears as a blinking underline or rectangle.

In Windows programs and on Macintosh computers, a vertical bar, called the *insertion point*, performs the same function.

cursor-movement keys   See *arrow keys*.

cut and paste   Many programs offer a cut-and-paste editing feature that allows you to copy or move information from one location to another. You cut or copy selected text or graphics to a temporary holding area and then paste it somewhere else.

cyberphobia   Fear of computers. Best overcome by sitting down with one of the beasts and discovering that it won't bite if you hit the wrong key. Graphical User Interfaces (GUI) were designed to reduce the intimidation factor by enabling inexperienced users to operate programs without having to remember which command to enter.

cylinder   Every disk is divided into tracks. Each track is a ring that is similar to a groove on a phonograph record. On a two-sided disk, a cylinder consists of a track and its matching track on the other side of the disk. With hard disks, the hard disk drive contains several *platters*. A cylinder on a hard disk consists of all the tracks that align on both sides of every platter.

When your computer stores information on a disk, it fills up an entire cylinder before moving on to the next one. This keeps the read/write head from having to move back and forth over the disk.

➤

If you are a dedicated decrypter, if you like to defragment at the end of the day, or if you enjoy carrying on dialogs with boxes, you will love the D words.

daisywheel printer A printer that uses a wheel made up of petals, each containing a single character. To print a character, the printer spins the wheel until that character is aligned correctly with the paper. The printer then slams the character against an ink ribbon which prints the character on the page. Daisywheel printers are more or less obsolete. To change type styles or type sizes, you must change the wheel. With dot-matrix, inkjet, and laser printers, you can change type styles and sizes simply by changing them in the document.

data Technically speaking, the facts and figures that you enter into the computer and that are stored and used by the computer. When data is put into some meaningful form, such as a document or report, it is called *information*. In short, you enter data, and the computer gives you information. In common usage, *data* and *information* are used interchangeably.

data bit When two computers communicate over the phone using modems, they transmit each individual character using a data bit. Each data bit contains a series of bits (0s and 1s) that represent a character.

The number of data bits used for each character must be agreed upon by the two modems. For example, if one modem is sending characters using a 7-bit scheme, and the other modem is expecting an 8-bit scheme, the data will not be transferred correctly.

data entry   Usually used when talking about a *database*. Data entry is the process of typing the facts and figures into your database. For example, once you've created a database for storing a list of names, addresses, and telephone numbers, you must enter each person's name, address, and phone number in the database. This is usually the most time-consuming and tedious part of creating a database, which is why there is a high demand for data-entry operators.

Modern advances in computers have made data entry more of a team effort. For example, in a manufacturing plant, a worker may have a computer right at his or her work area for collecting production data. Instead of filling out a form on paper showing how many parts were produced and sending it to the front office to have it keyed in, the worker types the information directly into the computer. The information can then be downloaded (copied) to the main computer at the end of the day.

With the advent of pen-based computers, data entry will become even more team-oriented. Workers will be able to carry around computer tablets and write information on the screen just as they write it on the form. The tablet converts handwriting into typed entries.

data file   An electronic file in which you store any work you've done on a computer. For example, if you type a letter, you can save the letter in a file on disk. Such a file is a data file. The other kind of file on disk is a *program file*. Program files contain the instructions that tell the computer how to perform a task.

data processing   Using the computer to work with data. All aspects of computing have to do with manipulating data, but data processing refers to information-intensive work, such as entering data (like the names and addresses in a database), manipulating it (alphabetizing the names), achieving desired results (printing them out in a format suitable for the tractor-feed mailing labels you've loaded into the printer), and storing the data (so you can use it next year when it's time to send Christmas cards again).

database   Have you ever wanted to speed up Christmas-card addressing? A database is the answer! It's a tool used to store, organize, and retrieve information. Say you wanted to save the names and addresses of all the people on your holiday card list. You could create a database for storing the following information for each person: first name, last name, street number, and so on. Each piece of information is entered into a separate *field*. All of the fields for each person on the list make a *record*.

A database is useful because it helps you organize and get bits of information from an immense sea of data. You can sort the records in the database alphabetically or numerically using the entries in any field. For example, you can sort alphabetically by last name or numerically by ZIP code. You can also extract a single record or a group of records from the database.

Databases are great for many projects, including customer lists, first-aid procedures, dictionaries, recipes, and more.

1	William	Kennedy	5567 Bluehill Circle	Indianapolis	IN	46224
2	Marion	Kraft	1813 Mockingbird Lane	Los Angeles	CA	77856
3	Mary	Abolt	8517 Grandview Avenue	San Diego	CA	77987
4	Joseph	Fugal	2764 W. 56th Place	Chicago	IL	60676
5	Gregg	Lawrence	5689 N. Bringshire Blvd.	Boston	MA	56784
6	Lisa	Kasdan	8976 Westhaven Drive	Orlando	FL	88329
7	Nicholas	Capetti	1345 W. Bilford Ave.	New Orleans	LA	12936
8	Allison	Milton	32718 S. Visionary Drive	Phoenix	AZ	97612
9	Barry	Strong	908 N. 9th Street	Chicago	IL	60643
10	Chuck	Burger	6754 W. Lakeview Drive	Boston	MA	56784
11	Carey	Bistro	987 N. Cumbersome Lane	Detroit	MI	88687
12	Marie	Gabel	8764 N. Demetrius Blvd.	Miami	FL	88330
13	Adrienne	Bullow	5643 N. Gaylord Ave.	Philadelphia	PA	27639
14	John	Kramden	5401 N. Bandy	Pittsburgh	PA	27546
15	Mitch	Kroll	674 E. Cooperton Drive	Seattle	WA	14236
16	Gary	Davell	76490 E. Billview	New York	NY	76453
17	Kathy	Estrich	8763 W. Cloverdale Ave.	Paradise	TX	54812

Record ← (points to row 1)

Field ← (points to ZIP code 12936)

database administrator   The person in an organization who takes care of a networked database so
everyone else can benefit from it. This person is
responsible for how the database is structured, what
information goes into it, who has access to the
information, and what reports will be generated
from it, as well as other administrative duties. The
challenge of this role is to meet the needs of the organization without sacrificing the integrity of the
database. The larger the database, the more complex
a task this can be.

database management system (DBMS)   A program
that controls the organization, storage, and retrieval
of data in a database. A DBMS also provides security
for the database to prevent unauthorized users from
changing the structure of the database or information that should not be changed.

dBASE   A popular database management program
developed by Ashton-Tate and marketed by Borland
International. This was the first relational database
program developed for personal computers. Despite
a buggy 1988 upgrade (dBASE IV Version 1) that took
over a year to be fixed, dBASE continues to be
popular because of its powerful capacity for handling large files, its flexibility in customizing dBASE
applications for specific company needs, and its
choice of a friendly menu-driven interface or the
original command line. See also *relational database*.

debug   To correct a problem in a computer component or in a program that causes the system to
respond erratically. Usually used to refer to correcting problems in a program.

decryption   Some utility programs let you encrypt a
file in order to prevent other people from viewing or
changing the file. With most encryption programs,
the program asks you to type a password. The program then scrambles the data contained in the file.
When you choose to decrypt the file, the program

will ask you to type the password you used to encrypt the file. When you enter the correct password, the program unscrambles the data to return the file to a usable form.

dedicated   A program or component used exclusively for a single purpose. For example, a dedicated modem line is a phone line used exclusively for your computer's modem. A dedicated modem line would have a different phone number from the one you use for your phone.

defaults   Initial settings or formatting. With defaults, the computer essentially tells you, "If you don't choose an option, I'll choose one for you."

Whenever you install a program, the program asks you a series of questions about your computer system and how you want the program to run. For example, you may be asked whether you have a color or monochrome monitor. The settings you specify are saved in a configuration file. Whenever you start the program, these default settings are in effect. In most programs, you can change one or more of the settings to customize the program for the current work session, or you can change the settings and save them to make them the new default settings.

Default settings are also used for the files you create. For example, if you start typing a letter in a word processing program, the program uses the default type style and type size for the characters you type. Unless you change the type style and/or size, the defaults will be in effect.

Fragmented file

Defragmented file

defragment   As you save files on disk, the files are saved in a series of neighboring clusters. If you delete a file, a gap is formed between clusters. The next time you save a file, the program will try to fit the file in the gap. If the file is too large to fit in the gap, the program stores as much of the file in the gap as can fit. The rest of the file is stored in the next free cluster. In such a case, the file is said to be *fragmented*; it is no longer stored in neighboring clusters.

File fragmentation is not a catastrophic occurrence. However, it can increase the amount of time it takes a disk drive to open the file, because the disk drive head must travel back and forth across the disk to read all the clusters that contain the file. You can purchase special programs for defragmenting files. These programs read files from the disk and rewrite the files so that they are stored on neighboring (contiguous) clusters.

Delete key   A key that erases the character above or to the right of the on-screen cursor. If you select a section of text or a graphic object before pressing the Del key, the selected text or object is deleted. Many programs store the most recent deletion in a temporary holding area. As long as you don't delete anything else, you can usually undo the delete operation or restore the deleted text or object. See *undelete*.

delimiter   A character or code that acts as punctuation in a series of commands or statements. The delimiter indicates where one command ends and another begins.

Dell Computer Corporation   A well-known manufacturer of IBM-compatible computers. Dell gained their fame by offering high-quality IBM clones directly to consumers at extremely low prices. Their speedy delivery and exemplary customer service turned many people's idea of mail-order computers from fly-by-night pariah into a convenient, money-saving alternative to retail shopping.

demo   Short for demonstration program. Because computer programs can be expensive, many companies offer demo disks for free. The demo disk provides a preview of the program's main features, but does not give you the entire program. You use the demo to determine whether or not you want to buy the program.

demodulation   When two computers communicate through the phone lines, each computer needs to be connected to a modem. Modem is short for MOdulator/DEModulator. That is, the modem translates the data from its digital form (the computer's signal) to an analog form (a signal that can be sent over the phone lines). The modem on the receiving end then demodulates the signal, translating it from an analog signal to a digital signal that the computer can understand.

density   Density is a measure of the amount of data that can be stored per square inch of storage area on the disk. Density is commonly used to refer to different types of floppy disks: single density (SD), low density (or double density, DD), and high density (HD).

To understand density, think of a disk covered with magnetic dust. Each particle of dust stores one piece of data. No matter how large or small the particle, it still stores only one piece of data. With single-density disks, the particles are large, so the disk can hold fewer particles (less data). With high-density disks, the particles are small, so more particles can be packed in less space, and the disk can store more data.

descender   The part of a letter that sinks below the baseline. In the word *park*, for example, the part of the *p* that sinks below the *a* is the descender. Think of it as being a foot below the rest of the characters. See also *ascender*.

descending sort   In many programs, you can sort lists or records in numerical and/or alphabetical order. Normally, the program sorts in ascending order (A, B, C or 1, 2, 3), but you can specify descending order (Z, Y, X or 10, 9, 8).

desk accessory   In a graphical user interface like Windows or System 7, a built-in utility that serves you the way physical accessories on a real desk do. Some common on-screen desk accessories include a calculator, a calendar, an alarm clock, and an address book. These vary from operating environment to operating environment.

desktop   Any program that provides an on-screen work area that is supposed to resemble your desktop. Common desktop programs come equipped with a set of desktop accessories items you commonly find on a desktop, such as a calculator, notepad, and phone number list. Most desktop programs also let you keep more than one file open at a time. If the desktop becomes cluttered, you can then remove items from the desktop or zoom in on the item you are working with.

desktop publishing (DTP)   A program that allows you to combine text and graphics on the same page and manipulate the text and graphics on-screen. Most people who do desktop publishing use three programs: a word processing program for preparing the text, a graphics program for drawing pictures, and a desktop publishing program for combining text and graphics.

Desktop publishing programs are commonly used to create newsletters, brochures, flyers, resumés, and business cards. If you have your own business, you can save hundreds of dollars by creating your own promotional materials. And you can add your own personal touch to any of your publications.

desktop video   A type of application used to edit videotape using a computer. Instead of using a mechanical editing system to cut and splice, introduce fades and dissolves, and color-correct and add other special effects, it's all done at the keyboard. First you import the images and sounds from the videotape footage, digitizing them in some cases so that the computer can manipulate them. (Not all programs require digitizing.) Later, after the editing process is complete, you output the new data back to videotape, and it's ready for the VCR.

destination You can often move or copy a file from one disk or directory to another. When you choose to copy the file, you must specify the source (where the file is currently stored) and the destination (where you want the file or copy to be stored).

device driver A program that tells the computer how to work with a device that's connected to the computer. For example, a print driver tells your computer how to talk in a language that your printer understands.

diagnostic program A computer program that tests the computer and helps you locate any problems that are causing the system to function improperly.

dialog box In many programs, you can enter a simple command to perform some task, such as saving a file. However, you may need to enter additional information before the program can perform the task. In such cases, the program may display a dialog box, which allows you to carry on a conversation with the program. Dialog boxes commonly contain the following elements:

Option buttons. In a group of option buttons, you can select only one button. Selecting a different button in the group unselects the currently selected button.

Check boxes. In a group of check box options, you can select any or all of the options. Selecting an option places an X or a check mark in the box and turns the option on. Selecting the option again turns it off.

Text boxes. A text box allows you to type text, such as the name of a file.

List boxes. A list box contains a series of available items, such as a list of files on the currently selected drive. You can select an item from the list.

Drop-down lists. To save space, some dialog boxes contain drop-down lists. Only one item in the list is visible, but you can pull down the list to see the remaining items.

Digital Equipment Corporation   A major manufacturer of personal computers, established in 1957. DEC, as they are commonly known, offered one of the first minicomputers in 1959, and today produces high-quality IBM-compatible PCs in addition to many other computer products and systems.

digitize   To convert an image on paper into a series of electronic dots that can be stored, displayed, and modified on a computer. This term is commonly used to describe the process of scanning an image into the computer. See also *scanner*.

dimmed   In many programs, any command that you cannot use appears pale on-screen. This allows you to read the command, but indicates that you cannot select it.

dingbats   Character-sized decorative symbols, such as squares (■), triangles (▲), snowflakes (✳), stars (✶), and so on, used to give a document pizazz. There are collections of dingbats in fonts, one popular one being Zapf dingbats.

DIP switch   Short for Dual In-line Package switch; pronounced dip. Tiny switches that allow you to turn options on or off on a computer component. Users most commonly use DIP switches to control the operation of a printer. For example, one DIP switch on my Epson printer activates a paper-saving feature. Whenever I'm done printing a document, the printer feeds some extra paper through the printer so I can tear the last page off. When I start printing my next document, the extra paper feeds back through the other way so the top of the page is correctly aligned to start printing. The lesson of this story? Get to know your DIP switches.

direct voice input   Spoken words that the computer can accept and process as data just as it processes keyboard input. Researchers have developed hardware and software that can digitize spoken words into computer text—there's even a TV remote control on the market that accepts voice commands—but you have to speak within a prescribed structure and at the right speed in order for the technology to work properly. Because spoken language varies so much from person to person, it will be some time before a microphone is as reliable as a keyboard for entering a lot of information into the computer.

directory   Because large hard disks can store thousands of files, you often need to store related files in separate directories on the disk. Think of your disk as a filing cabinet and think of each directory as a drawer in the filing cabinet. By keeping files in separate directories, it is easier to locate and work with related files.

directory tree A map of the directories on a disk. Think of a directory tree as a family tree.

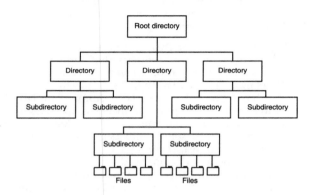

disclaimer A notice included in most software packages informing the consumer that if you experience any difficulties as a result of using the software—if you lose your data, say, or end up with an error-filled balance sheet—you're on your own. That doesn't mean the company won't fix errors in the product, but they won't reimburse you for any losses you've suffered as a result. Let the buyer beware.

disk See *floppy disk* and *hard disk*.

disk buffer When the CPU is saving data to a disk or requesting data from it, this small section of RAM holds the data temporarily until the data builds up to a sizable amount. This temporary holding area actually helps the computer system to work more quickly. Since RAM works so much more quickly than disk memory, it would slow things down to have to wait for the data to be written from or read to the disk by accessing it one byte at a time. By waiting until the buffer is full and then dumping or collecting a lot of data all at once, the disk only has to be accessed once.

disk cache   See *cache*.

disk capacity   The maximum number of kilobytes or megabytes of data that a disk can store. See the table of common floppy disk storage capacities under *floppy disk* for more details on specific disk capacities of common diskette types.

disk crash   The destruction of a hard disk. Also called a *head crash* because what usually happens is that either the read/write head of the disk drive physically collides with either the surface of the disk (it's never supposed to touch it) or a foreign object like a piece of dirt, or a hair lodges between the head and the disk. Just think, one potato chip crumb could get between you and all your invaluable files. Now you know why they tell you to keep the area around your computer clean—and back up your hard disk early and often.

disk drive   A device that writes data to a magnetic disk and reads data from the disk. Think of a disk drive as a cassette recorder/player. Just as the cassette player can record sounds on a magnetic cassette tape and play back those sounds, a disk drive can record data on a magnetic disk and play back that data.

disk maintenance   Although disks are generally reliable for storing information, you must maintain a disk to make sure it remains reliable and efficient. This is especially true for hard disks. To keep the disk in tip-top shape, get a disk maintenance utility, such as PC Tools or The Norton Utilities, and perform the following activities regularly:

> *Keep it organized.* Keep related groups of files in separate, logical directories. This way, you can find files easily. If you need to delete files, you can delete an entire group.

Keep it clean. If you don't use a file, copy it onto a floppy disk and then erase the file from your hard disk. If you don't use a program, back up the program's files and delete them from your hard disk.

Back up regularly. Get a backup program and perform weekly and/or daily backups of your hard disk. An up-to-date backup can protect you in case any files are deleted or damaged.

Defragment files. Over time, files become fragmented on disk; each file is no longer stored in one continuous area on disk. The result is that it takes your hard disk longer to read files from the disk, and it makes it more likely that parts of a file will get lost or damaged. Defragmenting rearranges the files on disk.

disk operating system   See *DOS*.

display   To show information on-screen. For example, a program may display a menu, allowing you to choose an option. The term *display* is also used as a noun to describe the image that is shown on-screen.

dithering   Smoothing the rough edges of curves produced by printers, or combining several dots of different colors or shades to produce what looks to the human eye like a new color or shade. This effect is available through many paint programs and graphics packages and is handy for creating half-tone images and enriching the color scheme of a design.

document   Any work you create using an application program and save in a file on disk. Although the term *document* traditionally refers to work created in a word processing program, such as a letter or a chapter of a book, *document* is now loosely used to refer to any work, including spreadsheets and databases.

document compare   To mark the differences between an edited version of a document and the original. Some word processing programs (such as WordPerfect) offer a document compare feature, but you can purchase separate programs that compare documents. Document compare programs usually compare two document files and create a separate file that shows where text was deleted, added, and/or moved. Deleted text is often printed in ~~strikeout~~; this makes it look as though a line was drawn through the text. Added text is usually <u>underlined</u> or highlighted.

document format   In a word processing program, you can often change the formatting (margins, type style, and so on) at three levels:

> *Default.* If you change the default formatting, you change the formatting for all new documents. Whenever you create a new document, the default formatting is in control.

> *Document.* You can override the default formatting for a single document by setting document formatting options. The document format is in control for all the pages in the current document.

> *Internal.* You can override the document formatting by changing the formatting within the document (internally). For example, you can change the type size and type style for a section of text.

document reader   A type of input device that "reads" printed words, scanning them in as digital signals so that a suitably equipped computer (one with an optical character recognition program installed) can transform the input into computer text which can be manipulated like any other text file. See also *optical character recognition*.

document window   In Microsoft Windows, you can run more than one program at a time. Each program is displayed in a separate application window on-screen. You can also open separate document windows within an application window. Each document window contains a separate file.

documentation   Most programs come with one or more books that tell you how to use the program. These books are called the documentation. Usually, you will get at least two books: a user's manual that tells you how to perform specific tasks, and a reference manual that provides an alphabetical list of features and commands and information on how to use them. The quality of the documentation varies widely from one program to another. If you need more help, many bookstores carry additional documentation, special books written by experts that will guide you through the more popular software.

More and more software companies are including on-line documentation with their programs. This documentation is accessible on your computer in the form of information screens or tutorials.

DOS   Short for disk operating system; sounds like dawss. In life, somebody's got to be the boss. That's true for computers as well. A computer is made up of a number of hardware components: a keyboard, disk drive, central processing unit, display screen, printer, and so on. But in order to function, this hardware needs a set of instructions—the software. There are two basic types of software: operating system software (the boss) and applications software.

The operating system provides the most basic instructions your computer needs to operate. It tells your computer how to interpret input (from the keyboard and mouse), how to process the data, and how to produce output (on the display screen, printer, and other output devices). Applications software uses the operating system to communicate indirectly with the computer.

The most commonly used operating systems for IBM and compatible computers are MS-DOS and PC DOS, commonly referred to as DOS. So would a biologist use a more special version? MOSS-DOS? Not!

DOS prompt   When you boot your computer using MS-DOS, you'll see various messages on-screen. The last thing that will appear is the DOS prompt, which looks something like C>. (This is assuming you don't have your computer set up to automatically run some other program.) The DOS prompt indicates that DOS is ready to accept a command. You type your command at the DOS prompt and press Enter.

dot-matrix printer   A common, inexpensive printer that produces low- or moderate-quality printouts. Dot-matrix printers produce characters and graphic images as a pattern of dots. Because these dots can be arranged in any number of patterns, dot-matrix printers can print graphic images and a variety of type styles and type sizes.

Dot-matrix printers are commonly distinguished by the number of pins they use. (The pins slam against the printer ribbon to form the characters and images on the page.) Common pin configurations include 7-, 9-, 18-, and 24-pin setups. Although you might think that the number of pins directly affects the quality of print, this is not always the case. Some printers can produce higher quality output with fewer pins.

When you are shopping for a dot-matrix printer (or any printer for that matter), be sure to find out how many *dots per inch* (*dpi*) it prints. The more dots it can print per character, the higher the resolution of the printout. To compare two printers, have the dealer print the same document on both printers, and compare the result.

dots per inch (dpi)   Text and pictures on-screen and in print are made up of a series of tiny dots. If you had a Lite Bright kit when you were a kid, think of displays and printouts in terms of that. You could create pictures by plugging little colored pieces into the Lite Bright board in various patterns.

With a Lite Bright, you get maybe four dots per inch, if you're lucky. On a computer screen and in print, you get hundreds or thousands of dots per inch, allowing the computer or printer to create much finer details. A typical printer, for example, will print 180 dots per inch. An advanced printer can print 3000 dots per inch or more.

double-click   To press and release a mouse button twice quickly without moving the mouse. Single clicking is usually used to select an object or command. Double-clicking is used to extend the selection or carry out the command. For example, in Windows, you can click on an application icon to select the icon, or double-click on the icon to run the program.

Keep in mind that two clicks do not equal one double-click. If you don't click twice in the time allotted (the double-click interval), the program will interpret your clicking as two single clicks. Some programs, such as Microsoft Windows, let you increase or decrease the double-click interval. This is useful if your mouse finger is slow on the double-click.

double-density   Density is commonly used to refer to different types of floppy disks. Early disks were rated as single density. Low-density or double-density disks store more data per square inch than single-density disks, but less data than high-density disks. See also *density*.

double-sided disk   A type of floppy disk that can store data on both sides of the magnetic wafer inside the plastic casing. This designation is still used but is not as significant as it used to be, when single-sided disks were standard and double-sided was considered pretty high-tech. Today, double-sided disks are the norm.

download   To copy a file from another computer or from an on-line service or bulletin board system. If you upload a file, you copy the file from your computer to another computer or to an on-line service or bulletin board system.

The term *download* is also used in reference to soft fonts. Soft fonts, also called *downloadable fonts*, are type styles and type sizes you can purchase and use on your computer; they are fonts that the manufacturer did not build into your printer. If you want to print a document in which you have used soft fonts, you must send the font information from your computer to your printer. This is called downloading fonts.

downward compatability   See *backward compatible*.

draft mode   Many printers allow you to create printouts that vary in quality. You can select draft mode to produce a low-quality printout quickly, or letter quality to produce a high-quality printout. High-quality printouts use more ink and take more time to print. See also *letter-quality*.

drag   To hold down the mouse button while moving the mouse. The dragging technique is often used to move a selected object or to extend the highlight over a section of a document.

drag-and-drop   A handy editing feature that has become widely available in Windows applications. Originally introduced by Microsoft, this feature allows you to move a block of text or an icon simply by selecting it with your mouse, holding down the mouse button, and dragging the object to where you want it. Your hand never leaves the mouse, so with one smooth motion you accomplish what would have taken at least a few steps without this feature.

draw program   A draw program lets you create line drawings using objects, such as circles, ovals, squares, and lines. Unlike paint programs, which keep track of every dot that makes up an image, draw programs treat each graphic object as a mathematical formula. The formula contains codes that tell the program how to display and print the object as a smooth line. For example, the formula for a circle contains the position and diameter of the circle.

Although you don't work directly with it, the formula makes it easy to work with objects on-screen. When you select an object, handles appear around it. You can then drag the object anywhere on-screen or change the object's shape, size, or dimensions without affecting surrounding objects.

drive   See *disk drive*.

drive designator   A letter that tells the operating system which disk drive to use. For example, the following DOS command:

COPY A:*.* B:

tells DOS to copy all the files from the disk in drive A to the disk in drive B. A: and B: are the drive designators (be sure to add the colon after the drive letter).

driver   See *device driver*.

drop cap   Originally a mechanical printing term, this is an oversized capital letter that dips below the baseline into the lines of text below, effectively bumping the text below to the right. It's often used to start a new chapter in a book or an article in a magazine. Most page layout programs and some word processing programs contain a drop cap feature.

drop-down menu   In GUI environments, a list of menu choices that appears when you click on the list heading and remains on-screen until you choose one of the options or close the box.

drop shadow   A special printing effect that makes an image appear to be floating above the page and casting a shadow on the page.

dump   To capture and save any data stored in memory as is, without formatting it in any way.

Dvorak keyboard   A keyboard layout that was designed in the thirties as an alternative to the QWERTY keyboard layout, which we still use today. The Dvorak keyboard is commercially available but has to be specially ordered. Its chief advantages are that your fingers spend much more time on the home row than they do on a QWERTY keyboard, and you type many common two-letter combinations with both hands, which is supposed to reduce errors. Its chief disadvantage is that most people are so used to the QWERTY layout they're just not motivated to give this alternative a chance.

dynamic data exchange (DDE)   In Microsoft Windows and OS/2 Presentation Manager, you can create a link that imports part or all of one file into another file. For example, you can create a link in a WordPerfect for Windows file that imports a spreadsheet created in Excel. Whenever you change the spreadsheet in Excel, the information is automatically updated in the WordPerfect document. If you plan to use DDE links, make sure the programs you purchase support DDE.

dynamic link   In programs that support DDE or OLE, this is the link connecting the two chunks of identical data, be it a chart, a block of text, or a graphic, so that when you update the data in one file, it is automatically updated in the other file. See also *dynamic data exchange* and *object linking and embedding*.

➤

Who said computers are no fun? With the E words, you will send electronic mail, expand your memory, encrypt your own files, and even explode a pie graph.

E-mail See *electronic mail.*

echo In DOS, you can create a batch file that contains a series of DOS commands. When you run the file, DOS reads the commands and executes them. As DOS reads the commands, it displays them on-screen, creating a visual echo. You can prevent DOS from displaying the commands on-screen by typing ECHO OFF as the first command in the batch file. You can have a message displayed on-screen by typing ECHO followed by the message you want to appear (for example, "ECHO Enter your name").

edit To change existing text, graphics, or other information in a file.

EGA See *Enhanced Graphics Adapter.*

electronic cottage The concept of an employee's home functioning as a satellite office of the company for which he or she works. Using a personal computer hooked up via modem to the company network, plus supporting equipment (such as a fax machine or fax board, a copier, a phone, and so on), people in many professions can perform their work efficiently—reducing commuting time and hassles, pollution, and office space expenses and substituting the distractions of chatty co-workers for the distractions of the well-stocked Frigidaire.

electronic mail   Here's mail that requires no postage. E-mail is a system in which people can send and receive messages through their computers. Each person has a designated mail box that stores messages sent by other users. He or she can then retrieve and read messages from the mail box.

Electronic mail is often used in large corporations that network their computers. Instead of sending paper memos, employees can send memos electronically through the E-mail system to a single user or to groups of users. If you are not connected to other computers on a network, or if you want to transfer messages electronically to someone outside the network, you can connect to an electronic mail service using a modem. These services require that you pay a subscription price, which usually covers the cost of a fixed number of messages.

electronic marketplace   The ever-expanding emporium of goods, services, information, and entertainment available through on-line service and electronic bulletin boards.

electronic publishing   Transmitting information electronically instead of on paper. People sometimes use the term to refer to desktop publishing, where you prepare a document to send to the printer using a computer instead of good old cut and paste methods. However, the term is used more often in the general sense, referring to information that makes it all the way to the consumer electronically. Computer-based training, on-line news services, and CD ROM-based databases are all examples of electronic publishing.

em dash   A dash that is twice the size of an *en dash*, or the width of a capital M. In this particular font, it's this size: —. Use an em dash instead of two minus signs when you want to interrupt yourself in the middle of a sentence. You won't find this dash on your keyboard, but it's usually available in the symbols menu of a word processing program.

embedded object   In programs that support object linking and embedding, this is a document or part of a document that has been embedded in another document. Whereas a *linked object* is just a copy of a portion of the source document that is automatically updated when the source document is revised, an embedded object can be fully edited within its new location (which is handy when that new location is in an entirely different program). See also *object linking and embedding*.

EMS   See *expanded memory*.

emulate   To imitate the way another component or program works. Often used to describe the ability of a less common printer to act like another printer. For example, in many programs, you must select the printer you intend to use with the program. Because there is such a variety of printers, no list can include all of the printers on the market. In the documentation that comes with your printer, there will usually be a list of common printers that your printer can emulate. You can then select that printer in order to set up your printer.

en dash   Many people mistakenly use the minus sign on their keyboard when they should really use an en dash. Don't let this happen to you. Use an en dash to indicate *to* or *through*, as in "We'll be there from January 2–15," or in a date: 15–Jan–93. It is generally accessible through the symbols menu or keycaps menu of your word processing program, and is half the width of a capital M in whatever font you are working in.

Encapsulated PostScript (EPS)   A page description language used by some programs and printers to control the printing of text and graphics (see *page description language*). If you create a file in a program that supports EPS files, the program adds the required PostScript codes when you save the file. If you print the file using a PostScript printer, the printer reads and interprets the codes to determine how to print each page. PostScript offers several advantages:

> *High quality.* PostScript files produce the highest quality output available on the printer you're using. If you print a PostScript file on a printer that can print 300 dots per inch, the file is printed in 300 dots per inch. If you print the same file using a printer that can print 3000 dots per inch, the file is printed in 3000 dots per inch.

> *Flexible fonts and scaling.* PostScript treats each character and each graphic object as an outline rather than as a collection of pixels or dots. Because of this, you have much more control over the size and dimensions of the object. For example, with non-PostScript fonts, you usually have a limited number of type sizes to choose from: 10-point, 12-point, 16-point, and so on. With PostScript fonts, you specify any size you want.

Portability. Because PostScript is a programming language, you can print a PostScript file using any printer that understands PostScript. You can also import PostScript formatted text and graphics into other PostScript documents.

encryption   The process of encoding a file or scrambling its data in order to prevent other people from viewing or changing the file. To *decrypt* the file, you must enter the correct password.

End key   In most programs, you use the End key to move to the end of a line, the end of a document, or the bottom of the current page.

endnote   If your word processing program or page layout program supports endnotes as well as footnotes, you have the option of listing all your footnotes in one place, instead of at the bottom of every page where they are referenced. The computer will number the notes consecutively throughout, and you'll end up with a tidy endnote section at the end of the document. Endnotes are preferable to footnotes in documents in which you are inserting several notes and references and want to encourage the reader to concentrate on the text instead of being distracted by every note as they go along.

Enhanced Graphics Adapter (EGA)   The second video adapter for the IBM that could display color and graphics. The first color video adapter, CGA (Color Graphics Adapter), could display four colors at the same time with a resolution of 200-by-320 pixels (dots of light on the screen), or one color with a resolution of 640-by-200. In comparison, the EGA can display 16 colors with a resolution of 350-by-640 pixels. A VGA adapter can display 256 colors with a resolution of 640-by-480 pixels. And a Super VGA adapter can display 256 colors with a resolution of 1024-by-768 pixels.

enhanced keyboard   The standard keyboard for the newer IBM and compatible computers. The enhanced keyboard layout differs from the previous PC and AT keyboard layouts in the following ways:

> *Function keys.* The function keys are at the top of the keyboard instead of on the left side, and there are two additional keys (which most programs do not use).

> *Cursor keys.* A separate cursor keypad is added between the main keypad and the numeric keypad. This allows you to use the numeric keypad exclusively for typing numbers, which is useful if you type a lot of numbers.

> *Esc key.* The Esc key is to the left of the function keys. On the PC keyboard, the Esc key is to the left of the main keypad. On the AT keyboard, the Esc key is in the upper left corner of the numeric keypad.

> *Alt keys.* There are two Alt keys. One Alt key is to the left of the Spacebar and the other is to the right.

Esc key   *12 Function keys at top*

                     Alt Key   *Separate cursor keypad*

Enhanced Small Device Interface (ESDI) A standard for connecting disk drives and tape drives to a computer. This standard enables the drive to transfer data at high speeds. ESDI drives can transfer data at roughly twice the speed as drives using the earlier ST-506/ST-412 standard. When shopping for a computer or hard disk, keep this in mind. A slow disk drive can slow down the fastest computer.

Enter/Return key Also known as the *bent arrow key*. A key on the keyboard that signals the end of input or the end of a paragraph. In general, you must perform two actions to enter a command: you must type or select the command, and then you must press Enter. In a spreadsheet program, you enter data into a cell by typing the data on the input line and pressing Enter. In word processing programs, you press Enter to start a new paragraph or to insert additional space between paragraphs.

entry A single unit of data. For example, to create a database, you must type pieces of information for each record. Each record may require a first name, last name, street address, city, state, and ZIP code. Each piece of information you enter is an entry.

entry line See *input line*.

environment The setting in which you perform tasks on your computer. For example, Microsoft Windows provides a graphical environment that allows you to enter commands by selecting icons rather than by typing commands.

Menus let you select commands.

Icon for running the calculator program

Epson   An extremely popular, widely available make of dot-matrix printers. Many smaller manufacturers of printers make them Epson-compatible because almost every IBM-compatible software program contains Epson printer drivers and so can support the lesser known Epson-compatible printer as well. See also *printer*, *driver*.

erasable storage   Any type of data storage, such as hard disks, floppy disks, and even RAM, whose data can be erased or replaced by writing new information over the old.

erase   To remove data in a file or to eliminate a file on disk. When erasing files, do not confuse *erase* and *delete*. When you delete a file from disk, the file's data remains intact until you save another file over it. As long as you don't save another file to disk or copy or move files, you can recover a deleted file. Several utility programs, such as PC Tools and The Norton Utilities, enable you to undelete files. However, when you erase a file, the file's data usually does not remain intact.

ergonomics   A literal translation from the Latin is the *study or management of work*. In practice, this is a science devoted to managing the work environment so people can be safe and comfortable—and therefore productive. Airplane cockpits are ergonomically designed so pilots can easily reach all the right buttons from where they're sitting. In computing, ergonomic considerations have helped shape computer furniture and peripherals. This field is receiving greater recognition as more people feel the ill effects of *not* managing their computing workspace properly. Sitting in a chair that doesn't support your back, working for too long without a break, not using a glare filter, and failing to give your wrists proper support, are just a few ergonomic no-no's that are showing up on a national level in lower worker productivity and higher medical bills.

error message   Information that appears on-screen when a program cannot carry out a given command. Error messages usually provide only enough information to help you find the problem, but not enough information to correct it.

Esc key   Short for Escape. The Esc key is usually used to cancel a command or operation. It lets you change your mind. In many programs, you can use the Esc key to back out of an operation or menu system one step at a time.

event-driven program   In comparison to older *command-driven programs*, this type of program caters to the user. It forces the computer to react efficiently to whatever choice we might make at any given time, instead of forcing us to remember what command to type in. It's the principle of the menu over the command line, first made popular by the Mac and now immortalized in Microsoft Windows. See also *command driven.*

execute   To carry out a command. Whenever you enter a command, the computer searches for and follows the instructions that correspond to the command.

expandability   The measure of how many extra expansion slots and extra room your computer has so that it can be added to in the future. For every peripheral you decide to add to your PC—fax board, external modem, CD-ROM drive, etc.—you need another expansion slot. When you find you need more megabytes of RAM to make your work go faster, you can't add them if your system doesn't have the correct expansion slots on the motherboard. Expandability is not the most exciting thing to consider when you're shopping for a PC, but it's like extra closet space when you're house-hunting: the lack of it doesn't seem important if the rest of the house is perfect, but just wait until you buy it and have to store your underwear out in the garage.

expanded memory system (EMS)   In DOS, the programs you run on your computer can directly access only up to 640 kilobytes of memory. However, many programs require much more memory to run efficiently. To get past the 640-kilobyte limit, several software companies got together and developed an expanded memory system.

   With expanded memory, additional memory is added to the computer in the form of memory chips or a memory board. You can add up to 32 megabytes of expanded memory, depending on the upgrade limitations of your computer. To access this additional memory, an expanded memory manager reserves 64 kilobytes of the standard 640 kilobytes as a swap area. This 64 kilobytes represents 4 *pages*, each page consisting of 16 kilobytes. Pages of data are swapped into and out of this 64 kilobyte region from expanded memory at a high speed.

The program you use must be written to take advantage of expanded memory. For example, both WordPerfect and Lotus 1-2-3 can use expanded memory.

expansion slot   When you purchase a computer, it usually comes equipped with several ports (receptacles) into which you can plug peripheral equipment (such as a printer, modem, and mouse). With many computers, you can add ports for plugging in additional peripherals, such as scanners and sound boards. The port is connected to a circuit board that you can plug into a receptacle inside your computer. The place where you plug the board in is called an *expansion slot*.

When purchasing a computer, it is important to find out the number of *open expansion slots* the computer has. Otherwise, you may be limited in the equipment you can add to your computer in the future.

expert system   A program that simulates the knowledge and experience of an expert in a given topic, like medicine, insurance risk calculation, or some other information-intensive topic, so that a nonexpert using the program can solve problems or make decisions without consulting the expert. See also *artificial intelligence*.

exploded pie graph   A graph used in presentation graphics and in spreadsheet programs that shows a pie with one of the slices cut away. By setting the slice apart from the rest of the pie, the data that the slice represents is emphasized.

export   To save a file in a format that another program can read, allowing two programs to share data. For example, if you create documents in WordPerfect for Windows and your colleague uses Word 5.0, you can save your WordPerfect documents in the Word 5.0 format. Your colleague can then open and work with the files in Word 5.0. You may also be able to *import* files created in another program.

extended character set   A standard code, called *ASCII* (pronounced Ask-key), is used for all characters you type. The first 128 characters in the ASCII character set are characters that almost all computers handle in the same way. This standard allows files that contain ASCII characters to be transferred between computers and programs. ASCII also contains an additional 128 codes that can be used in various ways by different programs to create an extended character set.

On an IBM computer, most programs acknowledge a specific extended character set. You can type a character from this set by holding down the Alt key and typing the number of the character using the numeric keypad (using the numbers at the top of the keyboard will not work).

extended filename   A filename that includes the letter of the disk, the directory, the filename, and the file extension all in its name. For example, the extended filename of a file named "Jordan" with the extension ".DOC" that was stored in a directory named "Clients" on a floppy disk in drive B: would be "B:\Clients\Jordan.DOC." The extended filename is also referred to as the full path name.

extended memory   In DOS, the programs you run on your computer can directly access only up to 640 kilobytes of memory. However, many programs require much more memory to run efficiently. To get past the 640 kilobyte limit, you can use extended memory.

With extended memory, additional memory is added to the computer in the form of memory chips. With most computers, you can add up to 32 megabytes of extended memory (depending on the upgrade limitations of the computer). It costs roughly fifty bucks per megabyte. To use this additional memory, you must install an extended memory manager (which is included with MS-DOS 5.0 and Windows), and you must have programs designed to use extended memory (such as Microsoft Windows).

Extended memory is the same sort of memory that makes up the one megabyte of base memory that most IBM and compatible computers are equipped with. Extended memory is directly available to the processor in your computer, unlike expanded memory (in which data must be swapped into and out of the base memory). Because of this, extended memory is faster than expanded memory. If needed, you can customize a portion of extended memory to act like expanded memory for use with programs that can use only expanded memory. See also *expanded memory*.

extension   In DOS, each file you create has a unique name. The name consists of two parts: a file name and an extension. The file name can be up to eight characters. The extension (which is optional) can be up to three characters. You cannot use any of the following characters:

. / \ [ ] : * < > | + ; , ?

The extension usually represents the type of file. For example, executable program files (the files you run to start a program) have the extension .EXE or .COM. Files that contain unformatted text have the extension .TXT. Document files often have the extension .DOC.

external drive   A disk drive that is not built into your computer system, but is encased in its own plastic cabinet and connected to the CPU with a cable.

external hard disk   A hard disk drive that sits outside the computer and is connected to the computer with a cable. External hard disk drives usually cost more than equivalent internal drives. However, if there is not enough room in your computer for an internal hard drive, an external drive may be the answer.

 If your computer has an open expansion slot, you may be able to add a 50 or 100 megabyte hard drive to your computer by plugging a hard card expansion board into the slot. Such a board provides a fast hard drive at a price that's competitive with that of internal and external hard drives.

external memory   Extra RAM or ROM, external to the CPU. It may be either on the motherboard or an expansion board.

external modem   A modem allows your computer to communicate through the phone lines with other computers. You can get either of two types of modems: internal or external. An internal modem comes on a card that you can plug into an expansion slot inside of your computer. You can then connect your phone line directly to the modem. An external modem sits outside the computer. It contains three cables. One cable plugs into an electrical outlet to provide a power supply for the modem. A serial cable connects the modem to a serial port on the back of the computer. A third cable connects the modem to a phone jack.

PC

Telephone (optional)

External modem

Phone line

Power source

Which should you buy? If you plan on using your modem on more than one computer, get an external modem. If you want to use the modem on only one computer, internal modems are better; they take up no desk space, require only one cable, and keep the serial port on the back of your computer open so you can connect a different serial device. However, if your computer doesn't have an open expansion slot into which you can plug a modem, you may have to settle for an external modem.

➤

Herein, you will learn just the fax about files, formats, fonts, and other interesting F words.

fax Short for *facsimile*. You can send and receive text and graphics through the phone lines. Most fax machines contain a scanner, a printer, and a modem-like component. When sending a fax, the scanner converts the print or graphics on the page into digitized electrical impulses. The modem-like device converts these digitized impulses into analog signals that can be sent through the phone lines to another fax machine. The receiving fax machine converts the incoming analog signals back into digitized signals. Its internal printer then prints a copy of the text or graphics it received.

You can also use your computer as a fax machine. To do so, you must install a fax card on your computer. If you intend to send and receive faxes, make sure you purchase a card that is capable of doing both. The drawback of fax cards, also called *fax boards*, is that you cannot send handwritten messages unless you have a separate scanner connected to your computer. You can send only files that you can produce on your computer.

feature Each thing that a piece of hardware or software accomplishes is a feature of that product. For example, the capability of a word processing program to insert page numbers in a document is one feature, and its built-in spell checker is another feature. However, the spell checker's tendency to take forever between checking one word and the next, would not be considered a feature unless it were being sold by an ingenious salesman who convinced you that this was a useful aspect of its operation.

feed   To supply data or material to a device. This term is commonly used to describe the process of supplying paper to a printer. For example, many dot-matrix printers use a tractor-feed mechanism that pulls a continuous sheet of paper through the printer. See also *tractor feed*.

female connector   When connecting your computer to a peripheral device (such as a printer or modem), you connect the units using a cable that plugs into a connector on the computer and a connector on the peripheral device. A female connector contains holes into which the pins of the male connector can be plugged.

field   To understand a field, you should first know a little about databases. A database is a tool used for storing, organizing, and retrieving information. It contains one or more records; each record is a collection of information about an individual person or thing. Each piece of information in a record is entered in a field. For example, a field may contain a person's last name, a telephone number, or a street address.

In most database programs, you are asked to assign names to each field. This helps you and the program identify the type of information that goes into each field.

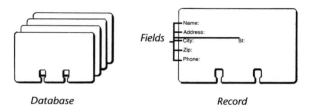

Fields

Database   Record

field upgradable   The capability of a computer to be upgraded at your home or office or at a local shop, as opposed to having to be sent back to the manufacturer. See *upgrade*.

fifth-generation computer   In the computer family tree, this is the next generation to come. As much as we love the integrated circuit technology that made microcomputers—not to mention calculators, programmable TV remotes, and talking shopping carts—a reality, we want more. The next technological revolution will make computers even smaller, faster, and easier to use. Fifth generation machines will be based on greater circuit integration, potentially making computers smaller. It will support parallel processing, which will speed computing time dramatically (assuming we've come up with radical new programming languages that make use of it). Artificial intelligence will play a major role in programming, enabling computers to accept human language input as a standard. These computers and languages are currently in development—but don't throw away your new 486 yet; it will be years before the fifth generation is ready for prime time.

file   Whenever you save a document, spreadsheet, or other item you create, the information is saved in a separate file on disk. You must assign each file a unique name to distinguish it from other files in the same disk and directory. The files you create and save are called *data files*. The disks you purchase to run programs contain *program files*.

file allocation table (FAT)   A map on every disk that tells the operating system where the files on the disk are stored. Think of a disk as a grocery store. Olives are stored in one section, bread crumbs in another, and Miracle Whip in still another. You shop every other day, so you have a good idea of where everything is—you have the store mapped out in your mind.

It's the same with disks. Every disk is divided into sectors that are grouped into clusters. The clusters are like grocery store shelves. When you save a file on disk, it is stored on one or more clusters. Whenever you open a file, your computer looks to the FAT to determine on which clusters the file is stored. It then pulls the required data off the shelves.

And if you're wondering how my grocery store example holds up under scrutiny, look at my grocery store. It has bread crumbs stored in three separate areas: near the Shake 'N Bake, near the bread, and near the bakery items, just as parts of a file are often scattered, or *fragmented,* around the disk.

file attribute   A set of characteristics that tells the computer how to treat a file. Files commonly have the following attributes, which you can turn on or off:

> *Archive.* Indicates if the file has been backed up recently (archive off). If the file has been backed up and has not changed, the archive attribute tells the backup program that it does not need to back up the file. If you change the file and save it, the archive bit is turned back on, so the file will be backed up the next time.

Hidden. If this attribute is on, the file's name will not appear in a directory listing.

System. If this attribute is on, the file is reserved for system use. If you try to use the file, you will receive an error message.

Read Only. If this attribute is on, you will be able to open a file and see its contents, but you will not be able to change the file.

file compression   See *compression.*

file compression utility   A program that compresses and decompresses files according to your commands, in order to save storage space. You can purchase a file compression utility in some utility packages or as a stand-alone program in such packages as PKZip. See also *compression.*

file conversion   See *conversion.*

file deletion   When you *delete* a file from disk, the file's data remains intact. The first letter of the file's name is deleted, the file's name no longer appears in any directory of files, and the area in which the file is stored is marked as free. As long as you don't save another file to disk or copy or move files, you can recover a deleted file. Several utility programs, such as PC Tools and The Norton Utilities, enable you to undelete files. DOS 5.0 also has an undelete feature.
    Do not confuse delete with erase. When you *erase* a file, the file's data usually does not remain intact.

file extension   See *extension.*

file format   Whenever you create a file (such as a memo or a picture) in a program, that file is saved with codes that tell the program how to display, print, and process the file. If you want to open the file in another program, you must first convert the file into a format that the other program understands. Many times, you can tell a file's format and/or function by its extension, as shown in the following table. In many programs, whenever you save a file, the program automatically adds an extension to the file's name that indicates the file's format.

Table F.1   Extensions commonly used for DOS files.

Extension	File Type
.BAK or .BK!	Backup file, the previous version of an edited file.
.BAT	Batch file. Contains a series of commands that can be executed by running the file.
.BMP	Bit-mapped graphics file. Contains a map of all the dots that make up a graphic image. These files are usually large.
.C	C programming language file.
.COM	Command file. A program file that can be executed by entering the name of the file without its extension.
.DAT	Data file.
.DBF	dBASE file. dBASE is a database program.
.DOC	Document file. Commonly used for files created in a word processing program, such as Microsoft Word.

continues

Table F.1 continued.

Extension	File Type
.EXE	Executable program file. The program can be run by entering the file's name without its extension.
.HLP	Help file.
.PCX	Graphics file for files created using PC Paintbrush.
.TIF	Tagged Image File Format. A format commonly used for bit-mapped graphics. Each file contains a map of all the dots that make up the graphic image. These files are usually huge.
.TXT	Text file. Text files usually have no obscure formatting attached, so you can open them in almost any application program.
.WKS, .WK1, .WK2, .WK3	Lotus 1-2-3 spreadsheet files.
.WP or .WPF	WordPerfect document file.
.WS	WordStar document file.

file fragmentation   As you save files on disk, the files are saved in a series of neighboring clusters. If you delete a file, a gap is formed between clusters. The next time you save a file, the program will try to fit the file into the gap. If the file is too large to fit in the gap, the program stores as much of the file in the gap as can fit. The rest of the file is stored in the next free cluster. In such a case, the file is said to be *fragmented*; it is no longer stored in neighboring clusters. See *defragment*.

file locking   If you have files that contain sensitive data, you may want to lock the files to prevent other users from viewing or changing them. With some programs, such as WordPerfect, you can lock a file by protecting it with a password. If your program does not have a password-protection feature, you can purchase a separate program that allows you to lock your files.

file manager   A program or a feature of a program that allows you to copy, move, and delete files on disk. Many file managers also allow you to manage directories on a disk; you can add, delete, or move directories to restructure the directory tree. The term is also used to refer to a flat-file database, because this type of database program works with information one file at a time. See also *flat-file database*.

file name   In DOS, you must give each file you create a unique name to distinguish it from other files on the same drive and directory. The name consists of two parts: a file name and an extension. The file name can be up to eight characters. The extension (which is optional) can be up to three characters. You cannot use any of the following characters:

" . / \ [ ] : * < > ¦ + ; , ?

Typically, the file name is used to identify the file, whereas the extension is used to indicate the type of file. For example, in the name JOHNSON.MEM, the file name tells me that the file concerns Johnson, and the extension tells me that the file is a memo.

file protection   Precautions taken to ensure that the data in a file is not erased or tampered with. An easy way to protect data on floppy disks is to activate the write protect feature. On a 3.5" disk, there is a tab in one corner that you can slide back, opening a little "window" and making it impossible to delete or record files on the disk. On a 5.25" disk, there is a notch you cover with a piece of tape or an adhesive tab provided in the box of disks. There are also file protection features built into some software, which enable you to assign a password to a file. The file can only be opened using the password.

file recovery   File recovery is a broad term used to describe any method for getting back a file that's been lost or damaged, including the following methods:

> *Undelete.* If you delete a file by mistake, only its name is deleted from any directory listing. The information contained in the file remains intact until you save or move a file onto the area that stores the file. You can purchase an undelete utility to rename the file and retrieve its contents.

> *Recover.* Sometimes an undelete utility cannot undelete the entire file as a single unit. Somewhere along the line, your computer lost track of the pieces of the file. With a manual undelete, you must piece the file together, which can take some time.

> *Restore.* If you've kept backup copies of your original files, either by copying the files or using a backup program, you can restore the files to disk. The drawback of restoring files is that the restored files will not contain any changes you've made since the last backup. But this is generally the easiest way to recover lost data.

file server   A large, central storage device in a network. The file server is a central computer in the network that stores data for all the users in the network. When an individual computer requests information, the file server delivers it. Think of it as an office gofer.

file transfer   Commonly used to describe the process of sending a file from one computer to another over the phone lines by way of modem or between two computers connected with a null-modem cable. However, in the broad sense, the term is used to describe any movement of a file. For example, in Word 5.0, you choose the Transfer command to open a file (from disk into memory) or to save a file (from memory to disk).

FileMaker Pro   A flat-file database program from Claris Corporation, which has won much popularity due to its ease of learning and use. Available for Macintosh and Windows.

fill   In graphics programs, the term *fill* describes the process of pouring color or shade into an enclosed object. Many graphics programs provide a paint roller or paint-can icon that you can move to the enclosed area and tip. The paint spreads out to fill the entire area.

In spreadsheet programs, you can use the fill feature to enter a series of values into a group of cells. You enter the starting value (such as the first date you want entered), the ending value (such as the last date), and the increment (such as every 7 days). The program enters all the values into a continuous sequence of cells.

filter   Any process that allows only specified information to be processed, displayed, or printed. The filter screens out unwanted values, names, or other data.

The most common filter you will encounter is a file list filter. This filter shows only the names of those files that match the entry you specify. For example, if you want to view a list of only those files that have the .DOC extension, you would specify *.DOC in the file list filter. The asterisk (*) stands in for any characters before the period.

fixed disk See *hard disk*.

flat-file database A database is a tool used for storing, organizing, and retrieving information. A flat-file database is similar to a Rolodex; each *record* contains the same type of information: for example, a person's name, title, phone number, and address. Each piece of information is stored in a separate, named *field*. Because flat-file databases have an overall structure, finding stored records is easy. However, if you need to create invoices or reports that pull information from more than one database, you should get a relational database. See also *free-form database* and *relational database*.

flatbed scanner A scanner allows you to transfer data on paper into electronic data that your computer can use. For example, you can scan a picture and then display it in a graphics program in order to modify it. A flatbed scanner allows you to scan a full page at a time; the process of scanning a page is similar to that of making a Xerox copy. See also *scanner*.

flicker The thousands of pixels that make up the image on a monitor don't stay consistently bright until a new image comes on the screen. They have to be constantly recharged so that they fool the human eye into thinking they're consistently bright. If the pixels aren't recharged quickly enough, your eye will notice the alternating dark and light areas on the screen, perceiving this as an annoying flicker. See also *raster display*.

floppy disk A wafer encased in plastic that magnetically stores data (the facts and figures you enter and save). Floppy disks are the disks you insert in your computer's floppy disk drive (located on the front of the computer). These disks owe their name to their early form; they were floppy—you could bend them. Now there are two kinds of floppy disks. The early version (the 5.25" disk) is still floppy, but the newer version (the 3.5" disk) is enclosed in a stiff plastic case. The term *floppy* is used to distinguish these disks from *hard disks*. Hard disks are typically fixed in position; you don't insert and remove them from the drive.

The wafer inside the disk casing is what actually stores the data. It is a round piece of mylar (plastic) that's covered with magnetic particles. When you insert the disk into the drive, the read/write head(s) in the drive can read and write information onto the exposed areas of the disk.

Just as you can store sounds on a cassette tape, you can store data on a floppy disk and later play back the data on your computer. The amount of data each disk can store depends on several factors: the disk's physical size (3.5" or 5.25"), the number of sides on which data is stored, its density (high density or double density), and how the disk is formatted (organized). The following table shows the various amounts of data each disk can store. Keep in mind that a kilobyte (1K) is equal to 1,024 characters; a megabyte (1M) is about 1,000 kilobytes.

Table F.2   Common floppy disk storage capacities.

Computer	Disk Type	Disk Size	Disk Capacity
Macintosh	Single-sided Double-density (SS/DD)	3.5"	400K

continues

Table F.2   Continued.

Computer	Disk Type	Disk Size	Disk Capacity
Macintosh	Double-sided Double-density (DS/DD)	3.5"	800K
Macintosh	Double-sided High-density (DS/HD)	3.5"	1.4M
IBM	Double-sided Double-density (DS/DD)	5.25"	360K
IBM	Double-sided High-density (DS/HD)	5.25"	1.2M
IBM	Double-sided Double-density (DS/DD)	3.5"	720K
IBM	Double-sided High-density (DS/HD)	3.5"	1.44M

Floppy disks are fragile. If you damage the magnetic coating on the disk, you destroy the data as well. Because of that, you should follow a few simple precautions when handling disks:

> Keep the disk in its paper sleeve except when using it. Dust, dirt, food, and drinks can damage the disk.

When labeling a disk, write on the label before sticking it on the disk. Any pressure from a pen can damage a disk. If you've already stuck the label on, use a felt-tip pen to write on the label.

Keep disks away from heat. Heat can warp a disk, just as heat can melt a cassette tape left on the dashboard of your car in mid-summer.

Keep disks away from magnetic fields. Because disks store information magnetically, a magnet can erase data from the disk.

floppy disk drive   See *disk drive*.

flow   In a program, *flow* refers to the progression from one instruction to another within the program. In word processing and desktop publishing, *flow* refers to the process of wrapping text around a graphic object on the same page. See also *wraparound type*.

font   Rhymes with Vermont. A font is any set of characters that have the same typeface and type size. For example, Helvetica 12-point is a font. Helvetica is the typeface, and 12-point is the size. For reference, there are 72 points in an inch. Following are some examples of fonts:

`Courier 12-point`

Helvetica 16-point

Garamond 18-point

Some programs refer to a font as a set of characters having the same typeface, type size, and type style. So Helvetica 12-point italic is considered a font separate from Helvetica 12-point bold. Other programs treat the type style as an attribute that can be added or removed to enhance the basic font. See also *bit-mapped font, built-in font,* and *outline font.*

footer   Any text that appears at the bottom of a page of a document.

footnote   A note at the bottom of a page that explains a word, phrase, quote, or concept mentioned on the same page. A superscripted number usually appears after the item being footnoted. This number corresponds to the footnote number at the bottom of the page.

footprint   The space that a computer takes up on your desk. Many computer manufacturers advertise computers with a small footprint. Although the small footprint may save a few inches of space, it may also restrict the number of devices (such as printers, modems, and memory cards) you can add to the system later.

forced page break   Most programs automatically divide the text into pages according to the page length settings you specify. At times, you may want to divide the pages differently to make sure two items appear on the same page. In such cases, you must create a forced page break.

forecasting   In spreadsheet programs, setting up scenarios that help plan for the future. If you provide the computer with past trends, data, and a series of conditions, it will extrapolate likely future scenarios. You can then use these in making more subjective predictions.

foreground colors   In many programs, you can control the colors of the display or printout. You control the colors by setting the *background color,* the *foreground color,* and the *foreground pattern.* The background color is the color on which everything else is set. For example, if you were coloring on a piece of paper, the background color would be the color of the paper. The foreground color would be the color of your crayon. And the foreground pattern would be the marks you made on the paper.

foreground operations   Many programs allow you to continue working while the program carries out some time-consuming task, such as printing a document or performing a series of complex calculations. In such programs, you are said to be working in the foreground, while the computer works in the *background*.

format disk   Before you can use a disk to store your data (facts and figures), the disk must be formatted. Formatting organizes the storage areas on disk so data can be stored in known locations.

If you do accidentally format a disk, don't do anything—particularly, don't panic. If you haven't turned off your computer, don't; turning the computer on and off may make things worse. You can usually recover an accidentally formatted disk if you know what you are doing and you have a good utility program, such as PC Tools or The Norton Utilities. If you don't know what you're doing, find someone who does. If all else fails, you can hire a data recovery service. It's well worth the price.

Most formatting operations destroy all data on the disk. Be careful not to format your hard disk by mistake or format a floppy disk that contains files you will need. In general, you format a disk only the first time you use it. If you want to use the disk to store a different set of files, delete the existing files instead of formatting the disk.

format file   Most files consist of both text and codes that tell the program how to handle the text. For example, a margin code tells the program where to set the margins, and a boldface code tells the program to print a set of characters in bold type.

Formatting a file, then, consists of laying out pages and styling the text.

formula   Formulas are used in spreadsheet programs to perform calculations. The spreadsheet consists of columns and rows that intersect to form cells. You can enter numbers into the cells and then use formulas to perform calculations using the numbers. For example, say you enter a series of values in cells A1, B1, and C1. You can determine the average of these values by entering the formula +(A1+B1+C1)/3 in cell D1. The formula in cell D1 tells the spreadsheet to add the values in cells A1, B1, and C1 and divide the total by 3. The result is then inserted in cell D1.

Spreadsheet programs typically perform a series of operations in a formula in the following order, giving some operators *precedence* over others:

1st	Exponential equations
2nd	Multiplication and division
3rd	Addition and subtraction

This is important to keep in mind when you are creating equations, because the *order of operations* determines the result. For example, if you want to determine the average of the values in cells A1, B1, and C1, and you enter +A1+B1+C1/3, you'll get the wrong answer. The value in C1 will be divided by 3, and that result will be added to A1+B1. To determine the total of A1 through C1 first, you must enclose that group of values in parentheses: +(A1+B1+C1)/3. In other words, you control the order of operations with parentheses.

FORTRAN A high-level language developed in the 1960s. As you might guess from the source of its name, formula translator, this language is used mainly to write scientific, mathematical, and other technical applications. See also *high-level language*.

fourth-generation computer We currently use fourth-generation computers. They replaced third-generation computers in the 1970s when the microchip was perfected. The microchip could hold thousands of circuits on its tiny surface and gave us the microcomputer.

fractals Groups of shapes that are not identical to each other but bear a patternlike similarity. These have always existed in nature—think of snowflakes, the leaves on a tree, the shape of a coastline—but they were endorsed with this official title in 1975 by a French mathematician. In computing, fractals can be created with software programs and are used by designers and illustrators to create interesting and beautiful patterns.

fragmentation See *file fragmentation*.

free-form database A database is a tool used for storing, organizing, and retrieving information. Free-form databases are similar to Post-it notes and scraps of paper on your desk; any piece of paper can store any type of information. Because of this, the database is very flexible. The hard part is finding information once you've stored it. See also *flat-file database* and *relational database*.

freeware Copyrighted programs that you can use for free. You cannot sell the software for profit.

Although freeware is free, there is sometimes a cost. Because it is rarely tested for computer viruses and Trojan Horse programs, using freeware is like riding a motorcycle without a helmet. Before using freeware, you should have a good backup of everything on your system, and you should check the source of the freeware. If you have a virus-detection program, run a check on the disk before using it.

full justification   In word processing and desktop publishing programs, you can have the program adjust the space between characters and words to make each line of text the same width. For example, in most newspapers and magazines, the text is laid out in columns of a uniform width. This is called *full justification*.

function keys   The 10 *F* keys on the left side of the keyboard or twelve *F* keys at the top of the keyboard. *F* keys are numbered F1, F2, F3, and so on. These keys are used to enter various commands in a program. The function of each key depends on the program in which you are working. For example, in most programs, the F1 key causes the program to display a help screen. In WordPerfect, however, F1 is used to cancel an operation. Most programs allow you to use the function keys alone or in combination with the Alt, Shift, and Ctrl keys to use additional functions.

Some keyboards are now offering a function key arrangement that puts the 12 function keys at the top of the keyboard and a duplicate set on the left side of the keyboard. And you thought you didn't have enough function keys!

fuzzy logic   A method of reasoning in which conclusions aren't always true or false. Sometimes they're probably true or probably false. It's an important development in artificial intelligence, because human reasoning often works this way, as opposed to the computer's rigid on/off, yes/no structure. Incorporating fuzzy logic into the way a computer processes data means the computer can accept natural language input more easily, and can reach more human-like conclusions in expert systems, such as medical prognosis and financial forecasting.

➤

If you're not afraid of ghosts, but gigabytes scare you to death, enter the gooey room of G words. One of the words might just grab you.

ghost If you crank the brightness control on your screen and leave the same image on the screen for a long time, the image can get burned into the screen, causing a ghost image to appear. To prevent this from happening, you can turn off your monitor or turn down the screen brightness whenever you leave your computer. You can also purchase screen-saver programs that blank the screen or display moving images on the screen when you don't use the keyboard for a specified amount of time. See also *screen saver*.

GIF A popular type of file, known by its .GIF extension, that saves graphics in a space-efficient format that can be easily copied, transferred, transmitted via modem, and read by many different software programs.

gigabyte A lot of bytes. A byte is eight bits, which are used to store information for a single character. A kilobyte is 1,024 bytes. A megabyte is 1,048,576 bytes (about one million bytes). A gigabyte is 1,073,741,824 bytes (about one billion bytes). This is nearly equivalent to a half-million pages of double-spaced text.

GIGO   Short for Garbage In, Garbage Out. An axiom of the savvy computer user, it means that the information you get out of your computer will only be as good as the information you put in. Although the computer is full of tools that can help speed up, simplify, or otherwise help you get your work done, it can't do the thinking for you.

glare   The distracting reflection of light off a computer monitor's screen. It can be reduced by using a glare filter and by adjusting your monitor so that it doesn't directly face or sit beneath a light source. I've heard that you can use a nylon stocking as a cheap subsitute for a glare filter, but if you can afford the computer, surely you can shell out another few bucks for a good filter.

global   A change or choice applied universally throughout an entire program or file.

global format   Most files consist of text and formatting codes that tell the program how to handle the text. When you change text, you are *editing* the document. When you change the way text is laid out or styled, you are making a *format* change. A global format consists of any settings that affect the entire document. For example, if you change the margins in a document or change the capitalization of a word throughout the document, you are entering a *global formatting change*.

glossary   A storage area in a program that contains text you often use. Say you are writing a contract and you use the name Marion Johnson throughout the contract. Instead of typing Marion Johnson each time, you can type it once and store it as a glossary entry represented by the letters MJ. To type Marion Johnson, you simply type mj and press a special key. The program automatically replaces the mj you typed with Marion Johnson.

Goto   Many programs offer a Goto feature which allows you to quickly jump to a specific place in a file. For instance, in a word processing program, the Goto feature may ask you to specify the page you want to go to. In a spreadsheet program, the Goto feature will ask you which cell or group of cells you want to go to.

grabber   In some programs, if you want to move an object (a selection of text, a group of cells, or a graphic element) from one area to another, you have to enter a move command that deletes the information from the source and pastes it in the destination. In other programs, if you have a mouse, you can drag the information where you want it. When you select the object you want to move and move the mouse pointer over it, the mouse pointer turns into a hand or some other icon that lets you grab the object. To grab the object, you hold down the mouse button, drag the object to where you want it, and drop it into place by releasing the mouse button.

grammar checker   A program that checks for incomplete sentences, passive voice, awkward phrases, subject-verb disagreement, wordiness, and other grammar problems. Many of these programs also provide some indication of the level of audience that will be able to understand the language in the document.

grandparent   The oldest backup file in a group of related files. It's used when you want to save a version of each stage of a file as it grows.

graphical user interface (GUI)   Pronounced gooey. Every computer needs an operating system that provides instructions telling the computer how to accept your input, produce output, and process data. Some operating systems, such as DOS, expect you to know what you're doing. The screen greets you with brief text-based prompts, requiring you to type the correct command.

Graphical user interfaces, such as Windows and GeoWorks, give your operating system a friendlier face. Instead of presenting text-based prompts, the interface provides windows, menus, and graphic icons that represent commands and programs. Instead of having to type a command, you enter the command by selecting an icon or by selecting an option from a menu.

Pull-down menu   *Icons represent programs.*

graphics Anything having to do with pictures rather than text. There are two types of programs that let you create graphics: draw programs and paint programs. Draw programs let you create line drawings using objects such as circles, ovals, squares, and lines. Draw programs treat each graphic object as a mathematical formula. This formula contains codes that tell the program how to display and print the object. For instance, the formula for a circle contains the position and diameter of the circle. Draw programs are effective for drawings that use geometric shapes, such as floor plans, city skylines, and flow charts.

Paint programs are much better than draw programs for creating freehand drawings, such as cartoons, portraits, or landscape paintings. With a paint program, you create a picture by turning a series of pixels (on-screen dots) on or off or by changing their color or shading. You can then modify the picture by changing individual pixels or by brushing pixels on the screen. This gives you much more control over the final product. Unlike draw programs, paint programs do not treat each shape you place on-screen as a separate object. For example, if you place a circle on top of a square in a paint program, you cannot choose to move or delete just the circle.

graphics accelerator board   A hardware add-on that revs up a computer's graphics capabilities. It handles all the graphics processing so the CPU can concentrate on other things, and enables the monitor to display and manipulate graphics faster. Even if you're not a computer artist, you can benefit from an accelerator board if you use a graphical user interface, like Microsoft Windows, because of all the power needed to redraw the graphics.

graphics editor   A program that contains tools for resizing, recoloring, rotating, and otherwise editing computer graphics.

graphics mode   Many programs offer two ways to display information on-screen: text mode or graphics mode. In text mode, all on-screen text appears basically the same. The program may use colors to distinguish between normal, bold, and italic text. In graphics mode, however, the program will attempt to show graphically how the text will appear in print. If you have a mouse, the mouse pointer will usually appear as a rectangle in text mode, but as an arrow in graphics mode. In graphics mode, it usually takes longer to update the screen when you page down or scroll, because with graphics, the computer must process much more data in order to generate the display.

graphics spreadsheet   A spreadsheet program that displays information graphically on-screen. This enables you to see what worksheets and charts look like before you print them, so that you can change font sizes, styles, background patterns, and chart formats umpteen times without wasting paper.

graphics tablet   An input device used for freeform drawing and for scanning images into a computer. It works with a stylus, which is a pen-like pointer with an electrical tip. At each point of the tablet's surface over which the stylus passes, the tablet receives an electrical signal that corresponds to a specific on-screen pixel position. The digitized image then appears on the screen.

gray scale   A series of shades from white to black. Graphics programs often specify the number of gray scales you can use: commonly 16 or 256. The more gray scales you use, the more realistic the image will look. However, as the number of gray scales increases, the amount of memory and disk space required to store the image also increases.

Greek text   To display text in such a way that the text cannot be read. Text is commonly displayed in pseudo-Latin or is displayed as gray bars. This focuses your attention on the design of the page rather than on its content.

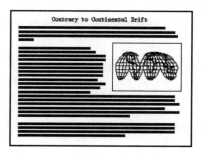

grid   A background that resembles graph paper and helps you position objects on a page on-screen. Many business presentation graphics programs and desktop publishing programs contain snap-to grids to help you position objects precisely. When you move the object near one of the grid lines, it snaps to the line.

grounding   Establishing a connection to a zero-voltage base in order to neutralize an electrical charge on a device so you don't zap it. If you ever repair or upgrade a computer, take the precaution of turning off and unplugging the machine before you mess with it. In addition, stick your *left* hand in your pocket whenever your other hand is down amongst the circuitry. That way, if an electrical current does pass through you, it will not take a path through your heart.

group icon   Windows jargon for an icon that represents several related program-item icons. Click on the group icon for Paradox for Windows, for example, and a window will open up containing six program-item icons: Paradox, Configuration Utility, Serial Number utility, Table Repair Utility, Readme, and Helpme. Group icons give you a good overall view of what programs are in your system without looking at every program item to find what you're looking for.

groupware   Software created especially for use on a network by a group of people working together, instead of by an individual user.

gutter   A printing term referring to the white space at the innermost edges of the facing pages of a book. In desktop publishing and word processing programs, you often have the option to increase the gutter in a document, in case you plan to have it bound in book form. That way, you won't lose all your inner margin space in the binding.

GW-BASIC   The version of BASIC that ships with IBM-compatible PCs bundled with MS-DOS. The GW stands for Gee Whiz; Microsoft gave it this name when they developed this version of BASIC, because it contained exclusive new programming features that other versions of BASIC didn't have. See also *BASIC*.

➤

If you don't know a hacker from a hocker, if you can't get a handle on halftones, or if you think it's barbaric to hang an indent, these definitions just might help.

hacker   Slang term for someone who is particularly skilled and knowledgeable about computers and who loves to play on computers. Often used to describe someone who can perform unusual tricks with a computer, such as breaking into other computers. Hackers are not always thought of as nice people.

half-height drive   A newer drive that is half as tall as its older brother. Early 5.25" disk drives were about 3.5 inches tall. Newer 5.25" drives, called half-height drives, are about 1 2/3 inches tall.

halftone   Take a close look at a photograph in a newspaper. You'll notice that the photograph is printed as a collection of dots. This is a *halftone image*. In dark areas of the photograph, the dots are large and close together. In light areas, the dots are small and far apart.

   In the old days, halftones were created by photographing an image through a mesh. The mesh made the image appear as a collection of small dots in the photo. With computers, photos are scanned in and then converted electronically into halftones. Dark areas in the image are transformed into collections of tightly set big, black dots. Light areas are transformed into loosely set small dots.

Why use halftones? Because photographs don't copy well. If you try to print a copy of a photograph, some of the light areas will get lost, and the dark areas may turn out completely black. With halftones, you have more control over the consistency of the dot patterns.

hand-held computer   A portable, battery-operated computer that fits in the palm of your hand. It may serve as a general-purpose computer, but is usually preprogrammed to perform a certain kind of task. Electronic dictionaries, language translators, and day planners are just a few of the popular hand-held computers on the market today.

hand-held scanner   A scanner that looks and moves sort of like a mouse. In addition to rollers on the bottom that enable you to move it over the image, there is a scanning head that digitizes the image into data the computer can understand and store as a file.

handle   In graphics and desktop publishing programs, you work with various *objects* on-screen, such as a line, a circle, a box containing text, or an entire graphic image. When you select an object (usually by clicking on it with the mouse), an outline appears around the object, and two or more black squares appear. These squares are called handles.

Handles allow you to resize or reshape an object. You move the mouse pointer over one of the handles, hold down the mouse button, and drag the handle to enlarge or shrink the object. Most lines have two handles; you can drag a handle at either end of the line to make it longer or shorter. Two-dimensional objects, such as circles and squares, have eight handles—one at each corner and one at each side. You can drag a side handle to change only one dimension of the object—its width or height. You can drag a corner handle to change the width and height at the same time.

Handles

handshaking   Before two computer devices can communicate, they need to acknowledge one another
and agree on the rules they will follow to transfer
information. The method they use to do this is called
handshaking. There are two types of handshaking—
hardware and *software.* With hardware handshaking,
the two devices send signals over a special wire to
indicate when they are ready to send or receive data.
With software handshaking, two programs send
signals to agree on the language and rules of communication.

hanging indent   In most word processing programs,
you can create indented paragraphs, usually for use
in lists. With hanging indents, the first line of the

paragraph is set against the left margin or tab stop and subsequent lines are indented. This format is useful for creating bulleted or numbered lists. The following example shows a hanging indent in action:

- In this example, the first line is set flush left so that the bullet hangs out from the left. The rest of the text is indented a few spaces in from the bullet.

Also, the entries in this dictionary are in hanging indent style.

hard copy   A printed version of a document, spreadsheet, or other piece you've created on the computer.

hard disk   A hard disk acts as a giant floppy disk drive that contains nonremovable disks. The hard disk drive is either internal (inside your computer) or external (connected to one of the computer's ports with a cable). The disk drive contains several stiff metal disks (usually aluminum) called *platters* on which data is stored. The platters are housed, along with the read/write heads, in a sealed unit—you cannot insert and eject the disk as you can with floppy disk drives.

Although a hard disk consists of several platters, the disk itself is treated as a single disk, and is assigned the letter C (the letters A and B are reserved for the floppy disk drives). However, you can partition the disk into *logical disk drives*. For example, you may have three hard disk drives—C, D, and E. Don't be fooled; the three drive letters apply to the same physical disk. They merely represent the various storage areas on the disk.

Even the smallest hard disk can store large amounts of data. For example, a 20-megabyte hard disk can store the same amount of data as sixty 5.25", double-density floppy disks or twenty-five 3.5" double-density disks.

Disk platters store data.

Head arms

Head actuator

Read/write head

hard disk backup   When you install a program or save a file on your hard disk, you can be fairly certain that the files will be there when you need them. In general, hard disks are reliable. However, as with any device, you have to be careful. You may unintentionally delete a file or several files, you may lose data in the event of a power surge or outage or some other natural occurrence, or the disk may wear out or fail for some unknown reason. Whatever the cause, you should have at least one copy of the files you need.

To create these copies, you should purchase a hard disk backup program. A backup program creates copies of specified files in a compressed form, so you can fit the copies on fewer disks than if you had simply copied files from the hard disk to floppy disks. If a file on your hard disk gets damaged or deleted, you can then restore the file using the backup program and the backup copies of your files. If you have DOS, you already have a backup program, but it's a little more difficult to use than any of the devoted backup programs on the market.

hard hyphen   Word processing programs automatically wrap text in a paragraph from one line to the next. If a hyphenated word is at the end of a line, the program may split the word at the hyphen. But what if you don't want a hyphenated word (or a date) to be split? Say you want the term Hewlett-Packard to appear all on the same line. In such cases, you can insert a hard hyphen. A hard hyphen acts as just another character in the word, telling the program to treat it as a single word.

hard space   Word processing programs automatically wrap text in a paragraph from one line to the next. If a word doesn't fit on one line, the program breaks the line at a space and moves the following word to the beginning of the next line. However, you may have a term that you want to appear on a single line, such as Barnum & Bailey. In such cases, you can insert a hard space at each place where you would normally enter a space. The hard space looks like a space but acts as a character, so the term is treated as a single word.

hardware   The physical equipment that makes up a computer, including the disk drive, monitor, keyboard, mouse, modem, printer, cables, and so on. These items are distinguished from software—the instructions that tell the computer what to do. Think of it in human terms. Your hardware is your body and mind; software is your education.

hardware platform   The structure of a specific computer system. For example, an IBM PC (Personal Computer) represents a hardware platform. This platform can run programs written specifically for this platform, but it cannot run programs designed for a different platform—for example, programs designed to run on Macintosh computers.

Harvard Graphics   A popular program from Software Publishing Corporation, that is mainly used to produce business presentation graphics like charts, slides, etc.

Hayes-compatible modem   Whenever you use a modem to communicate with another computer over phone lines, you must enter specific commands to dial the phone, answer incoming calls, and so on. The commands may vary depending on your modem and the program you use. The most common set of commands used for modem communications is the Hayes command set.

Why is this important? To communicate via modem, you need a modem and a communications program. Most communications programs use the Hayes command set. If you purchase a modem that is not Hayes compatible, you may not be able to use many of the communications programs on the market, such as Procomm Plus; you may have to settle for a second-rate communications program.

head crash   Also known as a *disk crash*. A head crash occurs when the read/write head in the disk drive falls on the disk. This would be like dropping a phonograph needle on a record. A disk crash can destroy any data stored where the read/write head fell on the disk.

A disk crash commonly occurs if the computer is bumped when it is turned off. With most newer computers, when you turn off the computer, it automatically *parks* the disk heads over an area of the disk that does not contain data. That way, if the disk heads fall, they won't destroy data. If you have an older machine, you may have to purchase a utility program (such as PC Tools or The Norton Utilities) to park the disk heads.

head seek time   See *seek time*.

header   Any text that appears at the top of every page of a document. Headers commonly contain the name of the document, the date, and a code that inserts the current page number.

Hercules Graphics Adapter   A board that plugs into the inside of your computer and gives a single color monitor the power to display pictures as well as text. With early monochrome monitors, you could view only text on-screen. By adding a Hercules graphics card to your system, you can display black-and-white graphic images on-screen.

hertz   Technically, hertz is a unit used to measure the number of times an electronic wave repeats each second. Practically speaking, hertz is used to measure the speed at which a unit operates. For example, computer speeds are often expressed in megahertz (abbreviated MHz). As shown in the following table, speed is related to the type of processor the computer uses.

Table H.1   Time needed to add 10,000 numbers.

Microprocessor	Speed	Time needed
8088	4.77 MHz	128 seconds
80286	12 MHz	32 seconds
80386	20 MHz	8 seconds

Hewlett-Packard   A major manufacturer of minicomputers, microcomputers, laser printers, and other computer-related equipment.

hidden codes   In word processing programs, you perform two basic operations: you type and style (format) the text. When you style the text (for example, change the margins or boldface a word), the program adds formatting codes that tell it how to display and print the text. Usually, these codes are hidden so that they do not clutter the screen and make the text difficult to read. In some programs, such as WordPerfect, you can view the codes on-screen and edit or delete them.

hidden file   Also called *invisible file*. A file whose name you cannot view in a normal directory list. Files are commonly hidden to prevent users from deleting or changing the files. For example, DOS hides two files:IO.SYS and MSDOS.SYS. If you were to delete, move, or change these files in any way, you could not boot your computer using the disk which contains these files. If you tried to boot your computer, you would get a message like

"INSERT SYSTEM DISK IN DRIVE A: AND PRESS ENTER"

How are files hidden? Files contain four attributes that tell the program how to treat the file. One of these attributes is the Hidden attribute. You can enter a DOS command or use a utility program to turn this attribute on (hiding the file) or to turn it off (revealing the file).

Hierarchical File System (HFS)   A system used to organize files on a hard disk in a Macintosh computer. The system allows you to store files in a series (hierarchy) of folders. For example, if you were a lawyer, you might have one folder that stored all the files for one of your clients. Within this folder, you may have another folder that contains only those files dealing with a particular case.

With the old MFS (Macintosh Filing System), you could organize your files into folders (using the Finder), but when you attempted to open or save a file, the names of all the files on disk would appear. With the introduction of hard disks, which are capable of storing thousands of files, the old method became impractical.

high density   Density is a measure of the amount of data that can be stored per square inch of storage area on the disk. Density is commonly used to refer to different types of floppy disks: single density, low density (or double density), and high density. See also *density*.

high-level programming language   Most of the programming languages you've heard of or used—

BASIC, C++, Fortran, Pascal—fall under this category, as opposed to being low-level programming languages.

This type of language is structured more like human language than like machine language, which is the computer's native tongue. One instruction in a high-level language corresponds to several instructions in a machine language. This means that you don't have step-by-step control over the micrprocessor, but you can still program even if you don't have intensive knowledge of the microprocessor. High-level programming language also makes it possible to write a well-organized program in far fewer lines than it would take using a low-level language.

It's sort of like being the Queen of England instead of a working stiff. If you decide you want to try wheat toast this morning instead of your customary crumpet, you tell the lady-in-waiting, who summons the butler, who goes back to the kitchen and tells the cook, who sends a maid to the pantry for the bread, etc., etc. If you just got up and made the toast yourself, you'd probably get it a lot faster and toasted just the way you like it—but it would take a lot more effort. See also *low-level language* and *programming*.

high/low/close graph   A graph used in presentation graphics and spreadsheet programs to display a stock's value. The graph shows the highest price of the stock on a given day, its lowest price, and its closing price (the price at the end of the day). Also called a high/low/close/open graph when it displays the value of the stock at the beginning of the day.

highlight   To select a portion of a document, spreadsheet, or database in order to work with that portion. The highlighted area typically appears in reverse video; that is, if text is normally white-on-black, it appears black-on-white when highlighted. The term *highlight* is often used to refer to the cursor, because in some programs the cursor displays the character it is on in reverse video.

holographic storage A hologram is a 3-dimensional image created by a pattern of light recorded on photo-sensitive material. As a medium for data storage, the 3-D nature of holography will enable extraordinary storage capacity once the technology is perfected. (If you think CD-ROMs can store a lot of data, wait until they put this on the market.)

home computer Historically, this term has been used to describe less expensive, less powerful computers, which were specifically designed to be used in the home. However, now that software designed for home use is demanding much more computer power, and business computers are coming down in price, many computers used in the home are actually business computers.

Home key Home is the beginning of the document, the left end of a line, or the upper left corner of the screen. The Home key is the key that takes you there. However, the function of the Home key differs depending on the program. In WordPerfect, for example, you press Home and the left arrow key to go to the left margin, and press Home twice and then press the up arrow key to go to the beginning of the document. In Microsoft Word, you press Home (no left arrow) to go to the left margin; pressing Home a second time does nothing.

host When two or more computers are connected (usually on a network), one computer is typically the host and the others are clients (or guests). Just as a host serves guests at a party, a host computer serves the computers that are connected to it. If you have a background in biology, you may prefer to think of the relationship between connected computers in terms of host and parasite.

housekeeping A variety of activities a computer carries out to prepare a program for use or to enable it to work smoothly. Depending on the computer system, it might include checking the internal clock, verifying that there is enough available RAM before loading a program, identifying available storage to maximize available space, and other transparent yet vital operations.

HyperTalk A language used to write instructions for HyperCard, an easy-to-use application-building program that ships with every Apple Macintosh.

hypertext Throughout this book, we've referred you to other terms in the book. For example, if you look up *3.5" disk*, you're told to look up *floppy disk*. So, you flip the pages looking for *floppy disk*. Wouldn't it be neat if you could go directly to that term by pressing a button?

That's the idea behind hypertext. A document is shown on-screen containing words or cues that link the document to other related documents. To skip to a related document, you simply select one of these hypertext links (usually by clicking on it with your mouse or tabbing to it and pressing Enter). Select the link, and *bam!*, you're there. No flipping pages. No searching through an index. Most newer programs use hypertext links in their help screens. Some CD-ROM disks use it to help you find information in a book. (See example on next page.)

hyphenation In most word processing programs, text is automatically wrapped from one line to the next. If a word does not fit at the end of a line, it is dropped down to the beginning of the next line. Most programs offer an automatic hyphenation feature, which allows you to even out the length of the lines. Instead of moving an entire word from one line to the next, the hyphenation feature breaks the word at the end of the line, adds a hyphen, and moves the rest of the word to the beginning of the next line. If you add text so that the word is not at the end of the line, the program automatically removes the hyphen and joins the parts of the word.

Selecting Basics opens a list of topics concerning basic operations.

Choosing Menus opens a help screen or menus.

The Menus help screen

Did you know that your computer is constantly being interrupted? That it is illegal to type some characters? And that your computer can get infections? The I's have this and more.

I-beam pointer In Macintosh programs and in Microsoft Windows, the mouse pointer turns into an *I* whenever you move it into an area of text. You can then click the mouse button to move the insertion point to that position (the *insertion point* marks the place where text will be inserted). Or, you can hold down the mouse button and drag the mouse to select an area of text. The idea behind the I-beam is that you can accurately position it between characters.

IBM Short for International Business Machines Corporation, the world's largest computer manufacturer. Their strength was built on manufacturing mainframes, but they have a central role in the development of personal computers, and are working to achieve a market share in this arena that matches their technological accomplishments. IBM set the standard for business PCs with the introduction of the IBM Personal Computer in 1981 and has continued to offer successive models that set the standard for personal computers among their competitors and PC users.

IBM PC-compatible computer   A computer that can run programs designed to run on the IBM Personal Computer. Although this term and the term *clone* are often used interchangeably, there's a difference: clones are designed to look and behave as much as possible like an IBM; compatibles, on the other hand, improve on the original, offering additional benefits, such as higher-quality parts, easier upgradability, or more computing power.

IBM Personal Computer   Also known as *IBM PC*. An early personal computer developed by IBM and released in 1981. The PC uses an 8088 microprocessor, which can process 8 bits of data at a time. Early versions of the PC came with 16 kilobytes of memory, which you could expand up to 64 kilobytes. Today, anything less than 640 kilobytes is inadequate. Compared to today's standards, the PC computer is anemic.

IBM Personal Computer AT   Also known as *IBM PC AT*. The AT (Advanced Technology), released in 1984, is a step up from the XT. It uses an 80286 microprocessor and a 16-bit data bus. (The 16-bit data bus allows the AT to process twice as much data at one time as the 8-bit XT.) This combination makes the AT handle data 50 to 75 percent more efficiently than the XT.

IBM Personal Computer XT   Also known as *IBM PC XT*. The XT (eXtended Technology), released in 1983, is a step up from the original PC. It uses the same microprocessor as the original PC (the 8088 processor), but comes with a hard disk drive, room for up to 640 kilobytes of memory, and room for additional expansion cards.

IBM Personal System/1   Also known as *IBM PS/1*. A series of home computers released by IBM in 1990. The PS/1 uses the 80286 microprocessor, and comes equipped with a keyboard and monitor and with

Microsoft Works and Prodigy. Microsoft Works is an integrated software package; that is, it includes a word processor, spreadsheet, calculator, and database. Prodigy is an information service you can connect to via modem over phone lines.

Although PS/1s are okay for casual users, you would probably be better off purchasing a 386SX IBM compatible computer.

IBM Personal System/2   Also known as *IBM PS/2*. IBM's early personal computers were designed with an *open architecture*. This means that IBM made public the specifications used for its system, thus allowing outside manufacturers to develop add-on products for the computer. Although this contributed to the success of the PC, it also allowed other manufacturers to eat into IBM's profits. So IBM introduced the PS/2, which has a *proprietary architecture*; that is, outside manufacturers can use the technology only if they get a license from IBM.

So what does the PS/2 offer? A 3.5" disk drive, VGA graphics display (a detailed color graphics display), and something called a *Micro Channel Bus*. To understand the Micro Channel Bus, think of the cables that connect a computer to its printer, mouse, and keyboard as multilane highways. Most computers are set up with 16 lanes, so 16 bits of data can be exchanged at a time. The Micro Channel Bus gives the computer 32 lanes—so 32 bits of data can be exchanged at a time. However, in order for the computer to communicate with a peripheral device (such as a printer), the device must also be able to handle 32 bits of data.

In answer to IBM's move, third-party vendors have designed a 32-bit bus design of their own called Extended Industry Standard Architecture (EISA). The EISA bus offers the benefits of the Micro Channel bus but also allows 16-bit peripheral devices to be connected to the computer.

icon In graphics environments, such as Microsoft Windows and the Macintosh interface, icons represent programs, windows, and files. Instead of typing a command to run a program or typing the name of a file to open, you select the icon (usually by clicking on it with the mouse).

idle time Any time that a computer or any of its peripherals is waiting to perform its specific function.

IF . . . THEN . . . ELSE A logical statement used in spreadsheets, databases, macros, and programming to determine a course of action. In a spreadsheet, for example, you can use the IF function in an invoice to determine whether a customer needs to pay sales tax:

> IF customer's state is IN
> THEN, multiply the subtotal by .05
> ELSE, multiply the subtotal by 0
> ENDIF

illegal character A character that cannot be used in a specific command or statement. For example, when naming files in DOS, you cannot use the following characters:

> . / \ [ ] : ; * < > | + < ? space

illustration program A program that enables you to draw images in vector format, so that they can be easily manipulated without a lot of distortion. These programs also contain tools for shading, coloring, resizing, and otherwise refining your images with great precision. Illustration programs differ from *paint programs*, which render images in *bitmapped format*, which can't be manipulated as precisely.

image enhancement   Fixing or improving the appearance of a graphic image. Depending on the situation, enhancement might include smoothing out jagged edges, increasing contrast between darks and lights, adjusting colors, and correcting distortions caused by faulty scanning. Some aspects of image enhancement can be done manually in an illustration or paint program. But comprehensive programs, such as Adobe PhotoShop, are designed especially for this purpose.

image processing   An umbrella term for any process that converts an image into digital data and then stores, manipulates, and/or outputs it. Scanning in a photo of yourself and adding a little hair on top could technically be called image processing, but it hardly does justice to the term. It's more commonly used to refer to sophisticated manipulation of digitized images, like examining a piece of forensic evidence using a dedicated image processing program that detects clues invisible to the human eye. In the business world, there are image processing programs that claim to rid your office of all those paper files by scanning in every piece of paper and logging it into a giant database, thereby enabling you to find any document simply by calling it up on-screen.

imagesetter   If you create something on your computer that you want professionally printed, a file of the piece has to be put through an imagesetter. This machine prints the file to paper or film at extremely high resolutions (1200 dots per inch or more, which is at least 300% better than the average laser printer).

Because imagesetters are such specialized and expensive pieces of equipment, you probably won't find one next to the office copier at work, but will have to take the file to a service bureau (a place that specializes in preparing documents to be printed).

impact printer   An impact printer is like a typewriter. It forms a character by slamming a series of pins or an imprint of the character against a print ribbon and onto the paper. The two types of impact printers are *dot-matrix* and *daisywheel*. Impact printers are especially useful for businesses that must print carbon copies of forms.

import   To bring a file created in one program into another program. In order to import a file into a program, the file must be in a format that is compatible with the destination program or the destination program must be able to convert the file into a usable format. If the file is not compatible, you may have to use a conversion program to convert the file from one format to another.

incremental backup   When you back up files, you copy the files, usually from a hard disk, to a removable storage medium, such as a floppy disk or a backup tape. If the original files become damaged, you can then use the backups to help restore the files to what they were when you backed them up.

There are two basic types of backups: *full* and *incremental*. When you perform a full backup, you back up all the files. As the program backs up the files, it marks them to indicate that they have been backed up. If you edit a file, that file is then marked as not backed up. Then the next time you perform a backup, you can perform an incremental backup to back up only those files that have changed since the last backup.

In general, you should perform a full backup every week and an incremental backup every day.

index Most word processing programs allow you to create an index for a book or manuscript. You mark the words you want included in the index and then tell the program to make the index. The program creates an index at the end of the document. The index lists all the words or terms you marked in alphabetical order and adds page numbers showing where the terms appear in the document.

In database programs, an index is used to point out the location of each piece of data. If you search for an item in the database or sort the database to list your entries in a different order, the program uses the index to speed up the operation.

index hole A small hole in the jacket of a floppy disk and the disk itself that lets the computer determine the starting point for the disk. This gives the computer a point of reference for reading the disk.

infection If a computer virus or Trojan Horse enters your computer system, your computer is said to be *infected*. As with any disease, you may not notice any symptoms of the virus at first. It can lay dormant for a long time, waiting for a particular date or waiting for you to press a certain combination of keys. Then it starts deleting your files and causing other problems. See also *Trojan Horse* and *virus*.

Info Select A popular free-form database from Micro Logic Corporation. See also *free-form database*.

information Technically speaking, information is data that has been put into some meaningful form. In common usage, *data* and *information* are used interchangeably.

initialize To prepare to use something. The term *initialize* is most commonly used to describe the process of formatting a disk. You initialize the disk before you can use it. The term is also used to describe the process of preparing a printer for a print job. You can select the type you want to use and then initialize the printer so that it knows which type you selected. See also *format disk*.

inkjet printer   A printer that sprays ink onto the page. Sound messy? It can be if you use cheap paper that sops up the ink. But if you use the right paper, an inkjet printer produces high-resolution output that rivals the output produced by expensive laser printers.

input   Any information you enter into a computer, including information you type, lines you draw, or images you scan. Contrast with output—the information that the computer gives back to you on-screen, in print, or through sound.

input/output system   Also known as *I/O system,* pronounced EYE-oh. The input/output system controls the flow of data between input devices (such as a keyboard and a mouse), output devices (such as a screen and a printer), and the central processing unit. This allows you to communicate with the computer and allows the computer to communicate with you.

Ins key   Also known as the *Insert key*. An editing key on the keyboard. This key is used in many word processing programs to turn Typeover (a.k.a., Overtype) mode on and off. If Typeover mode is off, anything you type is inserted at the cursor, and existing characters move to the right to make room for the inserted text. If Typeover mode is on, anything you type replaces existing text.

   In some word processing programs, the Ins key has a different function. For example, in Microsoft Word 5.0, the Ins key allows you to insert a block of text you copied or deleted. The program inserts the text at the cursor location.

Insert mode   In most programs, you can type text in either of two modes: Insert or Typeover (also referred to as Overtype). In Insert mode, anything you type is inserted at the cursor, and existing characters move to the right to make room for the inserted text. This allows you to insert words, sentences, or other material in the middle of a sentence or paragraph.

In Typeover mode, anything you type replaces existing text. Instead of deleting the current character and inserting a new one, you simply position the cursor on the character you want to replace and type the desired character. Although Typeover mode can be a timesaver, it can also be dangerous, especially if you're a skilled typist who doesn't often glance up at the screen.

insertion point   In Macintosh and Microsoft Windows word processors and desktop publishing programs, a blinking vertical line indicates the place where any characters you type will be inserted. The insertion point will appear anywhere you type text in the document, in a dialog box, or on the input line in the spreadsheet. This line is called the *insertion point*. The insertion point is comparable to the *cursor*.

installation program   When you purchase a computer program, you get one or more disks containing the files that make up the program. With simple programs or older programs, you could usually run the program directly from the floppy disk by entering the required command. With newer, more sophisticated programs, you must install the program files.

The term *installation* makes the process sound like a major ordeal, like installing central air conditioning. Actually, installing a program is simply a matter of copying the program files to another disk (usually a hard disk). Most programs come with a separate installation program that leads you through the process. This program is usually named

INSTALL.EXE or SETUP.EXE or INSTALL.BAT. The program copies the files as needed and asks you a series of questions about your system, such as what type of monitor you have and what type of printer you use.

Why can't you just copy the program files to your hard disk? In some cases, you can. In other cases, the manufacturer compresses the program files in order to fit more files on each disk. In compressed form, the files are unusable. To make the files usable, the installation program decompresses the files as it copies them to the hard disk.

integrated circuit   Also known as IC, and nicknamed *microchip*. A tiny chip (usually made from silicon) that holds a full network of electronic circuits working together to perform a function. It was this technology that made personal computers a reality, because it shrunk the size and increased the speed and reliability of computers so remarkably. See also *microprocessor*, a type of IC that contains a central processing unit for a personal computer.

integrated program   A collection of programs that runs under the umbrella of a single program. Most integrated programs contain a word processing program, a spreadsheet and/or database program, a communications program (for modem communications), and a graphics program. The names of integrated programs usually end with the word *Works*: Microsoft Works, Apple Works, and Lotus Works. Another popular program for IBM and compatible computers is PFS First Choice.

Integrated programs have three basic advantages. First, all programs in the group have a consistent look and feel, making it easy to learn each program. Second, the file formats used in each program are compatible, so you can cut and paste data from one file into another. For example, you can cut a picture created in the graphics program and paste it into a letter created in the word processing program. Third, you get several programs for the price of one.

The main disadvantage is that the several programs you get for the price of one are not the most powerful programs. The word processing program, for example, is usually not as powerful as one you could purchase separately. However, if you use the word processor only for typing letters, and use the spreadsheet only for balancing your checkbook, and you don't draw very complex pictures, an integrated program may be right for you.

integrity   Whenever you save, move, or change a file or any collection of data, there is an outside chance that the file can get messed up. A piece of the file can get lost, or the computer can lose track of an individual unit of data. It's rare, but it does happen. In such cases, the data is said to have lost its *integrity*— it is no longer a complete, unified collection of data.

Intel Corporation   A major manufacturer best known in the personal computing industry for their family of microprocessors. For a rundown of Intel microchips, see *microprocessor*.

intelligent database   A database program that goes beyond the call of duty to locate the information you're searching for, even if you don't ask in the most logical way. In addition to traditional search methods like seeking a match between the criteria you provide and the data in the database, an intelligent database also searches based on preprogrammed rules and conditions you established earlier for how to search.

For example, the database program Q&A is an intelligent database. It contains a feature called Intelligent Assistant, which understands about 600 words and phrases, and can be "taught" new words. So instead of using the unfriendly search options box, where you have to remember a slew of symbols (like *&A;B;C*, *<+C*, and *MAXn*), you can open the

Intelligent Assistant and type, "Who has the largest order?" or "How many customers named Carter live in Chicago?" If you type anything the Intelligent Assistant doesn't understand, it will ask you further questions about it. Intelligent Assistant takes some getting used to, to discover its range of vocabulary and to teach it any new words you plan to use a lot. But as you can see, it's a far more attractive proposition than the search box if you plan to request a lot of searches and create a lot of reports.

interactive program   A program that allows the user to control the direction that the program takes. Interactive programs commonly display on-screen *prompts* asking the user for input in order to decide how to carry out a particular task. Most modern programs are interactive.

I have recently seen interactive books for children that allow the child to determine the outcome of the story. For example, the story may have Goldilocks standing in front of a door; the child is given the choice of opening the door or running away.

interface   A connection that allows you to interact with the computer and allows the computer to interact with peripheral (external) devices. The following list explains the three most common interfaces:

> *Hardware.* Hardware interfaces consist of the cables, connectors, and ports that link the computer to peripheral devices, such as printers, modems, and mice.

> *Software.* Software interfaces consist of the commands, messages, and codes that two software programs use to talk back and forth. For example, a software interface exists between the disk operating system and any application you run on top of the disk operating system.

User. User interfaces consist of the devices that allow the user to communicate with the computer and vice versa. These devices include the video display, keyboard, mouse, and menus.

interleave factor   Think of a hard disk as a roulette wheel—you spin the wheel and roll a ball that eventually falls into one of the numbered holes in the wheel. Now, as the wheel is spinning, imagine trying to poke your index finger in each hole as the hole is spinning past. Unless you're the Flash, you won't be able to do it. You may get every third hole or every fifth hole.

A disk is the same way. The disk drive spins the disk very quickly—so quickly that the read/write head cannot read each division (sector) of the disk in consecutive order. Instead, the head can read maybe every third sector or every sixth sector. If the read/write head is not ready to read the sector, it must wait until the sector comes around again.

With some disk drives, you can change the interleave factor so that data is stored in noncontiguous (non-neighboring) sectors. With an interleave factor of 1 to 1 (1:1), data is stored in contiguous sectors. With a factor of 3:1, data is stored in every fourth sector. With an optimum interleave factor (this varies depending on the disk drive), the sector that the read/write head needs to read is properly aligned with the read/write head at just the right moment when the head is ready to read it.

internal hard disk   A hard disk mounted inside a computer's cabinetry. See also *hard disk*.

internal memory   Another name for *RAM* or *primary storage* that is built into the CPU. This is the computer's electronic storage area—the place where the computer loads information and instructions when you open a program or a file, so that the data can be accessed immediately. See also *memory*, *RAM*, and *primary storage*.

internal modem   A modem installed inside a computer's cabinetry. See also *modem*.

interoperability   The ability of computer equipment from a variety of manufacturers to work together and transfer data seamlessly.

interpreter   A routine used in programming to translate a program you've written into machine language so the computer can understand and attempt to execute it. Interpreters work fairly slowly because they translate your program one command at a time, let the computer carry out that instruction, and then move on to the next. This makes it easier to find errors in a program, so interpreters are great when you're just learning how to program. See also *compiler*, which interprets a program into machine language much more quickly.

interrupt   Computers can't do everything at once. If the computer is processing data and you start typing, the computer has to decide what to do. Should it continue processing or receive your input? Whenever you demand attention in this way (by typing or moving your mouse), you interrupt the program, forcing it to make a decision. Such an interruption is called a *hardware interrupt*. You interrupted the program by using a piece of hardware (the keyboard or mouse).

But programs can interrupt themselves, as well. For example, if the program constantly keeps track of the date and time, it may continually interrupt itself in order to check the time. This type of interruption is called a *software interrupt*.

inverse video   See *reverse video*.

I/O   See *input/output system*.

➤

In the J's, you will learn that you don't need a legal program to justify text, that you can avoid the jaggies, and that a joystick isn't all fun and games.

jacket   The casing of a floppy disk. It protects the magnetic wafer inside that holds your data. The jacket for a 3.5" disk is made out of hard plastic and offers better protection than the thin plastic or pressed cardboard jacket of a 5.25" disk.

jaggies   In computer graphics, you will notice that angled and curved lines look ragged. This effect is referred to as *the jaggies* (more formally known as *aliasing*).

Jaggies

To understand the jaggies, imagine the computer screen as a piece of graph paper with 1/4-inch squares. To draw a line on the graph paper, you must color a series of squares. If you draw a line straight across or straight up and down, the line is smooth. However, if you try to draw a curve, you'll get a ragged line. The computer display is the same way; you are turning pixels on or off in a grid to form an image.

Now, imagine that you have the same screen but instead of 1/4-inch squares, the squares are 1/16 of an inch. You can now form a curve that is much smoother. The same is true of display screens and printers—increase the number of pixels per inch or dots per inch, and you get a smoother curve.

job   A single task that you tell the computer to perform. The most common type of job is a print job. You tell the computer to print a document, and the computer takes care of feeding the necessary information to the printer when the printer needs it.

job queue   A series of tasks that you tell the computer to carry out. The computer performs the tasks in order until the last task is completed.

join   In a relational database program, you can join two database files in order to create a third file with all the information you need. Say you are in charge of calling all the members of the class of '89 to ask for an annual donation. You have one file (called MEMBERS.DAT) that contains a list of all members of the class of '89, along with their addresses and phone numbers. In another file (called DONATE.DAT) is a list of the members that tells how much each member donated during the fiscal year. You want to call only those members who did not yet contribute.

How do you do it? You join the files using what is called a *query*. The query tells the program three things:

> The *names* of the two files you want to join. In this case MEMBERS.DAT and DONATE.DAT.

> The *condition* of the join operation. In this case, the condition would specify that you want information for only those members who have donated zero dollars.

> The *specific information* you want to include in the third file. In this case, the member's name and phone number.

The program copies the requested information from the two files and spits it into a third file.

joystick   An input device with a lever that lets you move the cursor quickly in any direction on the screen. Joysticks are commonly used with computer games and with high-level graphics programs.

justification   In many programs, you can align text in the following ways: left-justified, right-justified, centered, or fully justified.

Left justification is the default setting for most programs. As you can see, each line is flush against the left margin, leaving a ragged right margin.

Right justification pushes the right end of the line against the right margin, leaving the left margin ragged. Although you probably won't use this justification often, it is useful for typing a date at the top of the page or a page number at the bottom.

Full justification adds space between words and/or characters to move the left end of each line against the left margin and the right end against the right margin. This gives the text the uniform look of newspaper columns.

Center positions the middle of each line of text at an equal distance from the left and right margins. This is especially useful for titles and headings.

➤

The K words destroy some established myths: Kermit is not just a frog, key assignments are not important missions, and kern is not just a grain grown in the Midwest.

Kermit   A set of rules (a *protocol*) used to govern the transfer of files over phone lines and between micro-computers and mainframe computers. Kermit was developed at Columbia University and is commonly used by universities. Although it is slow compared to other communications protocols, it is very good at detecting and correcting transmission errors over noisy telephone lines. (And, yes, Kermit is named after Kermit the Frog from the Muppets.)

kern   To tighten the space between characters in order to improve the appearance of neighboring charac-ters. Kerning is often used in word processing and desktop publishing programs to tighten the space between loose character pairs that appear in head-ings. The following examples show some loose char-acter pairs before and after kerning:

Unkerned	**Kerned**
W A	WA
T o	To
V A	VA

key   Each key on a computer keyboard consists of a plastic casing, called a keycap, that activates a tiny electrical switch to send data into the computer. You may also see *key* used in reference to sorting or searching data in a database. Here, it refers to the field (last name, first name, area code, etc.), that you want to sort or search on. See *sort key* for information on this type of key.

key assignments   Some programs allow you to customize the keyboard in a way that makes the keyboard more efficient for the way you work. The program comes equipped with a standard keyboard layout that assigns the program's functions to specific keys. You can then change the key assignments to assign the functions to different keys.

key field   See *sort key*.

keyboard   The main input device for most computers. The keyboard contains the standard character keys you would find on most typewriters, as well as the following special keys:

> *Enter key*. The Enter key, sometimes called the Return key, can be compared to the carriage return on a typewriter. It is used in word processing programs to end a paragraph. It is also used to confirm an entry or to select a command.

> *Insert key*. Used in some programs to turn Insert mode on or off. With Insert mode on, anything you type is inserted at the cursor position, and existing text shifts to make room. With Insert mode off, anything you type replaces existing text.

> *Del (Delete) key*. Erases a character or a selected object. With many programs, the erased character(s) or object(s) are held

temporarily in a buffer until you delete something else. So if you delete something by mistake, you may be able to undelete it.

Backspace key. Works like the Delete key to erase a character or a selected object. However, the Delete key erases the character that the cursor is on or the character to the right of the cursor. The Backspace moves the cursor to the left, erasing any character in its path.

Esc (Escape) key. Generally used to cancel a command or to back up step by step through a series of commands. In most programs, you can get out of trouble by pressing the Esc key.

Cursor-movement keys. A set of keys that allows you to move the on-screen cursor up, down, left, or right. These keys include the arrow keys, which move the cursor one character or one line at a time; the PgUp and PgDn keys, which move the cursor up or down one screen or page at a time; the Home key, which moves the cursor to the beginning of the line, the top of the screen, or the beginning of the document; and the End key, which moves the cursor to the end of the line, the bottom of the screen, or the end of the document.

Function keys. The 10 F keys on the left side of the keyboard or twelve F keys at the top (and sometimes on the left side) of the keyboard. F keys are numbered F1, F2, F3, and so on. These keys are used to quickly enter various commands in a program.

Ctrl (Control) and Alt (Alternative) keys. The Ctrl and Alt keys are used with other keys to make those keys behave differently. For example, you may press the F1 key to get help, but if you hold down the Ctrl key while pressing F1, the program may check the spelling in your document.

Num (Numeric) Lock key. Keyboards have a separate, numeric keypad that allows you to enter numbers. The keypad can be used in either of two ways: to enter numbers or to move the cursor. Pressing the Num Lock key locks the keypad so you can use it to type numbers. With Num Lock off, you can use the same keys to move the cursor.

keyboard template   A plastic or cardboard cheat sheet that tells how to use function keys and other key combinations to issue commands and get help in a particular software program. It fits around or above the keys on your keyboard. Some software packages come with a keyboard template, but they are also sold separately in stores or offered as incentives when you buy other computer accessories. You can even make your own template using a strip of heavy cardboard and colored markers, which code the key combinations according to the Shift key, Control key, Alt key, or Function key.

keypad   See *numeric keypad*.

keystroke   The action of pressing one or more keys to enter a single character or command. A keystroke can be as simple as typing a single character. However, some keystrokes require that you hold down one key while pressing another. The standard ways to show that you must press two keys are to join the keys with a hyphen (-) or plus sign (+). For example,

Alt+F3 or Alt-F3 tells you to hold down the Alt key and press the F3 key.

keyword   A unique word, phrase, number, or code that a program uses to sort a list of items or search the list.

kilobyte   Pronounced KILL-oh-bite. A standard unit used to measure the size of a file, the storage capacity of a disk, and the amount of computer memory. A kilobyte is 1,024 bytes, and because each byte represents a character, a kilobyte is equivalent to 1,024 characters. Kilobyte is commonly abbreviated as K, KB, or Kbyte.

You are about to enter the land of legends and lost clusters, a land where drives are logical and libraries have no books. So log on, look up, and try to find the missing link.

label The term *label* has several meanings depending on what you're talking about:

In a spreadsheet program, a label is any text you type into a cell (the smallest unit in a spreadsheet). Labels are distinguished from *values* (numeric entries), *formulas* (equations that perform operations on values), and *functions* (a shorthand for complex formulas).

With disks, you apply a physical label to the disk to indicate what's on the disk. You can also add a volume label to a disk when you format it. This volume label then appears whenever you view a list of files on the disk.

In programming and in macros, a label is used to link two parts of a program.

LAN See *local area network*.

landscape orientation Many programs and some printers allow you to print text in either of two orientations: *portrait* or *landscape*. In portrait orientation, text is printed as you would type a letter on a page—the page is longer than it is wide. In landscape orientation, text is printed sideways, making the page wider than it is long.

language   If you decide you want to program a computer, you have to learn a language that enables you to communicate with it.

There are two major types of programming languages. In a *low-level language*, you communicate using a code based on 1s and 0s that your microprocessor understands; in a *high-level language*, you get to use a more human-like set of rules, symbols, and natural language words that can then be translated into the 1s and 0s your computer understands.

Within these two levels are dozens of languages, each with its strengths and weaknesses for writing particular types of programs. A programmer might write a great Windows word processing program in C++, for example, but never think of using C++ to create an expert system that could help coordinate delivery routes for a fleet of trucks. For that task, PROLOG would be a much better choice. See also *high-level language, low-level language*, and *programming*.

laptop computer   A lightweight computer that you can carry around like a briefcase. The computer comes complete with a display, keyboard, and processing unit and is usually battery-operated.

laser printer   A printer that uses copy machine technology to print high-quality text and graphics. Although more expensive than dot-matrix and inkjet printers, laser printers are faster, quieter, and produce better-looking quality output.

LaserJet   A popular line of laser printers from Hewlett-Packard for IBM-compatible PCs. You can also adapt them to work with Apple Macintosh computers by installing a PostScript-compatible cartridge in the printer.

LaserWriter   A popular line of laser printers from Apple Computer. They can work with either Macintosh or IBM-compatible computers, although a special PostScript-compatible driver must be loaded in any IBM-compatible program using the printer.

launch   To start a program.

layer   In desktop publishing and graphics programs
and in some word processing programs, you can
assemble a page by combining graphics objects (such
as pictures and lines) and sections of text on the
page. Think of it as creating a collage. In some
programs, you can even overlap text and graphics
for special effects. This is called *layering*.

Layers are also used in some graphics and design
programs as transparencies. For example, if you are
designing a house, you might have one layer that
shows the overall structure of the house, another
that shows the wiring, and another that shows the
plumbing. You can then remove or add layers as
desired to focus on different aspects of the design.

Graphic image is layered on top of circle.

Kathryn M. Appleton

3345 West 56th Place
Chicago, Illinois 60629
Home Phone: (312) 434-2670
Work Phone: (312) 579-4532

Career Objective: To work in a progressive general acute care setting as
therapist responsible for direct patient care with develop
pediatrics.

Text is layered on top of rectangle.

layout   To arrange text and graphics on a page. Most
desktop publishing programs are specifically designed to help you position text and graphics on the

page. You create the text in a word processing program, create pictures in the graphics program, and then paste the text and graphics on pages in the desktop publishing program. The process of pasting text and graphics is called *page layout*.

LCD   See *liquid crystal display*.

leader   Also called *dot leaders*. A row of periods that leads the reader's eye from one bit of text to another. These periods are commonly used in tables of contents to lead the reader from the heading (on the left) to the page number (on the right).

> House Pets 10
> Cats 12
> Dogs 14
> Fish 18
> Birds 21

leading   Pronounced *LEH-ding*. The space between two lines of text. Leading is measured from baseline to baseline (the *baseline* is the imaginary line on which text rests; some characters, such as *y* and *g*, descend below the baseline). In most word processing and desktop publishing programs, leading refers to extra space you can add between lines. For example, you may single-space the text and then add a little more leading to increase the space.

Why call it leading? Because in the old days of printing presses, printers would insert strips of lead between lines of type in order to control the spacing between lines.

leading zeros   Zeros placed to the left of a number without changing the value of the number. Leading zeros were commonly used in older database programs that required a specific number of digits for each entry. The zeros would fulfill the requirements of the entry without changing its value.

LED   See *light-emitting diode*.

left justification   A way of aligning text so that each line of text is flush against the left margin, leaving an uneven right margin. (See also *justification*.)

legend   A separate section of a map or graph that helps the user interpret the map or graph. For example, if you create a graph to compare a student's grades for two quizzes, you may use a different colored bar for each quiz. The legend would match the color to the number of the quiz.

letter-quality   With many dot-matrix printers, you can control the quality of the printout. You might choose draft quality for a rough draft and letter quality for the final product. In this case, *letter-quality* indicates that this is the best quality the printer can produce. But a true letter-quality printer is one that uses a Daisy Wheel print head to produce letters that look like your secretary typed them on her IBM Selectric. Laser and inkjet printers also produce letter-quality output, but because they can do so much more than just print letters, it's kind of an insult to call them letter-quality.

library   A set of commonly used instructions that are stored in a single file. Libraries are used in programming to save time. Instead of entering a series of commands, you simply enter a command that tells the programming language to insert a given library. The entire set of instructions contained in that library is then inserted into the program. Many programming languages come with several libraries and allow you to create your own libraries.

light-emitting diode (LED)   Diode is pronounced DIE-ode. A small device that lights up when a current is passed through it. The disk drive activity lights on the front of a computer are LEDs.

light pen   A light-sensitive input device shaped like a pen. Instead of rolling a mouse around on a desk, you simply point to an item on-screen. The pen senses its position on the screen and sends the appropriate signal back to the computer. Pen-based systems are commonly used in hospitals and in other business settings that require lots of forms to be filled out. The pen allows the user to move from one area of the form to another very quickly and accurately.

LIM EMS   See *Lotus-Intel-Microsoft Expanded Memory System*.

line art   Artwork that consists only of solid blacks and whites, with no shades of gray. If you are creating artwork for a document you plan to print out on a low-resolution printer, stick to line art illustrations. Low-resolution printers don't print enough dots per inch to ensure clean consistent gray tones, and the muddy effect will spoil the look of the whole piece. See also *halftone*.

line feed   A code that tells the printer when to move to the next line. Many printers also have a line feed button that allows you to manually advance a page one line at a time in order to align the paper correctly in the printer.

line graph   In spreadsheet and presentation graphics programs, line graphs are used to show how data varies over time. Line graphs are often used on the news to show financial trends, such as the change in the inflation rate from one quarter to the next.

line spacing   The space between lines of text. In most word processing and desktop publishing programs, you can select a general line spacing, such as single spacing or double spacing, and you can add leading to adjust the spacing more precisely. See also *leading.*

link   To establish a connection between two computers, two devices, two programs, or two files. With computers, you can establish a link by connecting the two computers with the proper cable or with modems and then running a program on the two computers that allows them to communicate with one another.

   With data links, you can link files created in the same program or in different programs. For example, if you create an annual report in WordPerfect for Windows and create a spreadsheet in Excel, you can link the spreadsheet to the annual report. If you change the spreadsheet in any way, the changes will appear automatically in the report.

   Do not confuse linking with *importing.* If you import one file into another, the imported file becomes the property of the file into which it was imported, and it remains fixed. If you change the original file, the changes do not appear in the imported version. With linking, the link is dynamic; change the linked file and it automatically updates the link.

linked object   In programs that support object linking and embedding, this is a document or part of a document that is linked to the document you originally created it in.

   For example, say you create a spreadsheet in Excel to keep track of your tie-dyed shirt business, and you update it daily to record new sales. You also create a monthly letter to your Mom in Word for Windows that describes your continuing success. If you insert the Excel worksheet as a linked object in your Word document, you can really impress her. Each month when you open your letter document, the linked spreadsheet will automatically be updated, allowing you to print out the letter and send it off without another thought.

liquid crystal display (LCD)   A low-power display that is commonly used for laptop computers. An LCD functions like Venetian blinds. With Venetian blinds, you pull a cord and the blinds open so that you can see through them; the blinds themselves are barely visible. Pull the cord again, and the blinds turn sideways, blocking whatever is behind them.

With LCDs, long, rod-shaped molecules float on end in a liquid, so you cannot see them. When the computer passes a low current through the liquid, the molecules align in such a way to form a darkened character. It takes much less power to align these molecules than it would take to light up portions of the screen.

LISP   Short for List Processing. A high-level programming language used mainly to develop artificial intelligence programs and to write compilers and interpreters for other languages.

load   To transfer a program or file from disk into your computer's memory so that the computer can work with it. This is similar to the process of reading a passage of a book so you can think about it.

local area network (LAN)   Rhymes with van. A local community of computers linked with high-performance cables. LANs vary in size, but are always limited to a single geographical area, such as an office, corporation, or campus. This distinguishes them from WANs (wide area networks), which can connect computers that are miles apart. LANs offer the following benefits:

Hardware sharing. Several computers can be connected to a single printer, modem, or other device that's used only occasionally. By allowing computers to share equipment, a company can cut costs.

Electronic mail. On a network equipped with electronic mail software, network users can send and receive memos and notices over the network. This cuts down on waste paper and reduces the time it takes to print and distribute notices.

File sharing. Without a network, a user can send a file to another user by copying the file to disk and giving the disk to the other user. Hardly efficient. With a network, a user who has access to a file can get the file directly off the network. If two or more users are responsible for keeping a file updated, both users can edit a single file rather than editing separate versions of the same file.

Power sharing. Several workstations (microcomputers) can be connected to a powerful, speedy minicomputer, letting each user tap the resources of the minicomputer.

The structure of a network varies. The most common networks are structured either as peer-to-peer networks or as client-server networks. With peer-to-peer networks, each computer on the network is connected to the other computers in the network, allowing any two computers to communicate with each other. With a client-server network, all the computers on the network (the clients) are connected to a powerful central computer (the server).

local drive   A networking term that refers to the disk drive on the computer that you're sitting at, as opposed to any disk drive you may be able to access through the network (which is referred to as a *remote drive*). See also *networking*.

logical drives   When you purchase a computer with a hard disk, it comes with a single hard disk. However, the dealer may have *partitioned* (divided) the disk into separate storage areas called *logical drives* (or you may have done it). For example, you may have three hard disk drives—C, D, and E. Don't be fooled; the three drive letters refer to the same *physical* disk; they just represent different *logical* drives. The computer will treat each logical drive as a separate disk.

logical operator In programming and in spreadsheet and database programs, you can use conditional statements to determine whether a certain condition exists. Many times these statements contain a logical operator: AND, OR, or NOT. For example, in a database, you can tell the program to search for all records that have a last name entry of Johnson AND a state entry of IN (Indiana). Or, the search may specify a last name entry of Johnson OR a state entry of IN. In either case, the logical operator allows you to limit or expand the action. See also *relational operator*.

log off To break the connection with a network or another computer. This is similar to hanging up a phone.

log on To establish a connection and gain access to a another computer or to a network. In most cases, users are required to log on for security reasons. In a network, for example, a user must log on in order to gain access to the network's programs, files, and other resources. The log-on procedure requires that the user enter a name and type the correct password. This prevents unauthorized users from using the network and from changing any files without proper authorization.

Logo A programming language that teaches basic programming concepts. Developed at MIT in the 1960s as a teaching tool, it features a cartoon turtle who obeys your commands to create simple or sophisticated graphic images.

lookup function In a spreadsheet program, you can use a lookup table to store information that your spreadsheet needs to refer to. For example, say you're a teacher and you have a spreadsheet that calculates your students' grades. For each student, it adds the grades during the semester and divides the total to determine the final grade. However, at the end of the

semester, you need to assign a letter grade instead of
a percentage.

To have the spreadsheet do this automatically,
you can create a lookup table that assigns a letter
grade to each range of grades. You can then use a
lookup function that tells the spreadsheet to take the
percentage, find the corresponding letter grade, and
insert the grade into a cell.

Percentages   Letter grades   Lookup table
inserted from
lookup table

	Quiz 1	Quiz 2	Quiz 3	Quiz 4	Quiz 5	Grade	Final		Score	Letter Grade
3	86	82	91	92	88	87.8	B+		0	F
4	94	92	87	91	89	90.6	A-		60	D-
5	93	95	89	89	91	91.4	A-		63	D
6	79	76	87	88	80	82	B-		67	D+
7	67	79	81	82	83	78.4	C+		70	C-
8	86	83	89	89	90	87.4	B+		73	C
9	85	90	91	87	89	88.4	B+		77	C+
10	92	87	93	90	89	90.2	A-		80	B-
11	79	92	89	89	90	87.8	B+		83	B
12	100	98	97	100	97	98.4	A+		87	B+
13	86	90	92	88	93	89.8	B+		90	A-
14	79	86	76	85	76	80.4	B+		93	A
									97	A+

lookup table   See *lookup function.*

loop   In programming and in macros, a loop is used to
have the computer repeatedly perform the same
series of operations a specific number of times or
until a condition no longer exists. For example, say
you've created a document in a word processing
program and you want to make all occurrences of the

term *gadget* italic. You can create a series of instructions in a macro similar to the following:

1. Search for the word *gadget*.

2. If you find the word gadget, go to step 3. Otherwise, stop.

3. Select the word.

4. Make the word italic.

5. Go back to step 1.

The loop continues until there are no more occurrences of the word *gadget*.

lost cluster   A cluster is the smallest storage unit on a disk. When you save a file to disk, the file is stored in one or more clusters. Although computers generally do a good job of keeping track of which files are stored on which clusters, sometimes a cluster is misplaced. According to the computer's record, the cluster is in use, but it is not assigned to a specific file. When this happens, the cluster is said to be lost.

Lotus 1-2-3   A leading spreadsheet program from Lotus Corporation that combines spreadsheet, graphics, and database capabilities in one powerful business management tool. 1-2-3 was originally created for the IBM PC in 1982, and though today it is available on many platforms including the Macintosh and the Windows environment, it remains most popular as a DOS product.

Lotus Development Corporation   A software publishing company founded by Mitch Kapor in 1981. Lotus is best known for their flagship product, Lotus 1-2-3, but they have had some success in acquiring and refining other business applications, such as Ami Pro, a Windows word processor, to market under the Lotus name.

Lotus-Intel-Microsoft Expanded Memory System (LIM EMS)   A standard that allows programs to work with more than the 640 kilobytes of memory available under DOS. See *expanded memory*.

low end   Computerese for cheap, meaning at the low end of a hardware or software manufacturer's range of products. As long as you know what you're getting, buying a low end product can be a good decision. The mistake would be in neglecting to ask the questions that help you save money later. If you outgrow the limited feature set of a software program, can you trade it in for a good price on the next program up the line? If you're impatient with your new computer's slow speed once you've become proficient at using it, can you upgrade it or will you have to scrap the whole thing? Don't hesitate to ask the salesmen very specific questions about your computing needs. It's their job to save you money now *and* down the road.

low-level format   All disks are formatted at two levels: high and low. The low-level format lays out the sectors on the disk. The high-level format writes information on the disk that helps the operating system locate the various sectors.

The term low-level format is also used when referring to the process used to recover data from a damaged disk. For example, with PC Tools or The Norton Utilities, you can run a program that performs a low-level format. The program reads the data off each sector (if possible) and stores the information temporarily in memory. If the sector is bad, the program marks that sector to prevent it from being used, and then writes the information from that sector to a good sector on the disk. If the sector is good, the program writes the information stored in memory back onto the newly formatted sector. It proceeds this way, sector by sector, until the entire disk is reformatted.

low-level language   Of the two major types of programming languages, high level and low-level, this
type is for the hardcore computer geek. It enables
you to write extremely fast, memory-efficient
programs. "Low" refers to the fact that you're
communicating right down there at a level the
microprocessor can understand. This requires technical knowledge of how the system performs its
various tasks, which is not everybody's cup of tea.
That's why high-level languages (which send messages to the processor in the way that a queen
dictates work down to the kitchen staff) were developed to make programming a more reasonable proposition. Assembly language, which is very close to
machine code but contains words that correspond
directly to machine actions, is also considered a low-
level language. See also *high-level language* and *programming*.

low resolution   The text and images on your screen
and on your printouts consist of dense patterns of
dots. In general, the more dots you have per inch,
the higher the resolution and the sharper the image.
A low-resolution device outputs relatively few dots
per inch. For example, a 9-pin dot-matrix printer
prints at only 180 dots per inch, compared to a
higher resolution 24-pin printer, which prints at 360
dots per inch.

➤

Grab a stool at the menu bar, where the bartender is a robot that speaks only in machine language and directly from memory about topics exclusively covered by the magnetic media.

Mac See *Macintosh*.

machine language A computer doesn't understand English, or even French or Spanish. It understands only electrical impulses—on or off, electrical current or no electrical current. Because of this, the computer uses an alphabet consisting of only two characters—1 (for on) and 0 (for off). Each piece of information (a byte) that's sent to the computer consists of eight of these ones and zeros that turn a series of switches on or off in a particular order. The order in which the switches are turned on and off determines what the computer will do. This system is known as *machine language*.

  When you write a program (a set of instructions for the computer), you work with a programming language that you can understand. It uses the standard alphabet to construct logical commands, such as GO TO, ADD, and PRINT. Before the program can run on a computer, however, the program must be translated, compiled, or assembled into machine language—the language of 1s and 0s. See also *assembler* and *compiler*.

Macintosh A line of easy-to-use personal computers developed by Apple Computer. Several factors make Macintosh computers appealing:

WYSIWYG (What You See Is What You Get) Graphics. Shows you on-screen exactly what your text and graphics images will look like when printed.

Ease of Use. All programs and files on a Macintosh are represented by on-screen images, called *icons*. These icons look like small pictures that represent everyday objects, such as file folders and sheets of paper. To run a program or open a file, you simply select its icon. You don't have to type cryptic commands.

Consistency. All programs on a Macintosh have the same look and feel. For example, in any program on the Macintosh, you can print a file by opening the File menu and selecting the Print command. Once you learn how to use one program on a Macintosh, learning other programs is easy.

Macintosh II   Introduced in 1987, the first in a series of high-performance computers from Apple Computer. The Macintosh II (and all Mac IIs since) ran on a Motorola 68030 microprocessor; was color-capable; had a built-in hard drive, stereo sound, and expansion slots; and no longer included a built-in monitor. Later models include the Macintosh IIx, Macintosh IIcx, and IIci (each of which is progressively faster than the Macintosh II), and the esteemed Macintosh IIfx, an extremely fast computer running at 40MHz (over one and a half times faster than the Mac IIci), that is designed for serious graphics and computer-aided design.

Macintosh Classic   Introduced in 1990 for under $1,000, the Classic was Apple's first serious attempt to compete with IBM-compatible PCs in the mass market. Using a Motorola 68000 microprocessor, this model runs most Macintosh-compatible software, though not very quickly. The Classic has sold fairly well, but its sales and performance have been surpassed by faster, more powerful and competitively priced offerings from Apple. The Macintosh Classic II is a big step up from the Classic. Like the Classic, it does not contain color capabilities, but is about twice as fast, running on a Motorola 68030 microprocessor at 16MHz.

Macintosh LC   A color-capable, modular Macintosh introduced in 1990. The original Mac LC uses a Motorola 68020 microprocessor and runs at a clock speed of 16MHz. The Macintosh LC II, introduced in 1992, uses a 68030 processor and is much faster than the LC.

Macintosh Powerbook   Apple finally caught up with the rest of the portable computing crowd when they introduced the Macintosh Powerbook in 1991. Models include the 100 (jointly designed with Sony Corporation), 140, and the 170. All weigh approximately five pounds, and feature a built-in trackball instead of a mouse, a flat screen, a full-sized keyboard, Apple Talk remote access software (for easy access to your home or office Mac when you're computing on the road), and a built-in 20 MB hard drive.

Macintosh Quadra   This line of high-performance computers from Apple Computer are used as professional workstations and also are very popular with designers and artists. Quadras feature a new input-output technology that enables them to transmit data between peripherals and networked Macs at double the speed of other Macs, and they work about twice as fast as 386- or 486-based PCs. Models include the Quadra 900, which looks like an oversized desktop computer, and the conventional desktop-sized Quadra 700. Both run on the Motorola 68040 at 25MHz.

macro   A record of several commands assigned to a
keystroke or to a single command. Macros are commonly used in word processing, spreadsheet, and
database programs as a timesaving feature. The program records a series of keystrokes you press as you
carry out a task. You then name the record of
keystrokes or assign it to a single keystroke. For
example, you may need to perform the following
four steps to print a document:

1.   Open the File menu.

2.   Choose the Print command.

3.   Specify the name of the printer.

4.   Press Enter.

To save yourself time, you could record these
commands and assign them to a keystroke, say
Ctrl+P for Print Document. Whenever you want to
print a document, you would simply press Ctrl+P
instead of entering the four commands. You can use
macros to store complete addresses, commonly used
phrases, and other information you type regularly.

magnetic disk   A flat, round piece of plastic that
magnetically stores data (the facts and figures you
enter and save). Just as you can store sounds on a
compact disc, you can store data on a magnetic disk
and later play back the data on your computer.
Floppy disks are made of flexible plastic covered
with a magnetic coating; hard disks are made of
aluminium with a magnetic coating. See also *floppy
disk* and *hard disk*.

magnetic field   A magnet polarizes the items around
it with magnetic energy. This invisible area is called
a magnetic field, and its range differs according to
the strength of the magnet. If you're not careful,
these fields can undo hours of work put in at the
computer and saved to a floppy disk. The precious

information stored on a disk is merely an arrangement of magnetic particles on a sheet of plastic.
When those little particles get pushed and pulled by
the forces of a magnetic field, there's no going back.
To avoid this tragedy, keep disks away from computer monitors, televisions, radios, and other electrical devices, since most generate magnetic fields.

magnetic media   Any material that permanently stores
data magnetically. Types of magnetic media include
cassette tapes, compact disks, floppy disks, hard
disks, and backup tapes. When a disk drive or tape
drive stores information on a disk, it is converting
the electrical information from the computer into
magnetic information that is stored on disk. When
a disk drive or tape drive reads information off the
disk, it is converting the magnetic information back
into electrical information that the computer can
understand.

mail merge   See *merge*.

mailbox   See *electronic mail*.

mainframe   A powerful central computer designed to
service the needs of many computers in a large
corporation or a university. Mainframes generally
have a great deal of storage capacity, memory, and
processing power. The storage capacity allows corporations to store vast amounts of information in a
central location from which all authorized users can
access the information.

The power of the mainframe allows corporations
to cut costs, as well. Because the memory and processing power is housed in a central computer, the
corporation can purchase less powerful, less expensive computers for the users who need to hook into
the mainframe. These computers are often referred
to as *dummy terminals*, because they rely on the
mainframe to do all the processing.

male connector When connecting your computer to a peripheral device (such as a printer or modem), you use a cable that plugs into a connector on the computer and a connector on the peripheral device. A male connector contains pins which fit into the receptacles on a female connector.

management information system (MIS) A computer system that provides managers in a corporation with up-to-date information. MIS allows managers to access information about various departments in the corporation to determine problem areas and keep track of progress and performance.

manual recalculation In spreadsheet programs, you can create spreadsheets that use formulas to perform mathematical operations on values in the spreadsheet. In most spreadsheet programs, the program automatically recalculates the results of a formula whenever you change a value used in the formula. You must wait for the program to perform the recalculation before you can do anything else.

To prevent the program from recalculating each time you change a value, you can enter a setting that turns the automatic recalculation feature off. This puts the program in manual recalculation mode. In this mode, the program doesn't recalculate until you press the designated key.

map The structure of data or of an object. For example, a memory map provides the computer with a way of finding data that is stored in memory. Each piece of data has a unique address that tells the computer where that data is stored. With a bit-mapped graphic, the file stores the location and condition (on, off, and color) of every dot that makes up the graphic image. This bit map tells the computer how to display and print the graphic image.

margin   The space between the outer edge of a page and the start of the text. In many programs, you can choose how much blank space you want to surround your text by telling the computer how big to make the margins. An inch on every side is the average for most business documents.

marquee   This term is borrowed from the idea of a theater marquee, a big sign surrounded by a border of flashing lights parading around the edge to call attention to itself. The computer version of a marquee is not quite as flashy, but it serves the same purpose. Some programs use it to highlight an area of text that you can manipulate in some way. It looks like a line of small dashes encircling a block of text or graphics that you've cut, copied, or otherwise marked for action. If you use Windows, you'll notice there is a screen saver called Marquee, which parades the program name across the screen.

master document   In some word processing programs, you can link several individual documents so that the documents are treated as a single document. For example, say you want to write a 500-page book. If you create a single file that contains 500 pages, your computer will keep telling you that it's running out of memory, or it will begin to slow down considerably. So you divide the book into 20 chapters, 25 pages each. Each chapter is in a separate file.

Now, you have a new problem. You want the program to number the pages 1 to 500, but the program can number pages in only one chapter at a time. The pages in each chapter will be numbered 1 to 25. That's where a master document comes in handy. The master document allows you to link the files so they are treated as one file. You can then enter a page number code at the beginning of the master document to have all the pages numbered consecutively 1 to 500. Master documents also are useful for creating an index and a table of contents for the document.

math coprocessor   Every computer has a central processing unit (CPU) that processes data and performs required calculations. A math coprocessor is a processor you can add to a computer to increase the speed at which it performs mathematical calculations.

If you create spreadsheets that perform complex calculations, consider adding a math coprocessor to your system. Math coprocessors can also be helpful to speed up some graphics programs, because many graphics programs use mathematical calculations to determine how to display and print graphic objects.

megabyte (M or MB)   A byte is eight bits, which is used to store information for a single character. A kilobyte is 1,024 bytes. A megabyte is 1,048,576 bytes (about one million bytes). This is nearly equivalent to 500 pages of double-spaced text. Although that seems like a lot, by today's standards a megabyte of storage space is small. Many of the newer, more powerful programs require 5 to 10 megabytes of disk storage.

megahertz (MHz)   Pronounced MEG-a-hurts. Technically, *hertz* is a unit used to measure the number of times an electronic wave repeats each second. One megahertz is equal to a wave repeating itself one million times in a second. Sound fast? With computers, 1 megahertz is a turtle's pace—a slow turtle. Modern computers have speeds in the range of 16 to 50 megahertz, and if you've worked on a 33 megahertz computer, a 16 megahertz computer will seem mighty slow.

membrane keyboard   A keyboard without keys. It's a flat, pressure-sensitive surface with images of keys drawn on it. You use it as you would a regular keyboard, but since you don't get the sensation of pressing down and hearing the click of the keys, it's not suitable for situations in which there is a lot of typing. Membrane keyboards are used in factories, restaurants, and other places where dirt and dust are a problem, since they have no openings and can be easily wiped clean.

memory   Whenever you run a program or open a file, the computer reads the information from disk (the computer's permanent storage area) and copies it into memory (the computer's electronic storage area). Why? Because your computer's memory can work with the information much more quickly when it's stored in memory.

Think of it this way: Say you memorize a poem and someone asks you what the fifth line means. Because the poem is in your mind, you can begin to interpret it immediately. If you had to first find the poem in a book, read the line, and then interpret the line, it would take a lot longer.

It's the same way with a computer. A computer can quickly access information that's stored in memory. So, why use a disk? Because memory is electronic. Turn off the computer, and whatever is stored in memory is gone. The information stored on disk, however, is permanent; it stays there until you delete it. See also *RAM*.

memory address   A code number, letter, or name that identifies a specific location where data is stored in memory. The computer uses addresses to locate pieces of data.

memory cache   See *cache*.

memory management   The process of making efficient use of your computer's memory. For example, most IBM and compatible computers come with at least one megabyte of electronic memory (where programs and files are stored when you're working with them)—that's 1,024 kilobytes. Of this 1,024K of memory, 640 kilobytes can be used by programs. That leaves 384 kilobytes, which is reserved for system use where the computer stores its input/

output drivers, printer drivers, and other information it needs to communicate. Much of this 384-kilobyte chunk is not used.

When you start your computer, several programs may be automatically loaded into the 640-kilobyte chunk of memory. For example, the program that allows you to use your mouse may take up to 20 kilobytes. That eats into the amount of memory that's available for you to run your programs.

So what about that 384-kilobyte chunk that's just sitting there? A memory-management program may be able to load the mouse program into that portion of memory, freeing up some memory in the 640 kilobyte area. This makes additional memory available to your other programs.

Also, if your computer has additional memory (extended or expanded) the memory management program can organize it and control it so that your programs can use the memory to run more efficiently.

memory map   A map that shows how RAM is divided up in a computer. RAM is not just one big happy country at your beck and call, it's actually organized to allocate resources for such things as the keyboard buffer, display buffer, RAM cache, and so on. In some utilities programs, you can look at a memory map to see how the RAM in your computer is organized. See also *RAM* and *RAM cache*.

memory resident program   Also known as *TSR* or *terminate-and-stay-resident*. A program that remains on call after you leave it. With memory-resident programs, you can run the memory-resident program and then load another program on top of it. When you load the second program, the memory-resident program retreats to the background. Only a small portion of it remains in memory. To switch from the main program back to the memory-resident program, you press a designated key, called the *hot key*. A typical hot key requires the user to press two keys; for example, you may have to hold down the Ctrl key and press the Esc key.

menu   A list of options or commands from which you can choose.

Menu pulled down   *Pull-down menu bar*

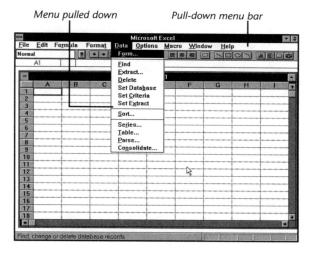

menu bar   Many computer programs let you enter a command by selecting it from a menu. Because display screens are so small, it wouldn't make sense to keep all the menus displayed on-screen at all times. You wouldn't be able to see what you were working on.

To get around this problem, many programs use a pull-down menu bar—a thin bar at the top of the screen that contains the names of all the available menus. When you want to enter a command, you choose the name of the menu from the bar. The menu then drops down from the bar to show a list of available options. Once you choose an option, the menu retreats into the menu bar.

menu-driven program   A program in which the user enters commands by selecting commands from a menu. This differs from a *command-driven program* in which the user must memorize the commands and keystrokes needed to perform specific tasks.

merge   Also known as *mail merge*. Have you ever gotten a letter from Ed McMahon, personally addressed to you? Well, Ed personalizes those form letters by using mail merge. He combines or merges a form letter with a list of names and addresses to create a series of letters all saying the same thing to different people.

How does he do it? Ed has a word processing program with a merge feature. He used the word processor to create two files: one containing the letter, and the other containing a list of people he wants to send the letter to. Instead of typing each person's name and address in separate letters, Ed types a single letter, inserting a code for the name, a code for the address, and a code for the city, state, and ZIP. These codes correspond to the codes Ed used to mark the names and addresses in the other file.

When Ed merges the two files, the program creates a series of letters by pulling names and addresses from the address file and inserting the information into the designated locations in the letter. Ed signs the letters, licks the envelopes and seals them, and drops them in the mail, just for his loyal fans.

microchip   A nickname for an *integrated circuit*.

microcomputer   Technically speaking, a computer that uses a single-chip microprocessor as its central processing unit. The following list will give you some idea of where the microcomputer stands in relation to other computers. Computers are listed from least powerful to most powerful.

> *Dumb terminal.* A computer that is connected to a more powerful central computer. The terminal relies on the central computer for its processing power and storage.

> *Microcomputer.* A personal computer—a computer that is small enough to fit on a desk and powerful enough to carry out necessary operations on its own.

> *Minicomputer.* A powerful computer often used as a central computer in a local area network. Minicomputers have a central processing unit comprised of more than one processing chip.

> *Mainframe.* A powerful computer with hundreds of megabytes of memory and hundreds of gigabytes of storage. Commonly used as the central computer in large corporations and at universities.

microfloppy   A 3.5" floppy disk. It's the standard disk size for Macintosh personal computers and is rapidly out-distancing the 5.25" as the disk of choice for IBM-compatibles. See also *floppy disk*.

microprocessor   A single-chip central processing unit (CPU) used in personal computers. The model number of a microprocessor tells a great deal about its computing power. The following list provides a brief description of the more common microprocessors.

> (**Note:** The Intel chips are generally used in IBM and compatible computers. The Motorola chips are used in Macintoshes, Amigas and NeXT computers.)

Intel 8088. The chip used in the original IBM Personal Computer. The 8088 (pronounced eighty eighty-eight) has a clock speed of 4.77 megahertz (which is fairly slow). It has an 8-bit external data bus structure and a 16-bit internal data bus structure. Later versions of the chip pushed the clock speed as high as 10 megahertz.

> **Note:** The data bus structure determines how much information the processor can process at one time. 8 bits is 8 units of information; 16 bits is twice as much. *Internal* data bus structure refers to how much data the computer can process within the main unit. *External* refers to the amount of data that can be transferred between the main unit and peripherals, such as printers.

Intel 8086. This chip was actually developed before the 8088 chip, but it has a 16-bit external data bus structure that prevented the computer from using many of the printers and other peripheral devices that were on the market when IBM released its first personal computer. The 8086 (pronounced eighty eighty-six) runs at a clock speed of about 8MHz. The 8086 can address only 1 megabyte of computer memory.

Intel 80286. Also known as the two-eighty six. This chip has the same 16-bit internal and external data bus structure as the 8086 chip, but it can address up to 16 megabytes of memory. It has a clock speed of about 12 megahertz. This processor can operate in two modes: *real* and *protected.* In real mode, the processor can use only 640 kilobytes of memory. In protected mode, the processor can use up to 16 megabytes of memory. In protected mode, programs are prevented from interfering with one another in memory. In order to run in protected mode, you need a special memory-management program.

Intel 80386 or 80386DX. Also known as the three-eighty six. A newer chip with a 32-bit internal and external bus structure that can access up to 4 gigabytes of memory. You can get a 386 that runs at any of the following clock speeds: 20MHz, 25MHz, 33MHz, or 40MHz. The most important aspect of the 386 is that it allows you to do *multitasking*— to keep several programs running at the same time and switch from one to the other. With multitasking, the computer can be performing operations in the background (such as calculating a complex spreadsheet), while you type a letter in your word processing program. In order to multitask, you need a multitasking operating environment, such as Microsoft Windows.

Intel 80386SX. Also known as the three-eighty six ESS-EX. A scaled-down version of the 80386 chip. It runs slower than a real 386 chip and uses a 16-bit data bus structure rather than the full 32-bit structure. However, this chip allows you to run programs designed specifically to take advantage of the 386 chip and allows you to do multitasking.

Intel 80486 or 80486DX. Also known as the four-eighty six. The 486 is basically a souped-up 386 with a math coprocessor. The math coprocessor allows the computer to perform mathematical calculations more quickly. If you create a lot of complex spreadsheets, a math coprocessor can be valuable. If not, a faster 386 may be a better buy. Runs at the following clock speeds: 20MHz, 33MHz, and 50MHz.

Intel 80486SX. A scaled-down version of a 486. Its a 486DX without the math coprocessor.

Pentium. Intel's successor to the 80486 chip is compatible with previous 8086 chips, so Pentium-based PCs can run all software developed for earlier computers. But the Pentium chip processes instructions between two and five times faster than the 486—that's nearly 150 times faster than an 8086 chip. It runs at clock speeds of 60MHz and 66MHz. Another significant advance is that whereas the 486 contains one 8-kilobyte read/write memory cache, the Pentium contains two 8K caches: one for data, the other for instructions. Data and program code don't compete for cache space, so the system can run faster.

The Pentium improves on the 486's 32-bit architecture with a 64-bit external data bus structure, which moves data to and from main memory twice as fast as a 486. Though it only contains a 32-bit internal bus architecture, there are two of them which can be combined, if necessary, to get better throughput. If you are thinking of upgrading, but plan to run only Windows 3.1 or another single-user operating system, it may not be worth the effort. However, if you plan to run with a 32-bit operating system like Windows NT, you can truly appreciate the improved performance. WARNING: Up-graders especially should be wary. The Pentium generates a lot of heat (about twice that of the 80486, due to the addition of about 2 million more transistors to its chip). You may either want to delay your purchase to see if the power required is reduced, or be sure to provide adequate internal cooling for your PC.

Motorola 68000. Also known as the sixty-eight thousand. This chip has a 32-bit internal data bus and a 16-bit external data bus. It can address up to 16 megabytes of memory and runs at a clock speed of 8 megahertz. Used in the Macintosh Plus, the Macintosh SE, and the Macintosh Classic.

Motorola 68020. Also known as the sixty-eight twenty. Similar to the 68000, but this chip uses a 32-bit data bus and can access up to 4 gigabytes of memory. It runs at a clock speed of 16 megahertz (twice as fast as the 68000). It was used in the original Macintosh II.

Motorola 68030. Also known as the sixty-eight thirty. This chip uses a 32-bit data bus and can access up to 4 gigabytes of memory. It runs at higher clock speeds than its predecessor, the 68020. Offers added memory management support that will prove valuable with the new generation of software.

Motorola 68040. Also known as the sixty-eight forty. This 32-bit bit microprocessor is significantly more powerful than the 68030.

It includes a built-in math coprocessor called a numeric, or floating-point, coprocessor. Used in the Macintosh Quadra line.

Microsoft Corporation   A giant among software publishing companies. Founded in 1975, Microsoft manufactures and markets a wide variety of software applications and programming language compilers.

Microsoft Excel   A leading graphics spreadsheet program, known for exploiting the graphical user interface in Windows and on the Mac to the great advantage of the user. It provides easy-to-use formatting and charting features, and handy on-screen shortcuts.

Microsoft Windows   A program that runs on top of your computer's disk operating system (DOS) and gives the system a friendly face. Windows is known as a *graphical user interface* (GUI). That is, instead of typing commands to perform tasks, you enter commands by selecting them from menus or by selecting a graphic symbol (icon) that appears on-screen.

One of the biggest benefits of Windows is that it provides a way for programs designed for Windows to use more than the standard 640 kilobytes of memory that the disk operating system can access. Also, if you have a computer with a 386, 386SX, 486, or 486SX microprocessor, you can keep more than one program running at the same time (see *multitasking*).

Microsoft Word   A popular word processing program. Word was the first major IBM-compatible program to feature a what-you-see-is-what-you-get interface. This enables users to format their work more easily as they write and edit it. Even in the heyday of DOS word processing programs, Word never unseated WordPerfect in popularity. But Word for Windows and Word for the Mac are market leaders. See also *WYSIWYG*.

Microsoft Works An integrated software program popular with DOS, Windows, and Macintosh users. Contains easy-to-use word processing, drawing, spreadsheet, database, and telecommunications programs, making it the only program some users ever need.

MIDI Pronounced MIH-dee, short for Musical Instrument Digital Interface. A set of rules that governs the exchange of information between musical instruments and the computer. With the proper equipment, a musician can compose music on-screen and then instruct the computer to play it. The musician can then go in and edit the music to change its pitch or tempo and other elements of the composition. Much of the music you hear in movies and on television uses MIDI technology.

migrate Computer jargon meaning to move from one computer platform or software program to another. Used mainly to describe major market switches from one product to another, as in migrating from DOS to Windows. Warms your heart, doesn't it, to be thought of as just another bird in the seasonal plan of some greedy marketing manager?

minicomputer A powerful computer often used as a central computer in a local area network. For the distinctions between microcomputers, minicomputers, and mainframes, refer to *microcomputers*.

minimize A Microsoft Windows term meaning to shrink a window down to an icon without exiting the program. You can do it by selecting Minimize in the Control menu (accessed by clicking the file drawer icon in the upper left corner of the screen), or by clicking on the Minimize button (the down-arrow box, second from the right in the screen's upper right-hand corner). See also *window*, *Microsoft Windows*.

mode   An operating state for a computer or program that you can switch on or off. The most common modes are Insert and Overtype modes in word processing programs. In Insert mode, anything you type is inserted at the current location without deleting existing text. In Overtype mode, whatever you type replaces existing text. In most word processing programs, you can press the Ins key to switch from Insert mode to Overtype mode and back.

Spreadsheet programs, such as Lotus 1-2-3 and Quattro Pro, operate in several different modes. In READY mode, for example, you can type entries into your spreadsheet. In EDIT mode, you can edit an entry. In WAIT mode, you must wait while the computer performs a task. Within a mode, a function key may enter a command that differs from a command it would execute if pressed in another mode. So it is important to know what mode the program is in (see *mode indicator*).

mode indicator   With programs that operate in different modes, the program usually contains a *status bar* or *status line* that displays messages. The messages often provide information telling you the next step you must perform or help for the feature you are using. The message may also contain a *mode indicator* or *status indicator*, telling you which mode you are in.

modem   Short for MOdulator/DEModulator, and pronounced mow-dem. A modem allows your computer to communicate through the phone lines with other computers. You can get either of two types of modems: internal or external. An internal modem comes on a card that you can plug into an open receptacle (slot) inside of your computer. You can then connect your phone line directly to the modem. An external modem sits outside the computer. It contains three cables. One cable plugs into an electrical outlet to provide a power supply for the modem. A serial cable connects the modem to a serial port on the back of the computer. A third cable connects the modem to a phone jack.

Which should you buy? If you plan on using your modem on more than one computer, get an external modem. If you want to use the modem on only one computer, internal modems are better: they take up no desk space, require only one cable, and keep the serial port on the back of your computer open so you can connect a different serial device. However, if your computer doesn't have an open expansion slot into which you can plug a modem, you may have to settle for an external modem.

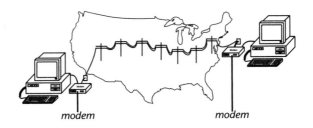

modem　　　　　　　　　　　　*modem*

modulation　The process of converting a digital signal into an analog signal. So what does that mean? The computer thinks and speaks in digital signals (1 or 0, on or off). However, if it needs to communicate through the phone lines, the signals must be sent as analog signals, which are wave forms. Modulation converts the computer signals into signals that can be sent over the phone lines. See also *modem*.

Moiré　Pronounced mwah-ray. An undesirable checkerboard effect created by overlapping shading patterns in graphic images. The effect usually appears when you reduce the size of a graphic image. Patterns that were clearly separate in the original image get pushed together, causing the Moiré distortion. (See also *monochrome*, *VGA*, *EGA*, and *CGA*.)

monitor   The display unit for a computer. The monitor allows the computer to communicate with the user.

monochrome   Literally, "one color." Monochrome describes a computer screen that displays only one color—usually white on black, amber on black, or green on black.

monospace   Literally, "same space." In a monospaced font, every letter gets the same amount of space, whether it's as wide as a *w* or as skinny as an *i*. *Courier* is one example of a monospaced font. It resembles a typewritten page, because typewriters allot a uniform amount of spacing to each letter, too. Compare with *proportional spacing*.

morphing   A special graphics effect that makes it look like one image is literally melting into the next. It's used to create special effects in desktop presentations, movies (remember the villain in the film *Terminator 2*?), and in print graphics, with such programs as MacroMind 3-D, MacTopas, and MorphIT!.

motherboard   The main printed circuit board in the computer. This board contains the processing chip, memory chips, support circuits, and bus controller. It's like the engine in your car; replace the motherboard, and you have a whole new computer.

Motorola   See *microprocessors*.

mouse   An input device that allows you to point to and select items on-screen. The mouse owes its name to its physical appearance; it looks like a little creature with a tail. The mouse tail is the cable that connects the mouse to the computer. Most mice have two buttons. The left button is used most often. If the mouse has three buttons, the center button is rarely used. You can press the mouse buttons and move the mouse in various ways to change the way it acts:

You can *point* to an item by moving the mouse so that the mouse pointer on-screen is positioned over the item. The tip of the mouse pointer must be touching the item; you cannot merely point in the direction of an item.

You can *click* on an item by pointing to it and pressing the mouse button once (usually the left mouse button).

To *double-click*, you point to an item and press and release the mouse button twice quickly. A double-click is not the same as two clicks. You have a certain amount of time to double-click (known as the *double-click interval*). Most programs allow you to change the double-click interval if you have a slow trigger finger.

You can *drag* the mouse by holding down the mouse button while moving the mouse. Dragging is often used in graphics programs to draw circles, lines, and other shapes. It is also commonly used to move items on the screen.

mouse driver   A program that tells the computer how to work with the mouse. If you purchase a mouse, it should come with a driver; if you don't install the driver, the mouse will not be usable.

MS-DOS   Pronounced Em-ess-DAWSS, short for Microsoft Disk Operating System. A disk operating system developed by Microsoft Corporation for use on IBM personal computers. See *DOS*.

multimedia   The combination of text, sound, video, graphics, and animation for use in presentations.

Multimedia PC (MPC)   A designation given by a group of computer manufacturers to an IBM PS/2 or any IBM-compatible PC that meets a set of minimum requirements the group has determined are necessary for multimedia computing. The minimum criteria include: an 80386SX microprocessor, with 2 megabytes of RAM, a clock speed of 20MHz, VGA graphics, a hard disk, a joystick, Microsoft Windows, a sound card, a mouse, and an MPC-compatible CD-ROM drive.

multisync monitor   With most monitors, you must make sure the monitor matches the display adapter that is installed on your computer. The display adapter tells the monitor how to display information. With a multisync monitor, the monitor automatically adjusts to the type of display adapter that's installed.

multitasking   The ability to run more than one program on a computer at the same time. This allows you to continue working in one program while the computer carries out tasks in another program. For example, you can have the computer calculate a complex series of formulas in a spreadsheet program, while you're writing a letter to your mom.

multiuser system   A computer system consisting of several computer terminals connected to a powerful central computer. This gives several users access to the same programs and data.

➤

Although the N's don't cover National Geographic, they do show you files in their native formats and the nesting habits of complex macros.

native file format   Whenever you create a file (such as a business letter or a picture) in a program, that file is saved with codes that tell the program how to display, print, and process the file. Each program uses a different set of codes, called a format. The format in which a program normally saves files is called the *native format*. Some programs can save files in different formats so you can open and use the files in programs that do not recognize the native format.

natural language   Any language—English, Gaelic, Swahili, etc.—that humans use to talk to other humans, as opposed to an artificial language, such as BASIC or Fortran, which is any language humans use to talk to computers.

natural recalculation   Say you own an auto shop, and you're figuring out how much one of your customers owes you. First, you would figure out the total cost of parts used. Then you would multiply the number of hours you worked on the car by your hourly rate. Then you would add the cost of parts and labor and add in the tax to figure out the total. You wouldn't add in the taxes first! In short, you have to perform the calculations in a specific order.

   The same is true of spreadsheet programs. Most programs allow you to specify the order in which you want the calculations performed: natural, row-wise, or column-wise. With natural recalculation, the program performs calculations in a logical manner. If any calculation requires the result from another calculation, the first calculation is performed first, just as you would do it. With row-wise recalculation, formulas are calculated left to right across each row, regardless of the logical order in which the calculations are to be performed. With column-wise recalculation, formulas are calculated top to bottom in each column. Most people rarely use the row-wise or column-wise method.

near-letter quality (NLQ)   With most printers, you can control the quality of the printout. You might choose a low-quality output for a rough draft and a high-quality output for the final draft. (Draft mode is usually faster and saves your ribbon from wearing out so quickly.) The high-quality output is called *letter-quality* because it is appropriate for a business letter. Low-quality output is called *draft*, because it is suitable for a rough draft. Between these extremes is *near-letter quality*.

nested   In programming and in developing macros, you can embed one set of instructions within another set. Say you want to create a set of instructions (call this set X) telling a program to open a file, print the file, and close it. Now suppose you already have a set of instructions (set Y) for printing the file. Instead of repeating the instructions from set Y in set X, you can enter a NEST command in set X that tells the program to go to set Y, follow the instructions, and then return to set X.

NetBIOS   Stands for Network Basic Input/Output System. A set of rules that applications must obey when they are used in networks connecting IBM-compatible computers working under DOS, UNIX, or OS/2. The rules have mainly to do with controlling the traffic of incoming and outgoing data among computers. The NetBIOS is invisible to people using networked computers, and is only important if you are writing a program to be used on a network.

NetWare The leading network operating system for IBM-compatible PCs. Novell's family of NetWare products includes NetWare 286 (the NetWare 2.x series), which supports up to 100 networked computers, and NetWare 386 (the NetWare 3.x series), which can handle up to 250. The popularity of NetWare products, which extends beyond PCs to Macintosh workstations, OS/2, and VAX networks, is due to their reliability, compatibility with other operating systems, and adaptability to many types of network configurations. See also *local area network* and *network operating system*.

network Two or more computers that are connected by a special communications link. Networked computers are usually connected by high-performance cables. In a local area network (LAN), the connected computers are in a single office or building (see *local area network*). In a wide area network (WAN), the connected computers can be thousands of miles apart (see *wide area network*).

network administrator A person who manages the network. A typical network connects many people and their computers to a central computer. This makes the system vulnerable. If a PC user wipes out his own files, that's his problem. If a shared file is wiped out on the network, that's everybody's problem. Hence, networks require administrators to control and protect the system. Administrators are in charge of installing programs on the network, assigning passwords to users, and controlling access to various files. They may also act as technical support, helping new folks learn how to use the network.

network operating system Just as a personal computer needs an operating system to tell it how to operate, computers linked by a network need another set of instructions to tell them how to work with each other—how to communicate, share files, figure out who gets to use the printer first, and so on. Some network operating systems, such as NetWare 286, effectively replace a PC's operating system, while others can co-exist with the single operating system.

network server A central computer in a network to which other computers (called workstations) are connected. The network server is usually a powerful computer with a large hard disk that runs administrative programs for the network. Servers contain the programs and files that various workstations share.

newspaper columns Many word processing and desktop publishing programs allow you to place your text in narrow columns, as in a newspaper. Programs automatically format the text so that it snakes from the bottom of one column to the top of the next.

NeXT A workstation developed by NeXT, Inc., which is a company founded by Steve Jobs (one of the co-founders of Apple Computer). The NeXT workstation uses a version of the UNIX operating system plus a friendly graphical user interface that makes it easy to use and even create applications in. The NeXT was originally developed for the education market, but is finding success as a low-end workstation in the business arena. See also *workstation*.

NLQ See *near-letter quality*.

node   A point at which two devices are connected. Often used in networks to describe the point where a workstation is connected to the network server (the central computer).

noise   Undesired signals that can interfere with communication between devices. Think of noise as static on a radio. Any static interferes with the music you are trying to listen to. In the same way, noise may interfere with data transfer over the phone lines or through network cables.

nonimpact printer   Any printer that works without touching the paper. Laser printers and inkjet printers are two common types of nonimpact printers. Compared with impact printers, they tend to print more quickly, quietly, and with better-looking results. However, they're not much good with duplicate forms. See also *printers* for a rundown of each major type of printer.

Norton Utilities   A utility program from Symantec Corporation. The utilities include an undelete program for files you accidentally erase, a benchmark program for testing your PC's performance, and other tools designed to take the worry out of your computing experience.

notebook computer   A compact laptop computer, weighing almost half as much but often costing more than a conventional laptop and named for the standard three-ring binder because it's about that size and shape. Although many models are as powerful as their larger cousin, their smaller keyboard and screen can make them less comfortable to use. However, innovations such as a built-in trackball instead of a mouse, and longer-lasting batteries make these invaluable when you're computing on the road.

null modem cable   A cable used to connect two computers directly—without using a modem. Such cables are often used with file-transfer programs to copy or move files from a desktop computer to a laptop computer and vice versa. For example, if you have a desktop computer at work and you use a laptop computer to work at home or on the road, you can use a null modem cable to copy files back and forth between the two computers.

Num Lock key   IBM and compatible keyboards have a numeric keypad that contains keys for entering numbers and for moving the cursor. If you press the Num Lock key, turning Num Lock on, the keypad is locked in number-entry mode; you use the keys to type numbers. If you press the Num Lock key again, turning (or toggling) Num Lock off, you can use the keys to move the cursor.

number crunching   A slang term used to describe the process of performing complex calculations. This term is usually used in reference to spreadsheet programs.

numeric coprocessor   See *math coprocessor*.

numeric format   In a spreadsheet program, you can enter values into the cells that make up the spreadsheet. But numeric values are usually more than just numbers. They represent a dollar value, a date, a percent, or some other real value. To indicate what particular values stand for, spreadsheet programs allow you to display the value in a certain numeric format. Some sample numeric formats are listed in Table N.1.

Table N.1   Numeric formats.

Format	Description	Example
Fixed	Displays numbers with a fixed number of decimal places from 0–15 places.	234.8431 78.34320 -234.00
Currency	Displays numbers in currency format, including currency symbol and decimal places from 1–2 places. Negative currency values appear in parentheses.	$999.90 $99,999,999.00 ($666.00)
Comma	Displays numbers from 0–15 places using commas to separate thousands. Negative values appear in parentheses.	99,999.00 (999)
Date		16-Mar-92 16-Mar Mar-92 Monday, March 16
Time	12:24:55 AM	12:24 AM 13:20:33

numeric keypad A separate section of the keyboard that contains keys for typing numbers. The numeric keypad is distinct from the number keys at the top of the keyboard. It is set up more like a keypad on an adding machine, allowing you to quickly type numeric entries.

You can also use the numeric keypad to move the on-screen cursor. If you type a lot of numeric entries, consider purchasing a keyboard that has a separate cursor-movement keypad. This allows you to use the numeric keypad exclusively for entering numbers; you won't have to keep pressing the Num Lock key to switch from numeric-entry mode to cursor-movement mode.

➤

The O's will help you get oriented with on-line informa-tion services, optical mice, and object-oriented graphics. You'll also learn how to find families for lonely orphans.

object linking and embedding (OLE)   A quantum leap beyond copying a block of text. In programs that support this technology, you can link or embed all or part of one file in one program within *another* file in a *different* program.

   For example, you might create a link by inserting a client list saved in Microsoft Access into a document in Word for Windows. From now on, every time you update the client list in Access, the list in the Word file will automatically be updated.

   Embedding doesn't sound quite as cool but can be equally useful. If, instead of linking, you embed the client list into the Word document, you will have a fully editable version of that file in the Word document. The embedded list won't be affected by any changes you later make to the original file, but that isn't the point of embedding; the point is that you can simply click on the list in Word and edit it without having to manually open the Access pro-gram where you created it. When you start creating fancy documents for which you want to pull in graphics and spreadsheets and mailing lists from all over the place, you will appreciate embedding—assuming, of course, that all your programs support OLE.

object-oriented graphics A graphics program that treats each graphics object (line, circle, square, and so on) as a separate object rather than as a collection of dots. Each object is stored as a set of mathematical instructions that tell the program how to draw and print the object. For example, the instructions for a circle may tell the program where to locate the center of the circle and how wide to make the circle.

Although you don't work with the instructions directly, they give you more control over sizing and shaping the object. For example, with bit-mapped graphics (the graphic is stored as a map of dots), if you double the size of the object, each pixel is doubled in size, making the object appear ragged. With object-oriented graphics, however, you can enlarge or shrink the object as desired without distorting it. The size of the pixels remains the same— only the arrangement of the pixels, as controlled by the instructions, is changed.

object-oriented programming A programming technology that treats each set of instructions as an object. Instead of writing a program line by line, you put objects together to form the program. The objects hide the complexity of the programming language and make it easy to copy a set of instructions from one program to use in another program. The copy is said to *inherit* the programming code from the original object; you can then modify the code to create a distinct object.

Although object-oriented programming languages are simpler to learn and use than other programming languages, object-oriented programs typically run more slowly. However, with today's faster computers, the difference in speed is becoming less and less noticeable.

odd parity   See *parity bit.*

off-line   Not ready to communicate with the computer. For example, a disabled workstation on a network is said to be off-line. A printer that is not ready to print is also said to be off-line. A device may be connected and turned on, but if it isn't able to send or receive data, it's off-line.

offset   In many word processing and desktop publishing programs, you can add space to the margins of each page to allow for the pages to be bound. This space is known as a *binding offset* or *offset.*

Why not just widen the left margin? This will work if you are binding pages that are printed on only one side. However, if you are preparing pages for printing on both sides, you will want the additional space inserted in the left margin on right-hand pages and in the right margin on left-hand pages. The binding offset adds the space where it is needed.

on-line   Ready to communicate with the computer. A device, such as a printer, must be connected to the computer, powered on, and in a state of readiness.

on-line help   Most programs allow you to press a key or select Help to get information and instructions on how to use the program. This is known as on-line help (as opposed to off-line documentation—the books that come with the program). Many programs also feature context-sensitive on-line help. With context-sensitive help, the program displays information and instructions for the currently selected command or for the task you are performing.

On-line help screen

on-line information service   A service that allows you to use your computer to buy and sell stocks, shop, make travel reservations, send and receive electronic mail, and access encyclopedias and newspaper or magazine articles. To use one of these services, you must have a modem connected to your computer and to a phone line, and you must pay a subscription price. Most on-line services cost about ten dollars a month, which pays for a set amount of on-line time and a set number of messages you can send.

operating system   See *disk operating system*.

optical character recognition   Also known as *OCR*. Your computer can read. It can't understand what it reads, but it can read text off a printed page and convert it into a form you can work with on your computer. In order for the computer to do this, it needs two things: a scanner and an OCR program. The scanner bounces light off the page and converts the printed characters into signals that can be brought into the computer. The OCR program converts these signals into characters.

What about handwriting? Most OCR programs recognize only characters that are produced on a typewriter or printer. They cannot recognize handwritten or hand-printed text. Some more advanced programs can recognize neatly printed text.

optical disk   A disk on which data is written to and read from by light. Optical disks can store vast amounts of data. However, optical disk drives typically access data more slowly than do hard disk drives. The most common type of optical disks are compact discs (CDs).

optical fiber   A thread of glass that uses light waves to transport data; usually bundled together within a jacket to form a cable. Because they can carry huge amounts of data and are not affected by electrical interference, optical fibers are used in many computer technologies, including digitizers and networking cables. Optical fibers are also replacing copper wires in telephone lines, and therefore setting the stage for a country-wide information superhighway.

optical mouse   A mouse that bounces a light beam off a grid in order to determine its position and control the position of the on-screen pointer. An optical mouse differs from a *mechanical mouse*, which has a ball that rolls as you move the mouse on the desktop. The ball moves a set of wheels inside the mouse to control the movement of the on-screen pointer. In general, an optical mouse moves the pointer more smoothly and precisely on-screen. With mechanical mice, the pointer movement can be affected by dirt on the desk or by the mouse sliding instead of rolling.

orientation   Many programs and some printers allow you to print text in either of two orientations: *portrait* or *landscape*. With portrait orientation, text is printed as you would type a letter on a page—the page is longer than it is wide. With landscape orientation, text is printed sideways, making the page wider than it is long.

original equipment manufacturer (OEM)   The company that manufactures a computer, a piece of equipment, or a part.

orphan   In word processing and desktop publishing programs, the first line of a paragraph that is stranded at the bottom of a page. The line is called an orphan, because it is left behind by its paragraph. If the line is stranded at the top of a page, leaving behind its paragraph, it is called a *widow*. An old printer's trick is to think of orphans alone at the beginning and widows alone at the end. (See also *widow*.)

Many programs offer a widow/orphan prevention feature that moves any orphan line from the bottom of the page to the top of the next page, so the line appears with its paragraph.

OS/2   Short for Operating System/2. This multitasking operating system was originally developed by Microsoft Corporation and IBM in 1987 and is now controlled by IBM.

OS/2 features a graphical user interface that looks similar to Windows, runs DOS and Windows applications as well as applications developed expressly for OS/2, and includes a network operating system. Furthermore, it takes full advantage of the available power in 80386- and 80486-based computers, so your programs run faster even when several are open at one time.

Despite its technological excellence, OS/2 still runs second to Windows in the marketplace, and will have a hard time catching up with their lead.

outline font   Also called *scalable font* or *PostScript font*. A type style in which each character is stored as a mathematical formula that tells the program how to form the character. Although you don't work with the formula directly, it gives you much more control over characters.

To understand outline fonts, compare them to bit-mapped fonts, where each character is stored as a separate pattern of dots. A 10-point version of the letter *B* is one pattern of dots, an 11-point version of *B* is another pattern, and a 12-point version is still another pattern. With outline fonts, you have one outline for the letter *B*; you can then choose the size of the outline. When you print, the program fills in the outline with the required pattern of dots.

outline utility   A feature of some advanced word processing programs that allows you to create and edit a document as an outline. You can type the outline as a series of headings and then type text under each heading to form the document.

If you need to view the outline, you can *collapse* text under headings so only the headings are shown. The text still exists, but the program hides it so you can work with the outline more easily. Move a heading in the outline, and all the text under that heading moves with it. This allows you to quickly rearrange sections of the document.

output   Information that the computer gives back to you. This includes printed material, on-screen displays, and beeps or other sounds. Contrast this with *input*—anything you enter into the computer, including characters you type, lines you draw, and images you scan.

overstrike   To type or print one character on top of another.

Overtype mode   Also known as *Typeover mode.* In most programs, you can type text in either of two modes: Insert or Overtype. In Insert mode, anything you type is inserted at the cursor; characters move to the right to make room for the inserted text as you type. In Overtype mode, anything you type replaces existing text. Instead of deleting the current character and inserting a new one, you simply position the cursor on the character you want to replace and type the desired character.

overwrite   Whenever you save a file, the file is stored on disk under the file name (the name you gave it). If you edit the file and save it again, the new version of the file replaces the old version. The new version is said to overwrite the old version.

Did you know that parking a disk is nothing like parking a car? That your physical drive is much different from that of any computer? And that you may have been a pirate in a former life?

pack You can purchase a program that compresses files so they take up less disk space (see *compression*). The program compresses or *packs* the designated files into a single compressed file. When you want to use the files, you must then decompress or unpack them.

   The term *pack* is also used to refer to the process of deleting records in a database. Normally, if you erase a record in a database, the record is removed from the database so it won't interfere with your work, but it still remains in the database file. To remove the record completely, you must pack the database file.

packaged software Also known as *off-the-shelf* software. Any program that is mass produced and sold— generally in a store or through mail-order or direct advertising as opposed to being custom developed for a client.

page In word processing programs, a page is either a *screen page* or a *printed page*. With a screen page, you typically flip pages by pressing the PgUp or PgDn key. Screen pages are usually shorter than printed pages, so you must flip two or three screen pages to flip one printed page.

page break   In most programs, you indicate the length of the page on which you intend to print. The program then divides the file you create into pages. Each page is separated by a page break, which is usually shown on-screen as a dashed or dotted line that extends across the screen. In most programs, you can enter your own page breaks as well; these are called *manual, or forced, page breaks.*

page description language (PDL)   A programming language, such as PostScript, that is used to tell a printer (that understands the PDL) how to print a page. Think of a PDL printer as a seasoned cook. You tell the cook you want a cheese soufflé. The cook knows what you mean and prepares the soufflé. Printers that don't understand PDL are like unskilled cooks. If you want a cheese soufflé, you'd better provide a detailed recipe or get ready to eat scrambled eggs with cheese.

The computer must send detailed instructions to a printer that doesn't understand PDL. For instance, to print a circle, the computer must convert the on-screen image into a bit map in order to tell the printer where to print each dot that makes up the circle. With a printer that understands PDL, the computer can send general instructions. Then, to print a circle, the computer tells the printer the location and size of the circle and the printer determines where to place the dots.

Because so much responsibility is placed on the printer, a printer that understands PDL must have its own processing unit and usually requires additional memory, which makes these printers more costly than other printers.

page layout program   See *desktop publishing.*

page orientation   See *orientation.*

page preview   In some word processing and page layout programs, there's a feature that lets you see a miniature version of what each printed page in your document will look like before you print it. You can save reams of paper by using this feature to check and refine margins, page numbers, headers, footers, and the basic design of the page before you print.

PageMaker A desktop publishing program from Aldus Corporation, the company that invented the term *desktop publishing*.

pagination Automatic page numbering. The variety of pagination options you might have (for example, where to place the page number, whether to print a page number on the first page of a document, and the option to start with a number other than 1) depends on the application program you're using.

paint program A program that allows you to create graphics objects that consist of a series of dots. When you create a picture in a paint program, you turn a series of pixels (on-screen dots) on or off or change their color. You can then modify the picture by changing individual pixels.

Unlike draw programs, paint programs do not treat each shape you place on-screen as a separate object. For example, if you place a circle on top of a square in a paint program, you cannot choose just the circle to move or delete. You would have to delete both objects and start over. However, in paint programs, you can add or delete individual pixels or change the color of a pixel. Because of this, paint programs are especially useful for creating irregular lines and shading patterns like those used in free-hand sketches.

palette In a graphics program, a menu of colors or patterns you can choose from.

palmtop computer See *hand-held computer*.

pane A Windows term for each window in a split screen.

Pantone Matching System A system used by many advanced graphics and print shops to ensure that the actual color printed matches the creator's intention. The Pantone system assigns numbers to about 500 colors. PMS colors can be used as is or can be mixed with other colors to form unique shades.

Paradox A relational database program marketed by Borland International. The DOS version of this program has long been popular because it makes asking complex questions comparatively simple. It also contains an application language (PAL) so people can create customized "apps" for their companies to access information just the way they need it. The long-awaited Windows version of Paradox, released in 1993, supports object-linking and embedding, accepts memo fields of any length, and contains tools for sophisticated document design. See also *relational database*.

parallel columns In many word processing and desktop publishing programs, you can set text in columns so that items in the left column align with items in the right column. The following list illustrates parallel columns:

1st line, left col.	The first line in the left column aligns with the first line in the right column.
1st line, next entry.	The first line in each left-column entry aligns with its corresponding entry in the right column.

parallel port   A receptacle at the back of a computer that provides a way for the computer to transmit output at high speeds. The parallel port is used most often to connect a parallel printer to the computer.

parallel printer   Printers can be classified in two groups—parallel printers and serial printers—depending on the computer port to which you can connect them. Because parallel printers typically print faster than serial printers, they are much more popular.

parallel processing   Two or more processors working together to process information and execute tasks at the same time. In order for this technology to be of any use to you or me, programming languages have to be invented which teach computers how to share tasks simultaneously among two or more processors. Today in Windows or OS/2 you can do multitasking, where one program does something in the foreground while you do something completely different in the background.

You can think of parallel processing as two or more processors doing different parts of the same task and talking with each other. It's quite different and requires a different kind of logic to create programs that take advantage of it. It's predicted that the next generation of computers and programming languages will be capable of parallel processing.

parameter   A value you can add to a command to specify what you want the command to act on. For example, if you want to format a floppy disk in DOS, you may need to specify the disk drive you want to use to perform the formatting operation. For example, if you enter the command **FORMAT A:**, FORMAT is the command, and A: is the parameter. See also *switch*.

parent directory   Think of the directory tree as a family tree; each person in a family tree has a parent.

In a directory tree, the parent directory is the directory one level above the current directory.

parent file   In a series of three successive updates of a file, the second-oldest version of the file.

parity bit   When data is sent over the phone lines by modem, it sends each unit of data as a byte (a collection of bits). To check data for errors during transmission, a parity bit is attached to each byte. The parity bit indicates whether the sum of the bits in a byte of data is odd or even. When the modem receives a byte of data, the program adds the number of bits in the byte to determine if the actual number is odd or even. The program then compares its count (odd or even) against the parity bit (odd or even) to determine if they match. If the parity bit says the number of bits is supposed to be odd but the actual count comes out even, the program signals a communications error.

park   Every disk drive has a read/write head that is used to read data from disks and write data onto disks. Hard disks have a read/write head for each platter included in the hard disk. When you turn off your computer, the read/write heads are suspended above the platters. If you move your computer or it gets bumped, the read/write heads can fall on the platters, destroying any data they fall on.

To protect the hard disk, the computer may have built-in instructions that tell it to park the disk whenever you turn off the computer. Parking consists of moving the read/write heads over areas on the platters that do not contain data. If the computer does not have built-in instructions, you can purchase a utility program, such as PC Tools or Norton Utilities, that has a disk-parking feature.

partition   A designated storage area on a hard disk. In DOS, the hard disk must be partitioned before being formatted. The disk can be partitioned into one or more storage areas.

Because hard disks can store hundreds or even thousands of megabytes of data, you may want to or need to partition the disk into several storage areas. For example, if you have a 100-megabyte hard disk, you may want to divide it into three 30-megabyte sections and one 10-megabyte section. Each storage area is called a *logical drive*, and is treated as a separate disk drive. In our example, the first storage area would be drive C, the second would be D, the third would be E, and the last would be F.

Hard disks were commonly partitioned on computers running under DOS version 4.0 or earlier, because these versions of DOS could handle hard disks of 32 megabytes or less. If you had a larger hard disk, you would have to partition the disk into smaller logical drives.

Pascal   Pronounced Pazz-KAHL. A high-level programming language invented in the 1970s and named after the Swiss mathematician Blaise Pascal, it was once used mainly in academic programming. A recent version of Pascal, called Borland Pascal, from Borland International, is now popular among PC application developers. See also *high-level language*.

password protection   Some programs allow you to protect a file by assigning a password to it. Whenever you want to open the file, you must enter the correct password.

paste   See *cut and paste* and *clipboard*.

path   In DOS, you can organize your files in directories and subdirectories. Whenever you want to open a file, you must tell DOS where the file is located. To do that, you must specify a path. The path tells DOS which drive to start with and which directories to follow to get to the file. The path statement might look like this:

C:\ZOO\LION\CUB

which tells DOS to go to drive C, then to the directory called ZOO, then to the subdirectory called

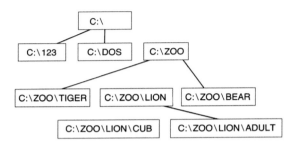

LION, and then to the subdirectory called CUB. It's sort of like telling a delivery person how to get to your house.

PC   See *personal computer.*

PC DOS   When IBM developed their first personal computer in 1981, they licensed MS-DOS from Microsoft to be its operating system. Because they're IBM, they had to make DOS their own, so they branded this licensed version PC DOS, even though it was actually no different from MS-DOS. As new versions of MS-DOS are released, PC DOS continues to be upgraded right along with it, with only an occasional utility or filename distinguishing one from another. For most practical purposes, they remain identical and fully compatible with each other.

PC Tools   An easy-to-use utility package from Central Point Software. This package is a good value because it offers anti-virus protection and a backup utility, in addition to standard PC management tools for undeleting files, repairing disks, protecting files, and checking your hard disk's performance. See also *utility program.*

peer-to-peer   Usually describes a local area network in which all computers are connected to one another, not necessarily using a central computer. A peer-to-peer network differs from a client-server network, in which all computers are connected to a central computer called the server.

pen computing   A computer with a touch-sensitive screen that can read handwriting (well, probably not your handwriting). But for those who print in a neat, consistent style with a stylus (a sort of plastic pen with no ink), pen-based computers can translate their marks into digital data and process them as if they were typed in on the keyboard. Most pen-based computers sold today are notebook-sized, and come with both a keyboard and a stylus; so you can impress fellow passengers on a plane by using your stylus to take quick notes, but switch to keyboard mode when it's time to get some real work down.

peripheral device   Any device that's connected to the computer's central processing unit but is not a part of that unit. Peripheral devices include printers, modems, mice, display screens, and keyboards.

personal computer   A computer that can stand on its own two feet. In the old days, computers were too expensive for businesses to plop one on every employee's desk. So businesses would set up a powerful central computer and connect weaker, inexpensive computers to it. However, as computers came down in price, businesses found that they *could* plop a powerful computer on every employee's desk. These individual, liberated computers are called *personal computers*. Although they are usually not as powerful as mainframe computers, personal computers provide individual users with all the power they need.

personal finance program   A type of program with several tools for managing your money: writing, logging, and printing checks, balancing a checkbook, managing a budget, and tracking expenses. As the market for this type of program becomes more competitive, some products are offering more extra features like financial advice, electronic bill paying, and investment-management tools.

personal information manager (PIM)   A program that allows you to keep track of notes, memos, names and addresses, dates, and other information.

physical drive   The actual drive that you can see and touch, as opposed to the logical disk drive. A physical disk drive can be *partitioned* into logical drives, so the computer will treat each logical drive as a separate storage area.

pie graph   In spreadsheet and presentation graphics programs, a graph that's shaped like a pie. Slices of the pie represent portions of a whole. For example,

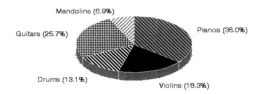

Mandolins (6.9%)
Guitars (25.7%)
Pianos (36.0%)
Drums (13.1%)
Violins (18.3%)

you could do a pie graph of your expenses to show what portion of your income goes for taxes, food, clothing, housing, automobile maintenance, child care, and so on. See also *exploded pie graph*.

PIF (Program Information File)   Pronounced piff. A file assigned to a particular program that tells Microsoft Windows how to run the program.

pin feed   See *tractor feed*.

piracy   The unauthorized use of a computer program. You're pirating software when you copy program disks from someone who has paid for the software. No one has the right to do this, including not-for-profit organizations, churches, or schools—let alone businesses. Software companies take this activity seriously and have been known to keel-haul even the meekest of offenders.

pitch   See *characters per inch*.

pixel   Also known as *picture element* or *pel*. Your computer screen is essentially a grid made up of thousands of tiny dots, called pixels. Whenever you type a character or draw a line on-screen, your computer turns the pixels on in a specific pattern to show you what you just typed or drew.

plasma display   Also called *gas plasma display*. A video display that uses charged gas to light characters and images on the screen. This type of display is used on many laptop computers.

platen   The roller on a typewriter or printer.

platform   See *hardware platform*.

platter   Metal disks that are used in a hard disk drive. Typical hard disk drives contain two to eight platters. However, the disk drive treats the collection of platters as a single disk. See also *hard disk*.

plot   To print an image using fluid lines, as opposed to creating the image as a series of dots. In spreadsheet and business presentation graphics, the term *plot* refers to placing data points on a graph. You type the values you want included in the graph, and the program plots the points for you.

plotter   A type of printer that uses pens to draw fluid, detailed sketches. Plotters are often used by architects and map makers to print complex drawings and layouts. Some plotters use a process similar to that used in laser printers to draw the lines.

point   The meaning of this term varies depending on what you're talking about:

With a mouse, you *point* by rolling the mouse on the desk until the on-screen mouse pointer is positioned on the item you want to select.

If you are talking about type sizes, the term *point* is often used to describe the height of a character. There are 72 points in an inch.

With programs and databases, you use a *pointer* to refer to data or commands located in another file or record.

point-and-click   A phrase where the whole is greater than the sum of its parts. Literally, it means positioning the mouse pointer over something on the screen, and then clicking on it to activate it (like clicking on the Word for Windows icon to start the program). Taken together as a phrase, though, as in "the point-and-click technology will blow you away," it sums up all that is great about graphical user interfaces, the ease of making things happen simply by clicking—without having to remember a lot of commands.

pointing device   An input device that allows you to move a cursor or pointer around on the screen. Common pointing devices include mice, pens (in pen-based computing), and graphics tablets.

pop-up menu   A list of options that appears on-screen when you enter a command. After you select an option from the menu, the menu disappears from the screen. Compare it to a pull-down menu, which you open by selecting it from a bar at the top of the screen.

port   A receptacle, usually on the back of the computer. A port allows you to connect various input and output devices to the computer, including a keyboard, mouse, display screen, and printer.

Pop-up menu

portable computer A personal computer that you can pack up and carry . . . if you happen to be Arnold Schwarzenegger. Portable computers weigh about 25 pounds and are comparable to lugging around a sewing machine. If you want true portability, get a laptop computer.

portrait orientation Many programs and some printers allow you to print text in either of two orientations: *portrait* or *landscape*. With portrait orientation, text is printed as you would type a letter on a page—the page is longer than it is wide. With landscape orientation, text is printed sideways, making the page wider than it is long.

POST Short for Power On Self Test. A little test your computer runs every time you turn it on, to ensure that the printer, keyboard, and other connecting peripherals are properly connected to the CPU, configured, and ready for action. If it encounters any problems, it will alert you with an error message.

PostScript   A page description language (PDL), developed by Adobe Systems, that controls the printing of text and graphics (see *page description language*).

You don't work with the language directly. You do your usual thing—selecting type styles, sizing the text, drawing pictures, and so on. PostScript works in the background, creating the instructions needed to form each character and graphics object. You will hardly notice PostScript. What you will notice is that you have more control over text and graphics. You'll be able to pick a type style and then change the type size one point (1/72 of an inch) at a time. Without PostScript, your selection would be limited; for example, you could choose only 6-, 8-, 10-, or 12-point type.

Another important advantage of PostScript is that files saved in PostScript can be printed on a wide range of PostScript printers. So you can create and save a publication, take it down to Wally's Print Shop, and have Wally print the publication on a high-quality PostScript printer that most people can't afford to buy.

power-down   To close all files and programs and switch off your computer. Most programs don't like having the lights turned out before they're tucked in. You should always quit any program you are working in before you flip the power switch.

power supply   An electrical device inside the computer that transforms standard voltage (115,120 volts of alternating current) from the wall outlet into low voltage (512 volts of direct current) that the computer can use. Power supplies are rated in watts. If you are purchasing a new computer, make sure the power supply is rated at least 200 watts. Otherwise, if you add devices to the computer later, you may end up overloading the power supply.

power-up   To switch on a computer with the operating system in place. The operating system consists of the files that contain the basic instructions your computer needs to operate. If your computer has a hard disk, these files are probably stored on the hard disk, and you can power-up by turning on the power. If your computer does not have a hard disk, you need to insert a floppy disk containing the operating system files (known as a *bootable disk*) in the floppy disk drive before turning on the power.

power user An advanced computer user who works with applications programs more than with programming languages. Power users understand and can make full use of a program's advanced features.

precedence Also known as *order of operations*. Spreadsheet programs allow you to enter formulas to have the program calculate values. For example, you can enter a formula to have the program calculate a student's grade point average. To use formulas effectively, you must understand that the program performs the calculations in a specific sequence. It gives some mathematical operators *precedence* over others:

1st	Exponential equations
2nd	Multiplication and division
3rd	Addition and subtraction

This is important to keep in mind when you are creating equations, because the *order of operations* determines the result. For example, if you want to determine the average of the values in cells A1, B1, and C1, and you enter +A1+B1+C1/3, you'll get the wrong answer. The value in C1 will be divided by 3, and that result will be added to A1+B1. To determine the total of A1 through C1 first, you must enclose that group of values in parentheses: +(A1+B1+C1)/3. In other words, you control the order of operations with parentheses. See also *arithmetic operator*.

presentation graphics program   Also known as *business presentation graphics*. A graphics program that is based on the assumption that most businesses require only a few graphics elements (usually called *charts*): graph charts, text charts, organizational charts, and flow charts. With business presentation graphics, you supply the raw data and choose how you want it displayed. The graphics program takes care of the rest, drawing the specified chart. You can then modify the chart for your own use.

With most presentation graphics programs, you can use the charts you create in any number of ways:

- You can print the chart on a separate page and then include that page in a report or presentation.

Presentation graphics programs let you select from many types of charts.

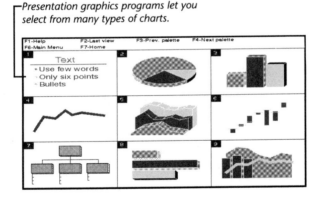

- You can save the chart in a separate file, and then pull the file into a document created in another program.

- You can create an on-screen slide show that presents one chart at a time.

- You can save the charts in separate files on a floppy disk and send the disk to a service which can convert the disks into actual slides.

primary storage Your computer's electronic memory (RAM). Because this memory relies on electrical power, it is described as volatile; turn off the power, and whatever was in memory is gone. Compare primary storage to secondary storage, such as magnetic disks, optical disks, and compact discs. Data is stored permanently in secondary storage.

print queue Pronounced cue. A list of files that is waiting to be printed. Many programs can print files in the background while you continue performing some other task on the computer. As you work, the program prints the files in the print queue until all the files are printed.

print spooling If you print without spooling, the program sends information required to print the file directly to the printer. Because the program is busy telling the printer what to do, you have to wait. Some programs provide a feature that lets you continue working while the program is printing a file. The program intercepts the information being sent to the printer and stores it in a temporary file on disk. As you work, the program feeds instructions in this file to the printer. When the program is finished printing the file, it deletes the temporary file.

printer A device that turns the masterpieces you create on your computer into paper documents the whole world can enjoy. There are a number of printers to choose from, each with a cost roughly analogous to the quality of the printing.

At the low end are dot-matrix printers, which combine patterns of dots to form images that resemble whole characters and graphics (kind of like an impressionist painting).

Thermal printers, also inexpensive, carry the impressionist technique to new lows by applying it to shiny, heat-sensitive paper that's hard to read and smells funny. You usually see these printers used in fax machines—not many people voluntarily buy them.

Letter-quality printers operate like daisywheel typewriters, so you get a clean, professional-looking document; but like typewriters, they can only print text, not graphics.

When used correctly, inkjet printers offer a good blend of affordability and quality, producing output by spraying ink onto paper in tiny jet streams, but you have to be sure to use them with the proper paper or the results can be messy.

At the top of the line are laser printers, which work sort of like a copier and produce slick, professional-looking results, making them worth the high price.

See also *resolution*.

printer driver   A miniprogram that converts printing codes generated by a program into codes that your printer can understand. When a program prints a document, it sends both the text and any formatting codes to the printer. These codes vary from program to program and from printer to printer. So you need a printer driver to perform the necessary translations.

printer font   The fonts (type styles) that a program uses to print text, as opposed to *screen fonts*, which the program uses to display text. Ideally, the screen font should match the printer font; that is, you want to see how the text will look on-screen before you print it. However, programs typically use one set of fonts for display purposes and another for printing. If the program does not have a screen font that matches the selected printer font, it displays the closest screen font available.

printer port A receptacle on the back of the computer that allows you to connect a printer to the computer. Most computers have two printer ports—a *parallel port* and a *serial port*. The parallel port is most often used as the printer port, because it allows data to be sent more quickly to the computer. The serial port is generally used to connect a mouse or modem to the computer.

processing Whatever the computer does to data between the input and output stage. Think of it in human terms. When you read, you are receiving input. When you write, you are producing output. When you are thinking, you are processing. Think about it.

PROCOMM Software that enables IBM-compatible computers to use their modems for communicating with other computers over phone lines. Initially a shareware program, PROCOMM is available for both DOS and Windows environments. It is now the program of choice for many users because it's easy to use, yet contains many popular features that automate the dialing and downloading processes.

Prodigy An on-line information service popular for its variety of consumer offerings, including shopping, airline reservations, multiplayer games, and discussion groups, and for its economical monthly price.

program Also called *application* or *software*. A program contains instructions that tell your computer what to do. There are two types of programs—operating systems and applications. The operating system gives the computer the general instructions it needs to operate. An application provides instructions for performing a particular task, such as word processing or desktop publishing.

programmable   Capable of being instructed to perform a desired task. A clear example of a programmable unit is the computer itself. You can program the computer to do any number of things, including balancing your checkbook or printing a series of form letters.

programming   The process of writing a set of instructions that tell the computer how to perform a specific task. Programming requires you to perform the following steps:

1. Come up with an idea for the program.

2. Form a general outline.

3. Write the program in a programming language.

4. Compile or interpret the program to convert it into machine language (a language the computer can understand).

5. Run and test the program.

6. *Debug* the program; find and eliminate any errors.

7. Revise the program.

project management   A type of software that helps to prioritize and track the process of successfully completing a complex project, assuming you can figure out how to use the program. Project management programs can be difficult to learn because they're based on complex management techniques that you have to understand before the software can make any sense. One of these programs is worth investing in only if you manage complex projects consisting of dozens of smaller projects performed by many people.

PROLOG Developed in the early 1970s by Alain Colmerauer and Philippe Russel, it's short for PROgramming in LOGic. A high-level programming language that's used mainly in developing artificial intelligence applications, which are programs that attempt to incorporate human-like reasoning into their processes.

prompt To request input from the user by displaying a symbol or message on-screen. Many programs will prompt you to type information or make a selection.

proportional sizing In most graphics programs, you can resize and reshape graphics objects on-screen. For example, if you have a picture that's an inch too tall, you can shorten it one inch. However, if you shorten the picture an inch and keep it the same width, you're going to end up with a short, fat

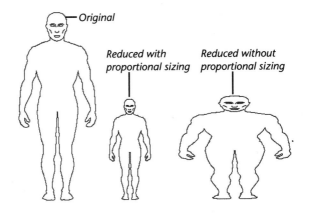

Original

Reduced with proportional sizing

Reduced without proportional sizing

picture. To keep the proper dimensions, most programs will allow you to scale the image a certain percent or size the image proportionally.

proportional spacing   In the old days of typewriters, each character had its own personal space. A skinny *i* was allotted the same space as a fat *m*. The carriage was set up to move a certain amount of space no matter which character you typed.

   With computers, you can use proportional spacing to give each character only the space it needs. The skinny *i* gets a narrow space, and the fat *m* gets a wide space. With proportional spacing, the printed words look much more uniform. Many programs may also provide *monospaced* type (such as Courier) that acts like the type on the old typewriters.

   Proportionally spaced font

   `Monospaced font`

protocol   See *communications protocol*.

PrtSc key   On IBM and compatible keyboards, you can press the PrtSc (Print Screen) key to print an image of the screen. If the image is a graphics screen, you must run the DOS program GRAPHICS.COM before pressing the PrtSc key.

   In Microsoft Windows, pressing the PrtSc key captures the screen and stores it on the Windows Clipboard. You can then paste the screen into the Windows Paintbrush program and print the screen from Paintbrush.

PS/2   See *IBM Personal System/2*.

public domain software   Free programs that you can legally copy and use. Often these programs are written by teachers or members of computer user groups. They are usually simple (written, for instance, to speed up file searches or the movement of the cursor) and rarely come with written instructions.

pull-down menu   A list of options that drops down from a menu bar at the top of the screen. The menu bar allows the menus to remain out of the way while you are creating or editing your file. When you select a menu, it drops down to cover a portion of the screen. When you are done with the menu, it retreats into the menu bar.

Pull-down menu

Although Q terms are nearly extinct, they offer some important revelations. First, you can query a database to get all the information you need. Second, not all BASICs are created equal.

Quadra See *Macintosh Quadra*.

Quattro Pro A spreadsheet program marketed by Borland International. It originally gained popularity by imitating and underpricing Lotus 1-2-3. Quattro Pro for Windows, however, is an innovative product in its own right, incorporating the 3-D concept of notebook pages (which make it easy to link information from several worksheets within the same file) and offering spectacular presentation graphics.

query In a database, you can use a query to pull specific information out of the database. Think of a database as a beach. Each record in the database is a grain of sand. Now, say you want a handful of sand, but you want only golden grains. That may take a while. With a database, you can set up a query that tells the database program which records you want. The program searches the database and pulls out the specified records.

query by example (QBE) A feature offered by many database programs that provides an easy way to pull records from a database. With QBE, you use a structure that matches the structure of the database containing the records you want to search. For example, if your database contains the following fields:

F_NAME   L_NAME   ADDRESS CITY   STATE   ZIP

you would use the same structure for your query. In each field, you would enter *search criteria* telling the program what to look for. For example, to find all records that have a last name entry of Smith, you would enter Smith in the L_NAME field.

You can also use wild-card characters to broaden the search. For example, to find all records for those people whose last name starts with *S*, you would enter S* or some similar entry in the L_NAME field. (The asterisk [*] is a wild-card character that stands in for other characters.)

Original list of records

	A	B	C	D	E	F	G
12	10	Chuck	Burger	6754 W. Lakeview Drive	Boston	MA	55784
13	11	Carey	Bistro	987 N. Cumbersome Lane	Detroit	MI	86667
14	12	Marie	Gabel	8764 N. Demetrius Blvd.	Miami	FL	86930
15	13	Adrienne	Bullow	5643 N. Gaylord Ave.	Philadelphia	PA	27639
16	14	John	Kramden	5401 N. Bandy	Pittsburgh	PA	27546
17	15	Mitch	Kroll	674 E. Cooperton Drive	Seattle	WA	14236
18	16	Gary	Davell	76490 E. Billview	New York	NY	76453
19	17	Kathy	Estrich	8763 W. Cloverdale Ave.	Paradise	TX	54812
20							
21	QUERY						
22	RECORD#	FNAME	LNAME	ADDRESS	CITY	STATE	ZIP
23			K*				
24							
25	OUTPUT						
26	RECORD#	FNAME	LNAME	ADDRESS	CITY	STATE	ZIP
27	1	William	Kennedy	5567 Bluehill Circle	Indianapolis	IN	46224
28	2	Marlon	Kraft	1813 Mockingbird Lane	Los Angeles	CA	77856
29	5	Lisa	Kaodan	6976 Westhaven Drive	Orlando	FL	88329
30	14	John	Kramden	5401 N. Bandy	Pittsburgh	PA	27546
31	15	Mitch	Kroll	674 E. Cooperton Drive	Seattle	WA	14236
32							
33							

Entry tells program to extract all records with a last name entry that starts with K.

Resulting list of records

query language   A set of language rules for searching a database and displaying the results to suit your purposes. Most query languages use standard English within a rigid structure. Query by example, or QBE, is a popular query language because it enables you to mimic the form of the information you want the database to find. See also *query by example*.

QuickBASIC   Whenever you write a program, you use commands that you can understand. For the computer to run the program, however, it must be translated or compiled into a language the computer can understand (machine language). QuickBASIC is an advanced compiler used to compile programs written in Microsoft BASIC, BASICA, and GW-BASIC, and versions of BASIC that come with many computers. See also *compiler*.

quit   To follow a prescribed set of steps when you decide to stop using a program. In Word for Windows, for example, you quit by selecting Exit from the File menu and then answering any questions it may ask about saving files you've worked on. Not to be confused with simply shutting off the computer when you get bored, a move which can really screw up your files if you haven't properly exited a program—files may not be saved and there can be other dire consequences as well.

QWERTY   Pronounced KWER-tee. The standard typewriter keyboard layout. The name QWERTY refers to the first six letter keys in the upper left corner of the keyboard.

➤

Contrary to popular belief, RAM cache is not money you pay for a male sheep, a root directory is not a storage area for turnips, and you can't run a program to make it lose weight.

radio button Also known as *option button.* Many programs display dialog boxes whenever they need your input. For example, if you enter a command to open a file, a dialog box may appear, asking you to name the file you want to open. Some dialog boxes contain buttons that let you select from a list of options. In a group of option buttons, you can select only one button. Selecting a different button in the group deselects the currently selected button, just as pressing a button on an old car radio deselects any selected station. See also *dialog box.*

You can select only one option button in each group.

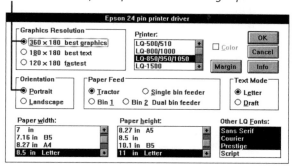

ragged-left alignment   Also known as *right justifica-tion*. With ragged-left alignment, all lines in a paragraph are pushed against the right margin, so the left ends of the lines appear uneven:

> *Ragged-left alignment* pushes the right end of the line against the right margin, leaving the left margin ragged. Although you probably won't use this justification often, it is useful for typing a date at the top of the page or a page number at the bottom.

ragged-right alignment   Also known as *left justification*. With ragged-right alignment, all lines of text are pushed against the left margin, making the right side of the paragraph look uneven:

> *Ragged-right alignment* is the default setting for most programs. As you can see, each line is flush against the left margin, leaving a ragged right margin.

RAM   See *random-access memory*.

RAM cache   Pronounced ram cash. A portion of a computer's electronic memory set aside to hold data frequently used by the current program. This increases the speed of certain program operations, reducing time the program spends getting data from a disk.

A RAM cache differs from a RAM disk, in that a RAM cache stores only chunks of data that the program needs. A RAM disk stores entire files, just like a disk drive.

RAM disk   A portion of a computer's electronic memory set up to work like a disk. Because computers can read and write to RAM much more quickly than to disk, a RAM disk increases the speed of certain program operations. Note that any changes you make to a file are saved only in RAM. You must carefully copy files from the RAM disk to a hard disk or floppy disk before turning off your computer, or your work will be lost.

random access   Anything but random, this is your computer's capability to get to a piece of information directly rather than having to sift through all the information that was stored before it. Consider the CD as opposed to the cassette tape. On the cassette, if you want to hear the fifth song, you have to fast forward through songs 1 through 4 first, stopping now and then to see if you're there. With a CD, though, simply enter track 5 and your favorite Gershwin tune starts up pronto. Like the CD player, the computer can work a lot faster with data stored in a random access source, like RAM, where it can move backward and forward, selecting any data you request, as opposed to the sequential search required by a tape backup.

random-access memory (RAM)   A computer's electronic memory, as opposed to the magnetic storage of a disk. Whenever you load a program into your computer or open a file, the computer reads information from the disk and copies it into its electronic memory. It then uses the information in RAM to interpret and carry out the commands you enter.

   RAM is made up of several electronic components called *chips* that store information electronically. The information remains in RAM only as long as the power to the computer is on. If you open a document in RAM and then turn off the computer and experience a power outage, RAM forgets the document. What you saved on disk is safe, but any changes you made to the document are lost. That's why it is so important to store information magnetically on disk.

   So, why not just use disks? The main reason is speed. If the computer had to play back instructions from your program disk every time you entered a command, it would take forever.

range   Also known as a *cell block*. A group of cells in a spreadsheet. A spreadsheet is made up of a series of columns and rows that intersect to form rectangles called cells. You type entries into the cells to create your spreadsheet. If you need to perform some operation on two or more cells, you must select a range of cells.

Range of cells C20..F31

A range is typically specified by the cell address in the upper left corner of the group and the cell address in the lower right corner. (The address specifies the column letter and row number of the cell, such as A3.) For example, the range A1..C3 specifies a rectangular group of cells starting from A1 (Column A, Row 1), going over to C1, and down to C3.

range name   A name assigned to a group of cells in a spreadsheet. Many spreadsheet programs let you name groups of cells to simplify group selection. Instead of selecting the cell group with the mouse or typing a range, such as C6..M44, you can type the name you've assigned to the block, for example SALES.

raster display   The display style of most desktop computer monitors. The screen of a desktop computer monitor is made up of tiny rows of dots. Each line is called a raster. In order to show an image on the screen, the rasters have to be constantly charged so that the dots light up. A device called an electron gun charges the rasters one line at a time, from the top line down to the bottom line, so quickly that it gets back up to recharge the top raster before your eye can notice that it's started to fade out.

read   To get data from a disk and store it in the computer's electronic memory, where the computer can work with it.

readme file   A type of file found in many DOS and Windows programs, that you're supposed to read before you use the program for the first time. It usually contains useful information that didn't make it into the manual or, if the program didn't come with a manual, all the instructions you're going to get. If you find a README file in the directory of files in a new program and it has the extension .EXE, .BAT, or .COM, you can open it just by typing the filename. If it has an extension .DOC or .TXT, you have to open it from within a word processing program.

read-only attribute   A characteristic assigned to a file, making it impossible to change the file's contents. See also *file attribute*.

read-only memory (ROM)   Rhymes with prom. A memory chip used to permanently store instructions. ROM's main function is to carry out the central processing unit's management functions. Most of ROM is used by the ROM BIOS (Basic Input /Output System) that directs the traffic between the computer and the keyboard, printer, and monitor. ROM may also contain a set of instructions installed by the manufacturer to perform a series of tests whenever you start your computer.

ROM chips are also used in printers to store information the printer needs to print characters. With printers that allow you to plug in font cartridges (cartridges that contain additional type styles), the cartridges contain ROM chips that store the instructions for creating the type styles.

read/write head   Every disk drive has a read/write head that reads information off of a disk and writes information onto the disk. The read/write head works a lot like the recording head in a tape recorder. Whenever you save a file to disk, the read/write head applies a series of electrical charges to the disk as the disk spins under the head. This changes the orientation of the magnetic dots on the disk, storing information magnetically. To read information from the disk, the read/write head senses the orientation of the magnetic dots and converts the data into electrical impulses that the computer can understand.

real mode   An operating state for IBM and compatible computers that allows programs to use only the standard 640 kilobytes of memory available through DOS. Some operating environments, such as Windows, allow programs to access memory above the 640 kilobyte limit by running in *protected mode*. In protected mode, programs are prevented from interfering with one another in memory, so you can keep two or more programs running at the same time.

real time   In transactions, *real time* means the program responds in the same time frame as a human being would expect it to. Flight simulators, for example, are considered real-time instruments, because they respond immediately to certain conditions (just as a real airplane would respond to a gust of wind). If you were to create a real-time animated sequence on the computer, the characters would move across the screen at the same speed as they would if they were alive.

reboot   Also known as *warm boot*. To reload the computer's operating system when the computer is already running. In DOS, if your computer is locked up, you can usually reboot by holding down the Ctrl key and the Alt key and then pressing the Del key, or instead, by pressing the reset button on the computer (if it has one). Rebooting is preferred over restarting the computer, because it doesn't require you to switch the power to the components inside the computer off and on.

recalculation method   You can create spreadsheets that use formulas to perform mathematical operations on values in the spreadsheet. The spreadsheet program performs the calculations and then recalculates whenever you enter new data or change a formula. Most programs let you choose from the following recalculation methods:

> *Automatic recalculation.* The program immediately recalculates the spreadsheet whenever you change or add values or formulas. You must wait for the program to perform the recalculation before you can do anything else.

> *Manual recalculation.* The program recalculates the spreadsheet only when you press the designated function key or enter the appropriate command.

recalculation order   In a spreadsheet, you can enter formulas that perform calculations on values in the spreadsheet. For example, you can set up an invoice that determines total cost of several products being shipped to a customer and then adds sales tax. The spreadsheet usually performs calculations in the most logical order, but many spreadsheet programs let you choose one of the following recalculation orders:

Natural recalculation performs calculations in a logical sequence. In the example above, the spreadsheet would calculate the total cost of products before determining the sales tax.

Row-wise recalculation performs calculations left to right across each row, regardless of the logical order in which the calculations are to be performed.

Column-wise recalculation performs calculations top to bottom in each column.

Most people rarely use column-wise or row-wise recalculation.

recognition logic   The type of software you have to use with an optical character reader. It enables the device to make sense of what it sees and turns it into computer data.

record   A collection of information about one person, place or thing. A database contains a series of records, each of which contains one or more field entries. For example, if you had a database containing the names, addresses, and phone numbers of all the members on your kid's baseball team, the name, address, and phone number for just one kid would be a record.

recover   To get out of trouble. The term *recover is* commonly used to describe the process of restoring lost or damaged files. You can recover files in either of two ways:

Undeleting. When you delete a file, the actual file contents remain on disk. Only the name is changed to prevent it from being displayed. In other words, the file is there, but you can't see it. As long as you don't store another file on disk overwriting

the contents of the deleted file, you can
undelete the file using a special program,
such as PC Tools or Norton Utilities.

Restoring from backups. If you create backup
copies of your files, you can use the backup
program to restore the backed up files to
their original form. However, the file will
not contain any changes you've made to the
file since the last time you backed up.

redlining Some word processing programs provide a
feature that compares two versions of a document
and marks the differences. Any text that has been
deleted appears struck out in print. Any text that has
been added appears with redlining. The appearance
of redlined text varies; it may appear shaded or with
a double-underline, or the program may allow you
to select a style.

reformat If you're talking about reformatting a disk,
it means to format the disk again, erasing all data
that's on it, once you no longer need the data and
want to use the disk for something else. If you are
planning to erase all the files from a disk because you
don't need them anymore, it's a good idea to reformat instead of just erasing, especially if the disk is
kind of old. If you reformat, you can check the disk
for bad sectors, dropout, and any other problems
that may have developed over the ages.

  If *reformat* is used in reference to a document, it
means to change the design elements—the font,
margins, placement of graphics, and so on.

refresh To update the display or the information in
memory. The display on a computer monitor is
constantly being refreshed by a beam of light that
illuminates the screen. If the beam stopped moving
and refreshing the screen, the characters would fade
from the screen.

The term *refresh* is also used to describe the activity of redisplaying data after the user enters a change. For example, if you change the margins in a document, the program may not show the effects of the change until you start moving through the document or until you enter a command telling the computer to refresh or redisplay the screen. This speeds up your work because you don't have to wait for the program to refresh the display each time you enter a change.

relational database   A relational database lets two or more database files exchange information. For example, you can create one database that stores customer information and another that stores inventory information and prices. You can then create a report (say an invoice) that pulls a customer's name and address from the customer database and pricing information from the inventory database, and then updates the inventory database to show the quantity of a particular item sold.

relational operator   In programming and in spread-sheet and database programs, relational operators allow you to compare two values. For example, say you own a company and you want a list of all the customers who owe you money. You would want to search your database for all those customers who have a balance greater than 0. The term greater than is a relational operator. It determines a condition by comparing two values: the balance and 0. Relational operators are commonly expressed using the following symbols:

=	Equal to
>	Greater than
<	Less than
<>	Not equal to

    <=   Less than or equal to

    >=   Greater than or equal to

relative cell reference   In a spreadsheet program, rows and columns intersect to form cells. Each cell has an address consisting of the column letter and the row number. For example, the address of the cell in the upper left corner of the spreadsheet is A1. You can use these cell addresses along with mathematical operators to create formulas. For instance, insert the formula A1+B1 in cell C1 to have the program add the values in cells A1 and B1 and insert the total in cell C1.

    If you copy the formula in cell C1 into cell C2, the addresses in the formula change; the formula in C2 will be A2+B2. Why? Because the addresses in the formula give relative locations. In this case, the formula A1+B1 tells the program to add the values in the two cells to the left of the current cell. When you copy the formula to cell C2, the formula still tells the program to add the values in the two cells to the left of the current cell. Now that the formula is in cell C2, however, the two cells to the left of it are A2 and B2. If you want the references to remain the same when you copy or move the formula, you must mark the addresses as absolute. See also *absolute cell reference*.

release number   The number to the right of the decimal point in a program's number. When a software company performs a major overhaul of one of its programs, it changes the version number of the program. The version number is the number to the left of the decimal point. For example, in WordPerfect 5.0, 5 is the version number. When WordPerfect updated version 5.0, for example, it released the new version as WordPerfect 5.1. When the company performs a minor revision of a program, it keeps the original version number, but it changes the release number.

Some software companies (WordPerfect is again a fine example), release revised versions that are marked with a certain release date. So, not all releases of WordPerfect 5.1 are equal.

removable storage   A magnetic tape, disk, or cartridge on which you can store data and then remove it from the drive. Contrast this with nonremovable storage, such as a hard disk. Removable storage units are commonly used to store backup copies of files that are stored on a hard disk.

rename   To change the file name on disk. Contents of the file remain the same, only its name is changed.

repaginate   To change the page numbering in a document. Most word processing and desktop publishing programs offer automatic repagination. If you add a page in the middle of the document, the program automatically adjusts the page numbering.

repeat key   A key that you hold down in order to repeatedly type a character. On newer keyboards, most character keys automatically repeat if you hold them down. For example, if you want to type a row of periods, you can hold down the period key. On older keyboards, you have to hold down a repeat key and then press the key you want to repeat.

repetitive strain injury   See *cumulative trauma disorder*.

replace   To substitute new data in place of old data. The term *replace* is commonly used to refer to either of the following actions:

> *Replace file.* When you save a file for the first time, you have to name the file. If you try to copy or save a file of the same name to the same drive and directory, the new file will replace the old file.

Replace text. Many programs offer a feature that searches for one string of text and replaces it with the text you specify. For example, say you created a training manual to teach new hires how to make gadgets. Later, the company decides to call gadgets *widgets*. You can have the program search through the manual for every occurrence of the word gadget and replace it with widget.

report   In general, any presentation of information that appears in print complete with page numbers and headings—for example, an annual report.

In database programs, *report* has a special meaning. You generate reports to assemble information from the database into some meaningful form. For example, you may create an inventory report that pulls together a list of items that are out of stock. See also *relational database*.

reset button   Some computers have a reset button you can press to reboot the computer. Don't confuse the reset button with the on/off button. The on/off button actually turns off the computer. The reset button keeps the computer on, but clears its memory and causes the computer to reread the instructions it needs to get started.

Printers may also have a reset button. On a printer, the reset button clears any printing instructions from the printer's memory and reorients the printer. This button is useful if you stop printing in the middle of a print job. Sometimes the printer continues printing long after you tell it to stop.

resident program   See *memory resident*.

resolution   The detail and sharpness of an image as displayed on-screen or in print. Imagine the computer screen as a piece of graph paper. To create a character or a line, the computer colors the squares on the graph paper in certain patterns. If the screen consisted of large squares, the characters and lines would look ragged, as they do on low-resolution monitors. High-resolution monitors use tinier squares, making the text and graphics much smoother.

With display screens, resolution is measured in *pixels* (the tiny squares on-screen). A VGA monitor has a resolution of 480 by 640 pixels—307,200 total pixels. A Super VGA monitor has a resolution of 768 by 1,024 pixels—786,432 total pixels (more than 2 ½ times the number of pixels as the VGA monitor). With printers, resolution is measured in *dots per inch* (dpi). Low-resolution printers print at about 120 dpi, while most laser printers print at about 300 dpi. Advanced typesetting printers can print up to 3,000 dpi.

resource   Any programs, data, or devices that you can get at while using a program.

restore   When you create backup copies of your files using a backup program, the program compresses the copies of your files so they will take up less disk space. If an original file is lost or damaged, you must use the backup files to get the lost file back. Because the backup file is compressed, it is not usable in its backed up form. The restore operation decompresses the backed up file, making it usable.

retrieve   To get stored data so you can work with it. Whenever you write a letter, draw a picture, or create any other work, you save it to disk in a named file. Whenever you want to work with the item in that file, you must open or retrieve the file.

Some programs distinguish between opening and retrieving. When you open a file, the file appears on a fresh screen by itself. When you retrieve a file, you retrieve it into the currently open file.

Return   See *Enter/Return key.*

reverse video   Programs usually display text as white text on a black background or black text on a white background. If you select the text, the text appears opposite of normal. That is, if text normally appears white-on-black, the program displays selected text as black-on-white. This is called reverse video, and is also known as inverse video.

RGB   Most color monitors use the RGB system of producing color on the screen. It's short for *Red Green Blue*. Back in art class, you learned that these three colors are called the additive primaries because combined together, they produce white. Combined in paint you get black, but on a monitor you get white because a full color signal (RGB all on at max setting) turns the intensity of the 3 color guns to max and this produces the white on the screen. Try it in the Windows control panel for colors, adjust color palette, define custom colors. If you're shopping for a color monitor, make sure to purchase an RGB monitor over the cheaper kind, a composite monitor. The colors will look better and print will be more readable.

right justification   A way to align text so that each line of text is flush against the right margin, leaving an uneven left margin. See also *justification*.

ringback system   A system for calling a remote computer, either as a security measure or as hassle saver for somebody running a BBS who has to share their phone line with the computer modem.

   If you call a computer system using ringback for security purposes, you have to supply your modem's number when you call and then that system will call your modem back. This way it has your number in case you do anything dastardly like break into the office payroll files and raise your salary or otherwise access and manipulate restricted data.

If it's simply being used in a BBS whose owner only has one phone line, you have to call the computer system twice, once to activate the remote modem and again to connect your modem.

RISC   Stands for Reduced Instruction Set Computer. It's a different kind of computer system than the typical personal computer, because it sacrifices general speed for greater speed in a specific activity.

With a general purpose personal computer (say an IBM-compatible 386), before you take it home and load stuff into it, its microprocessor is already preprogrammed with over 100 instructions for how to input and output information and handle other mundane tasks. It doesn't run quite as fast as it would if there were only ten instructions preprogrammed into it, but it can also handle any compatible software you load with fairly consistent speed and dependability. It's a great general purpose machine.

A RISC system, though, would be useful to a big company that wants it to do one thing, like computer-aided design. If the company's main concern is that the computer be fast in computer-aided design (not that it be adaptable to any program under the sun you may choose to load into it), the RISC system is a good choice. So the CPU is preprogrammed with only 50 or so instructions, meaning it can handle computer-aided design as fast as lightning, but it's not very handy with other programs. So you probably don't want a RISC system in your den at home, but you might want one in your design firm.

ROM   See *read-only memory.*

ROM BIOS   See *basic input-output system.*

root directory   Because large hard disks can store thousands of files, you need to organize the disk into directories. Each directory stores a group of related files. Together, the directories form a directory tree. Directories branch off from one another as in a family tree. The first directory in the tree is called the *root directory*.

row In spreadsheet programs, each spreadsheet is comprised of alphabetized columns (which run down) and numbered rows (which run across). The columns and rows intersect to form cells, the basic unit of the spreadsheet.

run To start a program. When you run a program, the computer reads the instructions from disk and stores them in electronic memory. Once the instructions are in memory, the program can perform its required work.

run-time version A pared-down version of an operating environment that allows only one program to run in that environment. For example, say a programmer develops a program that requires the GeoWorks environment in order to run. However, most users don't have GeoWorks. The programmer can purchase a run-time version of GeoWorks from the creators of GeoWorks and include it with the program. The run-time version will work only with this program and will not offer the full features of the GeoWorks package.

➤

Do you want to split your screen without using an axe? Scale a picture instead of a fish? Capture a screen without using a net? The S's will show you how.

sans serif A plain-Jane type design. Serifs are the wispy little details that appear in some type designs. *Sans serif* means without serifs. Sans serif type designs are typically used in headings and headlines. The following examples show the difference between serif and sans serif type designs:

Serif

Times Roman

Sans Serif

Helvetica

save This could be the most important thing you do all day. It means storing information in a secondary storage place, like a hard disk or a floppy disk, so that you can use it again when you need it. The first time you save a new file, you have to go through a procedure of deciding what to name it and what drive and directory you want to save it to; every time thereafter, it's a speedy command that's well worth the trouble. Power failures and other acts beyond your control can occur at any time, and any time the power goes out, everything in RAM is erased. The more often you save your work, the less work you will lose.

scalable font A font that will display and print nicely at any size you choose. Scalable fonts differ from bitmap fonts, the other common type, which only print and display nicely at the sizes they are loaded in at. That also means that instead of each point size (8-, 10-, 12-, 14-, and 16-point) taking up the space of one font, one typeface (in all point sizes) takes up the space of one font. PostScript and TrueType fonts are two of the most popular scalable groups of fonts for PCs. If you have a Macintosh, you can see an example of a bitmapped font—Macintosh screen fonts are bitmapped fonts, so they look funny in some sizes on-screen.

scaling   If you've ever assembled a plastic model, you know what scaling is. If you get a scale model of a B-52 Bomber, the dimensions of the model match the dimensions of the original. Of course, the model has to be quite a bit smaller to fit in your house. Scaling on the computer is the same thing. You can take an original graphic object or text (if you are using scalable fonts), and change its size without changing its dimensions.

Scaling is also used to refer to the range of values in a graph. For example, you could use a graph to show your movie ratings on a scale from 1 to 10.

scanner   Have you been to a grocery store lately? They have some fancy new gadgets in the checkout lane. Your groceries pass over a light beam, and the price is automatically entered into the register. The device used here is a *scanner*. It bounces light off the bar code label, takes note of the reflection it sees, and enters the code into the computerized register. In other words, the scanner *reads* the bar code into the computer.

Scanners that operate with personal computers work in much the same way. They bounce light off an image and take note of the reflected light. The scanner converts the signals it picks up into a map of dots (a bit map) that represents the shape of the scanned characters or objects. Once you've saved the image, you can open the file in a paint program and edit its dots.

The two most popular scanners are hand-held and flatbed. Hand-held scanners are the least expensive. They are best for scanning small pictures and irregular shapes (such as a pop can). A flatbed scanner resembles a photocopying machine. You place the image face down on top of the scanner, and the scanner takes a picture of the image.

Scanned image

Paper image

Scanner

scrapbook A computer file in which you can store pictures and pieces of text you commonly use. Unlike a clipboard, the scrapbook stores permanently anything you place in it. With the clipboard, any items placed in it are wiped out when you quit the program or turn off the computer.

screen capture To take a picture of your computer screen and save it to a file on disk. When I say take a picture, I don't mean that you need a special camera. To capture a screen, you use a special program that runs in the background. When the screen you want to capture is displayed, you press a key combination, such as Shift+Print Screen, which activates the screen capture program.

With screens that display only text, the screen capture program records the text. With screens that display graphics objects, such as icons and windows, the program saves the screen as a graphics file. You can then treat the captured screen as you would treat any picture.

screen dump   A "snapshot" of something displayed on a computer screen, created using a *screen capture* program, and saved as a graphics file.

screen fonts   The fonts (type designs and sizes) that a program uses to display text, as opposed to *printer fonts*, which the program uses to print text. Ideally, the screen font should match the printer font; you want to see how the text will look on-screen before you print it. However, programs typically use one set of fonts for display purposes and another for printing. If the program does not have a screen font that matches the selected printer font, it displays the closest screen font available.

screen memory   A portion of RAM that stores data needed to display whatever is output to the screen.

screen saver   If you stare at a fixed object for a long time and then look away, you may be able to see an outline of the object. The same thing happens with the computer screen. If a fixed image is displayed on the screen too long, it can get burned into the screen. To prevent this from happening, you can purchase a screen saver program that displays moving images on the screen, preventing any one image from being displayed continuously. Screen savers can provide a creative art form for your work surroundings, turning your computer screen into an acquarium complete with swimming fish, or into a modern painting featuring flying toasters and toast!

ScreenPeace can transform your screen into an aquarium.

script   A series of instructions commonly used to automate the transfer of information over the phone
lines. To get daily stock quotes from the Dow Jones
News/Retrieval, for instance, you would dial a phone
number, enter your name and password, and then
work through a series of menus to find your investment portfolio. Scripts automatically place the call,
navigate through the Dow Jones service, and then
obtain the latest quotes for your portfolio stocks.

scroll   Imagine that your computer screen is a small
window. Behind this window is a long sheet of paper on which your document is typed. To see more
of your document, you hand-scroll the paper up or
down, or back and forth. On computers, scrolling is
done electronically, taking advantage of the Page Up
and Page Down keys and the arrow keys.

Many programs display a scroll bar at the right
side and sometimes at the bottom of the screen. The
scroll bar contains an arrow at each end and a sliding

scroll box. To scroll text one line at a time, you can click on one of the arrows with the mouse. To scroll one page at a time, you click inside the scroll bar on either side of the scroll box. To move to an area of the document, you drag the scroll box inside the scroll bar. For example, to move to the middle of the document, you drag the scroll box to the middle of the bar.

Scroll Lock key   Normally, when you use arrow keys to move in a document, the cursor moves, but the text remains in place. If you turn scroll lock on (by pressing the Scroll Lock key), the cursor remains in place, and the text moves. The Scroll Lock key is a toggle; that is, pressing the key once turns scroll lock on, and pressing the key again turns it off.

SCSI   See *Small Computer System Interface*.

search and replace   See *replace*.

second-generation   When the transistor replaced the vacuum tube as a data processor, the second generation of computers was born. This was a revolutionary innovation because the transistor was far smaller, more power efficient, and required fewer moving parts than the vacuum tube. The species flourished in the early 1960's until the transistor was replaced by the integrated circuit. See also *first-generation*, *third-generation*, *fourth-generation*, and *fifth-generation*.

secondary storage   A system that permanently stores program and data files. Secondary storage includes magnetic disks, optical disks, compact disks, and storage tapes. This differs from primary storage— your computer's temporary memory. See also *random-access memory*.

sector   When you format a disk, you organize it into tracks and sectors. If the disk was a grocery store, each shopping aisle would be one track. Each 10 feet or so of shelf space would be a sector, and each complete shelf would be a cluster. When you save data to the disk, it divides the data into sector-sized portions and shelves them neatly away, filling up each cluster as it sees fit. To find out how the groceries get off the shelf, see *file allocation table*.

security Preventing the wrong people from viewing or copying computer files that contain sensitive information. Just as you might lock a filing cabinet to prevent people from reading what they shouldn't, you can lock computer files and assign passwords to prevent others from looking at or copying the files.

seek Whenever the computer stores data on disk or reads data off the disk, it has to position the read/write head to a specific location on the disk. This is called *seek* and is like moving a phonograph needle to a certain groove in a record. The time it takes the read/write head to move to the proper location is called *seek time* and is measured in milliseconds (thousandths of a second).

selection Also known as a *block*. A portion of a document, spreadsheet, or database that you choose (highlight) in order to work with that portion. The highlighted area typically appears in reverse video; that is, if text is normally white-on-black, it appears black-on-white when highlighted.

serial communications A way to transfer data one bit at a time over a single wire. Think of serial communications as a one-lane street. The eight bits of information that make up a byte (a character, for example) have to proceed down the street in single-file to their destination. With *parallel* communications, you have an eight-lane highway. All eight bits that make up the byte can travel down the highway side-by-side. Parallel communications are typically used for fast data transfer over a short distance. Serial communications allow for long-distance data transfer.

serial mouse   A pointing device that you can plug into the serial port on your computer. This type of mouse is distinguished from the *bus mouse*, which plugs into a special board that you insert into an expansion slot in the computer. The choice of which type of mouse to use depends on whether you have a free serial port or expansion slot in your computer.

serial port   A receptacle at the back of a computer that allows you to plug in a serial device, such as a serial printer, a serial mouse, or a modem.

serial printer   Printers can be classified in two groups—*parallel printers* and *serial printers*—depending on the computer port (receptacle) you can connect them to. Because parallel printers typically print faster than serial printers, they are much more popular.

serif   A fancy, easy-to-read type style. Serifs are the wispy little details that appear in some type designs, such as Times Roman. See also *sans serif*.

server   In a network, computers play either of two roles: client or server. The client is the computer on which you work. The server is the central computer and/or disk drive that provides information to the client. Whenever the client requests information, the server supplies that information.

service bureau   A business that provides printing preparation, data entry, or payroll production services using technology that would be too expensive for most individuals and companies to purchase and operate on their own. These services include: key-entry typesetting, high-resolution printing, and scanning. For printing preparation, they usually charge by the page, based on the type of work done: black and white, 4-color, camera-ready printout, separated color film, and so on.

shareware   Programs that you can test-drive, but that you are legally obligated to pay for. You can purchase shareware from dealers, such as The Software Labs, for the price of a disk and shipping: usually three or four bucks. You try the program and share it with your friends. If you like the program and want to continue using it, you must send money to the programmer who developed the program.

sheet feeder   A sheet feeder is like a paper tray in a copy machine. You load a stack of paper in the tray, and the sheet feeder feeds the paper into the printer one page at a time.

shell   Any program that stands between the user and another program, making the other program easier to use. One of the most common shells is the DOS Shell, a program that lets you select files from a list and enter commands by selecting them from menus.

A graphic representation of the directory structure on a disk

The DOS Shell lets you enter commands from menus.

A list of files in the current directory

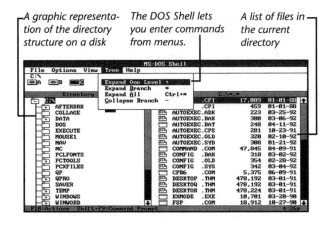

Shift key   Just like the Shift key on a typewriter; when you hold down the Shift key and type a character, the character is inserted as an uppercase rather than a lowercase letter. The Shift key can also be used in

combination with the Function keys (F1, F2, F3 etc.) to make the keys enter different commands than they would enter if pressed alone.

side-by-side columns   See *parallel columns*.

silicon   The stuff most computer chips are made from. It's a natural semi-conductor (halfway between being a conductor of electricity and an insulator of it), and is found in many minerals, including rocks, sand, and clay.

Silicon Valley   A nickname for an area in California south of San Francisco and north of San Diego, where a huge concentration of computer-related companies are located.

single density   A type of disk that stores very little data. The earliest floppy disks were single density. Most newer disks are double density (low density), which store twice the amount of data as single density, or high density, which store about four times the amount of data as single density. See also *density*.

single in-line memory module (SIMM)   A small, narrow circuit board that contains eight or nine memory chips (the electronic devices that store data while your computer works with it). SIMMs plug into special sockets inside the computer to give the computer extra memory.

single-sided disk   A disk that stores data on only one side. Think of a disk as a piece of canvas. On double-sided disks, you can paint on both sides of the canvas. On single-sided disks, you can only paint on one side.

site license   If there are 200 people in your company who need to use WordPerfect, you could either buy 200 packaged copies of it or enter into a site license with WordPerfect Corp. or an authorized dealer. For a far lower price than the 200 packages, you get one package plus the right to make 200 copies of it for your employees to use. In network situations, site licenses authorize a certain number of people to use a program on a network.

slide show   With the introduction of VCRs, slide shows are losing their popularity. Instead of sitting through a boring slide show of your relatives' summer vacation in Greece, you now have to sit through a boring movie of your relatives' summer vacation in Greece.

However, computer-driven slide shows are becoming more popular in business presentations. Using a presentation graphics program, such as Harvard Graphics or Freelance, you can create a slide show for the computer screen. The slides may contain graphs, lists of items, pictures, and other elements that you would commonly use to present your ideas to a group of people. Most of these programs allow you to save the slides to disk and send them to a vendor for conversion into bona fide slides.

slot   See *expansion slot.*

small caps   Capital letters that are smaller than regular-sized capital letters. They are based on the same font and font size you are working in, but are slightly smaller than normal. In this typeface, here's what small caps look like compared to regular-sized caps:

SMALL CAPS

REGULAR CAPS

Small Computer System Interface (SCSI)   The abbreviation is pronounced scuzzy. A connection that allows high-speed information transfer between the computer and any external devices, such as a printer or hard drive. SCSI offers the additional advantage of allowing you to connect several devices, such as printers or external drives, to a single port (receptacle). Each device is assigned an address, and only one device can talk at a time.

soft font Type designs and type sizes that come on disk just like software. Soft fonts are also known as *downloadable fonts*. If you want to print a document in which you have used soft fonts, you must send the printer the information it needs to print that font. This is called *downloading fonts*. Many programs download fonts automatically as needed during the printing process.

soft hyphen Some word processing and desktop publishing programs offer a feature that automatically hyphenates words as needed to make the lines of text appear even. If a long word doesn't fit at the end of a line, the program splits the word, adds a soft hyphen at the end of the first part of the word, and moves the second part of the word to the next line. If you add or delete text so that the word is no longer at the end of the line, the program automatically removes the soft hyphen and joins the parts of the word. See also *hard hyphen*.

soft page break In most programs, you tell the program the length of the page on which you intend to print. The program then divides the document you create into pages. Each page is separated by a soft page break, which is usually shown on-screen as a dashed or dotted line that extends across the screen. If you add or delete text on a page, the program automatically adjusts the position of the page breaks. Contrast with *hard page breaks*, which remain in a fixed position even if you add or delete text.

soft return When you type on a computer, most programs automatically insert a soft return at the end of each line. This causes the text to *wrap* from one line to the next. If you add or delete text later, so the soft return is no longer at the end of a line, the program automatically removes the return and places it where it's needed. On the other hand, when you press the Enter key, the program inserts a hard return. This return remains in place until you delete it.

In some programs, such as Word, you can manually enter a soft return that lets you start a new line of text without ending the paragraph.

software   Also known as *programs* and *applications*. The human-developed instructions a computer needs in order to operate. Think of the computer as you would a human body complete with brain cells. Before a human being can function on its own, it needs some instructions; it needs experiences and an education of some sort. The same is true of a computer. Without instructions, a computer has no life of its own and is just a lump of circuitry in a metal case. The computer needs software in order to tell it what to do.

There are two basic types of software: operating system software and applications. The operating system gets the computer up and running. Application software tells the computer how to perform a specific task.

software license   In most commercially sold software, you'll find a software license. Often the license is printed on the envelope that holds the disks. Essentially, it's a contract you enter into with the software publisher simply by opening the envelope and installing the software on your computer. In return for your use of the product, you agree not to copy it for others to use (usually you are allowed to make one backup copy for your own protection).

software piracy   See *piracy*.

software publisher   A publisher of software programs. This type of company functions similarly to a book publisher, in that it distributes and markets products which it may have come to control through a variety of ways. Like a book publisher, a software publisher might develop the product in-house, might find a talented individual or group of individuals to create it out-of-house, might get closely involved with its development, or might not have any interest in reviewing it until it's complete. Large software companies like Microsoft Corporation have extensive facilities in-house and have a tightly controlled development plan for their product line. But smaller houses often seek products from a variety of outside sources, hoping to find the one breakthrough product that will put their name on the map.

sort   You group things every day, or at least every week. You sort white clothes in one basket and colors in another. Maybe you arrange your VCR tapes in alphabetical order. Wouldn't it be nice to be able to do that by pressing a button? Some programs offer a sort feature that allows you to create and arrange lists of items. You create the list and then have the program sort the list alphabetically (A, B, C) or numerically (1, 2, 3). You can also have the program sort in ascending order (A, B, C or 1, 2, 3) or descending order (Z, Y, X or 10, 9, 8).

sort key   To group items in a list or records in a database, you can give sort instructions with *sort keys*. For example, say you have a customer file that contains the following information for each customer:

Last   First   Address   City   State   ZIP   Phone #
Name   Name

With a sort key, you can tell the program to sort the customers by last name. If any two customers have the same last name, sort by first name, as well. The first sort instruction is the *primary key*; the second is the *secondary sort key*.

sort order   The order in which a list of items is ranked or grouped. For example, numerically in ascending order (1, 2, 3) or alphabetically in descending order (Z, Y, X).

sound board   A device that dramatically improves the sound quality on an IBM or compatible computer. Most PCs don't come with a sound board as standard equipment; they contain a speaker that transmits only beeps and tinny music. But a sound card reproduces sound digitally, like a compact disk, and sends that quality of sound to speakers (which are usually sold separately from the sound card). You can even hook the system up to your home stereo. For aspiring computer musicians, multimedia enthusiasts, and PC game aficionados, a sound card is a must-have.

source code   In programming, this is the stuff a programmer writes in a programming language and types into the computer. He or she then uses a compiler or an interpreter to translate it into machine language the computer can understand and obey.

SPARC   Short for Scaler Processor ARChitecture. A type of microprocessor different from the one that's probably running your computer, unless you happen to be sitting at a RISC workstation. This type of chip was developed and is sold by Sun Microsystems. It's designed for computers that are generally dedicated to a high-powered activity, like computer-aided design, so its circuitry is designed to process that type of information at least twice as fast as a PC. See also *RISC* and *workstation*.

speech synthesis   The process of transforming typed text into words that the computer can say. Although speech synthesis makes the computer speak, the tone of voice is robotic. See also *voice recognition*.

spell checker   A program or feature that proofreads your document. The spell checker compares each word in the document to words contained in the spell checker's dictionary. If it comes across a word that is not in the dictionary, the spell checker displays a message asking what you want to do next. You may be given the chance to skip the word, choose a word from the spell checker's dictionary, or type your own correction.

Although spell-checkers are a big help, they can't do everything. If you typed "too" when you meant to type "to," the spell checker will skip the word because too is a correct spelling. Be sure to proofread your work before sending it out.

split screen   Newer TVs allow you to split the screen so you can watch two or more programs at once. Not that there are ever two programs on TV at the same time that are worth watching, but the technology is there should the need ever arise. With computers, there is a definite advantage to being able to split the screen; you can work with two documents at the same time, cutting and pasting sections from one document to the other. In split screens, the program usually divides the screen into *windows*. Each document is kept in a separate window.

Split screen shows two documents.

spool   See *print spooling.*

spreadsheet   If you've ever balanced a checkbook, you've worked with a spreadsheet. A spreadsheet consists of the same sort of layout: a series of boxes, called *cells*, into which you enter text and numbers. The only difference with a computerized spreadsheet is that the spreadsheet can do the math for you. You enter formulas telling the spreadsheet which values to add and subtract, and it does the rest. A spreadsheet can even perform complex calculations, allowing you to figure out loan payments and terms and perform other financial and statistical operations.

The spreadsheet consists of rows and columns, which intersect to form *cells*. You can type any of three entries into a cell:

> *Labels.* Labels are text entries. In a checkbook spreadsheet, for example, the name of the person you wrote a check to would be a label.

> *Values.* Values are numeric entries, such as dollar values, percentages, or quantities.

> *Formulas.* Formulas perform calculations on the values.

How does it work? Each cell has an *address*, consisting of the column letter and the row number. For example, the address of the cell in the upper left corner of the spreadsheet is A1. You can use these cell addresses along with mathematical operators to create formulas. For instance, if you inserted the formula +A1+B1 in cell C1, the program would add the values in cells A1 and B1 and insert the total in cell C1.

startup disk   Also known as *boot disk* and *system disk.* A disk that contains instructions (operating system files) the computer needs to get started. If you have a computer with a hard disk, the hard disk is probably the startup disk. When you turn on the computer, the operating system is loaded from the hard disk. If your computer does not have a hard disk, you must insert a system disk in one of the floppy drives before turning on your computer.

startup screen   Also called the *opening screen*. The first thing that's displayed when you start your computer or run a program. The opening screen usually shows the name of the program and its version number. It remains on-screen for a short time, and then disappears, allowing you to start working.

status line   Most programs like to keep you informed by displaying important information at the bottom of the screen, in a place called the *status line*. This line often provides information like the name of the file that is currently open, and the position of the cursor. Or this line may display the mode in which you are working: for example, OVR means you are typing in Overstrike mode—anything you type will replace existing text. That's a good thing to know. If you ever run into trouble, check the bottom of the screen; it may provide just the help you need.

stickup initial   A capital letter that starts a word and is taller than the other capital letters in the document. Designers usually use stickup initials sparingly, maybe in the first letter of a chapter or an article, though it's not as commonly used as a *drop cap*.

stop bit   Stop bits are used when two computers are talking over the phone lines using a modem. A stop bit acts as a space between words. It tells the computer where one byte of data stops and the next one begins.

storage   A data warehouse—a place where data is kept so the computer can work with it. There are two types of storage: *primary* and *secondary*. Primary storage is the computer's electronic memory. It temporarily stores data in an area where the computer can get it in a hurry. Secondary storage is the computer's magnetic storage. It is a permanent storage facility where files can be stored while the computer is not actively using them. Primary and secondary storage work together to provide the computer with the information it needs.

Think of primary storage as your memory and secondary storage as a book. If you read a passage from the book and then forget it, it's gone from your memory, but it is still in the book.

street price   The price at which you can actually buy a piece of hardware or software, as opposed to the price the manufacturer recommends (the manufacturer's suggested retail price, or SRP). Street price is calculated by averaging the product's retail price at several outlets. Since the computer industry is so competitive, the street price of a product can be much lower than the SRP, and the retail price may vary greatly from store to store, and from mail order house to mail order house. Shop around.

strikeout   Some word processing programs have a feature that compares two versions of a document and shows where text has been added and deleted. The deleted text is shown with a line drawn through it—as if you had typed hyphens over the characters.

string   A series of characters which can include letters, numbers, and symbols. Many programs offer a feature that allows you to search for a word or phrase or for the name of an item by entering a *search string*. The search string tells the program what to look for. For example, you might type "book" to find all occurrences of the word *book*.

structured programming language   A programming language, such as C, Ada, and Pascal, that facilitates top-down programming. See *top-down programming* and *language*.

style sheet   A file that contains a set of styles but no text. Style sheets are used mainly in word processing and desktop publishing programs when you plan to format more than one document in the same way. You can create a stylesheet for a newsletter, an annual report, or any other frequently produced document. When you apply a style sheet to a file, it automatically formats it using all the formatting instructions—font style and size, margins, paragraph indentations, and so on—contained in the style sheet.

styles   Imagine you are making a book, and each chapter title is to be set in 24-point Helvetica bold italic, centered, with .5 inch between the bottom of the title and the first paragraph. Rather than change the font, style, indentation, and point size each time you enter a chapter title, you can create a style called Chapter Title. This style would contain all the specified text attributes (24-point, Helvetica, bold, and italic), the alignment (centered), and the space following the title (.5 inch). Next time you need to format a chapter title, you type the title, select it, and choose the Chapter Title style from a list of styles, completing the operation in one or two keystrokes.

Another advantage of using styles is that you can quickly change the formatting of all text formatted with that style. Suppose you decide that the chapter title should be larger, for example, 36-point type. Simply change the point size in the style, and the type size is changed for all headings formatted with that style.

stylus   An input device that functions much more precisely than a mouse. It looks like a plastic pen without any ink. You "write" with it on a graphics tablet, or use it to highlight fields directly on the monitor screen. Its electronic tip inputs a signal that the graphics tablet digitizes so that the computer can process it. The corresponding image appears on your screen.

subdirectory Because large hard disks can store thousands of files, you often need to store related files in separate directories on the disk. Think of your disk as a filing cabinet and think of each directory as a drawer in the filing cabinet. A subdirectory is equivalent to a group of files in the drawer—for example, all files under the letter *K*.

submenu A menu that opens out from another menu and provides a list of additional commands or options.

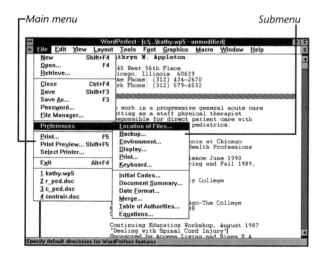

⌐*Main menu*　　　　　　　　　　　　　　　*Submenu*

subscript Text that is printed slightly smaller and lower than surrounding text, as is the number in the following example:

$$H_2O$$

Super VGA See *Video Graphics Array*.

superscript Text that is printed slightly smaller and higher than surrounding text, as are the numbers in the following example:

$$X^2 + Y^2 = Z^2$$

surge protector Also known as a *surge suppressor*. A football helmet for computers. The surge protector stands between the computer and the electrical outlet to prevent any sudden increases in power from damaging the computer. It works by allowing a fixed amount of electricity to flow to the computer. It never allows that amount to be exceeded. The surge protector regulates only the maximum current—it does not protect against power drops or outages. Do not confuse surge protectors with cheaper outlet strips. Outlet strips look like surge protectors (they have several outlets into which you can plug your computer and printer) but they offer no protection.

switch A value you can add to a command to control the manner in which the command is carried out. For example, if you want to format a floppy disk in DOS, you may need to specify the disk drive you want to use and the storage capacity of the disk. For example, if you enter the command

FORMAT A: /SIZE:720

FORMAT is the command, A: is the parameter, and /SIZE:720 is the switch.

syntax error Rude language in front of the computer. When you program or use a command-driven program, the computer expects you to construct instructions using words, spelling, and grammar in an expected format. This expected format is called syntax. Any violation of the format is a syntax error. For example, if you want DOS to display a page by page list of files, you should type, "DIR/P." If you accidentally type "DOR/P," the computer would not be able to figure out that your finger just slipped and you really meant to type an I. You would have committed a syntax error.

SYSOP   Pronounced SISS-opp; short for *system opera-tor.* A person who manages a Bulletin Board System (an electronic bulletin board you can connect to using a computer and modem). The SYSOP is typically responsible for keeping the bulletin board organized, for helping users get the information they need, and for ensuring that only authorized users are allowed into the BBS.

System 7   The latest major upgrade of Apple's operating system for all Macintosh computers. It's made up of two components, System, which is the operating system, and Finder, the graphical user interface. To the user, these appear and function as one integrated environment. Important new features in System 7 include:

> *TrueType fonts.* Also included with Windows 3.1, this technology produces scalable fonts that are identical on screen and in printed form.

> *Balloon help.* A system of help screens that pop up in cartoon-like balloons to explain any topic—menu choices, dialog box options, and so on—when and where you need it.

> *File sharing.* This enables networked Macs to share files without using a file server.

> *Publish-and-subscribe.* Apple's version of dynamic linking. It enables you to copy a file or portion of a file in one program to a

file in another program. For example, you might import a spreadsheet into a newsletter document, so that the spreadsheet in the newsletter is instantly updated when you update it in the original document.

32-bit addressing. For newer, more powerful Macintoshes such as the Mac LC, Quadra, and IIsi, this enables the computer to take advantage of the faster running speed, resulting in programs that run significantly faster.

system date   The day's date as kept by the computer. Some computers have a battery-operated clock that keeps the date current. With other computers, you may have to type the current date when you start the computer.

The most useful aspect of the system date is that many programs allow you to insert the date directly into your documents. This saves you the time it takes to type the date. Some programs even let you enter a code that keeps the date current. If you open the file the next day, the date is changed!

system disk   See *startup disk*.

system prompt   In an operating system such as DOS, text appears on-screen, showing that the system is ready for you to enter a command. For example, if you start your computer with DOS, DOS displays a system prompt that looks something like this:

C:\> or C>

system software   All the software your computer needs to keep it up and running. This always includes an operating system, such as DOS. It may also include a graphical user interface (such as Microsoft Windows) and a network operating system (such as Netware). System software—or operating system software, as it's sometimes called—differs from application software, which is all the software your computer needs to perform the tasks you want it to perform (like word processing, database management, desktop publishing and so on). See also *software*.

Time for T. Set the table, and put it on my tab. And let's not get into a TIFF if I forget to pay; otherwise, I might call in reinforcements from technical support.

Tab key Similar to the Tab key on a typewriter, this key moves the cursor to the next tab stop to the right. In most programs, tab stops are initially set at every five spaces. You can move the tab stops to change the place where the cursor moves when you press the Tab key. See also *tabs*.

table A collection of information that is laid out in rows and columns, making it easy to find related information. You've seen tables in books. In fact, this book contains a few tables.

In the old days, if you wanted to create a table, you would use tabs or spaces to set up the columns. If you had a long entry that took up two lines or more, you had to do some tedious manipulation with the tabs to get everything aligned.

Many word processing programs now offer a table feature that takes care of the alignment for you and allows you to place lines in the table to give it a more professional look. You specify the number of columns and rows you want in the table, and the program creates it. As you enter text in the table, the program automatically wraps the text from one line to the next within the column, if needed.

Each cell is a box.   Columns

	1st	2nd	3rd	4th	5th	6th	7th	8th	9th	Final
Home	1	0	0	3	0	2	1	2	2	11
Visitors	0	2	0	1	0	0	0	3	0	6

Rows   A table

tabs   Similar to tabs you would enter using a typewriter, tabs in word processing programs are used to align entries in a column or to indent text. However, computer tabs give you much more control over text alignment. The following examples show the different types of tabs in action:

Left Tabs	**Right Tabs**
Entries are aligned on the leftmost character.	Entries are aligned on the rightmost character.

Centered Tabs	**Decimal Tabs**
Entries are centered in the column.	100.34 23876.987 1239.8 546.784

Tagged Image File Format (TIFF)   A common file structure used for storing graphics images. A TIFF file contains a map (bit map) of all the dots that make up the image. The file contains information that shows the location and shade of each dot. Graphics programs use the bit map to determine how to display or print the image. On a typical VGA monitor, the map can include information for over 300,000 dots; that's a lot of dots. Because of this, TIFF files are usually huge.

Tandy Corporation   A major manufacturer and retailer (through its Radio Shack stores) of personal computers and electronics. It introduced one of the first personal computers, the TRS-80, in 1977. But since 1984, it has built IBM compatibility into its models, which are geared to home and small business use, and to portable computing.

tape   A mode of secondary storage that can store far more files per tape cartridge than a floppy disk. Whereas a floppy disk is a disk of plastic with magnetic coating, tape is a thin ribbon of plastic (like an audio tape) that's magnetically coated. It's used mainly for backing up an entire hard disk, since its sequential format makes accessing individual files a hassle. It's like the difference between searching for a song on a cassette and selecting a song on compact disk.

tape backup   A system that allows you to store backup copies of your files on a tape cartridge. Most people store their backups on floppy disks. If they have a lot of files to back up, a backup may require several disks. With tape backups, you can store many files on a single tape, so you don't have to swap disks during the backup.

target   The desired destination. For example, if you are copying a file from one disk to another, the disk from which you are copying is the *source*, and the disk to which you are copying the file is the *target*.

technical support   A question/answer hotline that provides people with technical advice and helps them solve problems they're having with a program or device. Many computer companies offer technical support to registered users for the products they manufacture. Some companies charge for calls; others answer your questions for free.

telecommunications   Transmitting sound, video, and computer data electronically over telephone wires.

telecommuting   Instead of commuting, where you move your body to the office to get your work done, this means doing your work at home and sending it to the office via modem. This is one of those buzzwords you always read is sweeping the country, but when you suggest the idea to your boss he just looks at you funny; however, statistics show that it is becoming more common as society grows more computer-savvy, traffic and pollution problems escalate, and the cost of office space goes through the roof.

template   If you're talking about a keyboard template, it's a reference card that sits on your keyboard. The template contains a list of commonly used commands and/or a list of keys you can press to perform certain functions.

A keyboard template

F6	F7	F8		F9	F10	F11	F12
Prev Document •	Double Indent •		Ctl+Sh	Document •	Stop Macro •	Vertical Line •	Sort •
Next Document	Hanging Indent	Margins	Ctrl	Tables	Record Macro	Horizontal Line	Merge
Prev Window •	Decimal Tab •	Special Codes •	Alt+Sh	Columns •		Text Box Edit •	
Next Window	Flush Right	Styles	Alt	Page	Play Macro	Text Box Create	Generate
Prev Pane	Center	Select Cell	Shift	Line		Figure Edit	Define ToC, etc.
Next Pane	Indent	Select		Font	Menu Bar	Figure Retrieve	Mark Text

If you're talking about a template in a word processing, desktop publishing, or spreadsheet program, this template is a basic structure that you can quickly fill out to form a complete document. You may have a template for a business letter that includes the date, your name and address, and maybe a pretty picture. Whenever you want to type a letter, you just open the template and type the inside address, the salutation, and the body of the letter.

terminal   A computer that connects to a central computer and takes advantage of the central computer's power and advanced processing capabilities. A terminal consists of a keyboard and monitor. The keyboard lets you talk to the central computer, and the monitor lets that computer talk to you. What's missing in some terminals is the processing unit—the computer's brain. Terminals are often used in local area networks to provide people with a connection to the central computer. Typical terminals differ from personal computers, which can think for themselves, although a personal computer is sometimes used as a terminal.

There are two types of terminals: *smart* and *dumb*. Dumb terminals can do no processing on their own. They rely totally on the central computer. Smart terminals do some processing on their own and may have a floppy disk drive that allows the user to copy files to and from the central computer. Some terminals have a special card that lets you switch back and forth between the mainframe computer and the terminal.

terminal emulation   A technique that uses special software to allow one type of computer to act like another. Some mini- or mainframe computers will interact with only a specific type of terminal. If you want to connect to that mainframe computer using your personal computer, you must make your computer act like the required terminal.

terminate-and-stay-resident (TSR)   See *memory resident*.

text chart   A poster that contains only text. In business presentation graphics programs, text charts are commonly used to show a list of bulleted items or to display small chunks of text. Text charts differ from other charts, such as pie graphs, bar graphs, and organizational charts, which are more graphic.

text editor   A bare-bones word processing program often used for creating and editing *batch files*. (A batch file contains a series of commands you can enter by running the batch file.) Text editors do not allow you to enhance text (for example, by making it bold or italic), because such enhancements require codes that could interfere with the operation of the batch file.

text file   Also known as *ASCII file*. A file that contains only text—no formatting codes, such as codes for making text bold or italic. Many programs allow you to save a file as an ASCII, or text, file, which strips out any special codes and saves only text. You can then open and use the file in various programs, allowing you to transfer data easily from one program to another. However, this plain-vanilla file will contain only text; you will lose any special formatting you used in the file.

   Program files and batch files are commonly saved as text files to prevent formatting codes from interfering with the operation of the file.

thermal printer   A printer that heats specially treated paper to form characters and graphic images. Instead of slamming keys or pins against a print ribbon, thermal printers heat the paper with small patterns of dots. This discolors the paper to form characters and graphics. Thermal printers are fast and quiet, but many users dislike the feel of the specially treated paper. Many fax machines are equipped with thermal printers.

thesaurus   You know what a thesaurus is, a book that lists synonyms in dictionary format. In computing, it's an electronic version that often comes bundled with word processing programs. When you need to find a synonym, you type it into the thesaurus dialog box. The program comes up with a list of synonyms, allows you to select the one you like, and then automatically replaces the old word in your document.

   For example, you might be sick of the word *example*, so you look it up in the thesaurus for an alternative. You find:

pattern

standard

exemplar

archetype

guide

standard

original

You could select one of these choices and the computer would delete *example* in the sentence and replace it with the new word. Or, if none of those words is quite right but you're intrigued by *archetype*, you could select it and choose the Lookup command again. A new list appears:

model

example

ideal

exemplar

mold

original

prototype

Sometimes you can spend all day just going from synonym to synonym, but the idea is to find a suitable choice and get back to work.

third generation   Computer history's equivalent of
the industrial revolution. The third generation was
born in the early 1960s when integrated circuits
replaced transistors in computer design (though
they still relied on many discrete parts).

   This advance reduced the size and increased the
reliability of computers. But yet another generation
was born, the fourth generation, when scientists
achieved a computer that was made up almost
entirely of integrated circuits. See also *first generation*, *second generation*, *fourth generation*, and *fifth
generation*.

third-party vendor   A computer middleman. This type
of company buys equipment directly from a manufacturer, repackages it, and sells it to another company. This term also refers to companies that sell
hardware accessories, such as mice, glare screens,
and modems.

three-dimensional spreadsheet   Also called a *spreadsheet notebook*. A spreadsheet that consists of several
related spreadsheet pages. The page system is used to
help you manage the spreadsheet. For instance,
suppose you want to use a spreadsheet to keep track
of your income and expenses. You have interest
income and income from your job, and you have
expenses for your car, groceries, utilities, rent, and so
on. You can keep each source of income and each
expense on a separate spreadsheet page to prevent a
single spreadsheet from getting cluttered.

   Now, suppose you want to determine the amount
of money you'll have left over at the end of the
month. With a three-dimensional spreadsheet, you
can enter a formula that refers to values on all the
pages. The formula will determine the total income
and the total expenses, and then subtract expenses
from income to determine what's left . . . or what you
owe.

throughput A measure of the computer's overall performance. Think of it in human terms. Say a person is smart but lazy. Such a person might know a lot, but does as little as possible. A highly motivated blockhead, likewise, will get little done. The same is true with computers. If the computer has a high-speed central processing unit, but a low-speed disk drive, the disk drive will slow down the overall performance of the computer.

So what? A measure of a system's throughput is important when you are looking to purchase a computer. The computer manufacturer may advertise a computer with a quick disk or a powerful microprocessor, but what is really important is how fast the computer can perform the required operations.

TIFF See *Tagged Image File Format.*

time-sharing A technique that allows several people to use the same computer, program, and/or file at the same time.

timed backup A feature offered by many programs that saves the file you are working on at specified intervals—for example, every five minutes. When you are creating or changing a file, whatever you enter is stored in your computer's electronic memory. If you turn off the computer or if the power goes out, your changes are lost. To make your changes permanent, you must save the file to disk. The timed backup feature regularly saves the file for you, so you can continue working worry-free.

title bar In graphical user interfaces like Windows and the Mac's System 7, this is a bar along the top of the screen that shows the name of the file you're working in.

toggle An option that you can turn on or off by performing the same steps. For example, if you press the Caps Lock key, any characters you type will be uppercase. If you press the same key again, you turn Caps Lock off; any characters you type are now lowercase.

toner   Powdered ink that's used in copy machines and laser printers. The ink is applied to the page, and then the page is heated to make the ink stick.

toolbox   A collection of commonly used instruction sets that a programmer can insert in a program. Think of a toolbox as a programmer's shorthand. Instead of entering an entire series of commands one by one, the programmer inserts the required set of commands from the toolbox.

Some applications feature a toolbox that appears on-screen and contains several instruments to help you do your work. For example, a toolbox in a graphics program may contain several drawing tools, including a line-draw tool, a circle tool, and a paint brush.

top-down programming An approach to programming that starts with the general and ends with the specifics. You start writing your program at the highest level of the idea, its purpose. Next, you outline each major function. You save the details, like how the program will handle each eventuality, for the end.

This method is much praised for the way it forces programmers to look at the big picture and produce a well-organized program that's easier to review, debug, and upgrade. Structured programming languages, such as Pascal and FORTRAN, are well-suited to this type of development process.

touch-sensitive display A technology that makes the computer screen respond to the human touch. A clear, pressure-sensitive panel is laid over the computer screen. The panel consists of a grid of half-inch squares—about as wide and tall as a person's index finger. Each command on the screen is aligned with one of the squares. When a person presses the screen to choose a command, the pressure-sensitive panel tells the computer which square was pressed. If you can't stand seeing fingerprints on your computer screen, touch-sensitive displays may not be for you.

track A track on a computer disk is similar to a groove in a phonograph record. A read/write head in the disk drive writes information onto the sectors in a track, and reads information off the sectors.

On a storage tape, tracks are parallel lines that run the length of the tape. The tape is drawn past the read/write head, which either reads information from the tape or writes information on the tape.

trackball Kind of like a joystick—without the stick. An input device involving a ball and two or more buttons. You roll the ball with your hand to move the on-screen cursor, and you click the buttons to enter commands. Think of it as an upside-down mouse. With a mouse, the ball is on the bottom. You slide the mouse over a table or mouse pad to make the ball move. With a trackball, you move the ball directly with your hand.

If the work area around your computer is often cluttered, a trackball may be better for you than a mouse. With a mouse, you need some desk space to slide the mouse freely. If you run out of room, you have to pick the mouse up, move it, and roll it some more. A trackball does not need to move on the desk, and you don't have to pick it up and move it.

tractor feed   A special part on some printers that pulls or pushes paper through the printer. Continuous-feed paper with holes on both sides fits onto the feeder's sprockets. This special paper is one long sheet divided into pages by perforations. Tractor-feed mechanisms are commonly used on dot-matrix printers.

transfer   To exchange data between devices or to copy data from one area to another within a computer or network. The term is commonly used to describe the process of reading a file from disk into the computer's memory, or saving the file from memory to disk.

translate   To convert a file that has been saved in one file format into another, so the file can be opened in a different program. See also *conversion*.

tree structure   The organization of directories on disk. Think of the structure of directories as a family tree. The ultimate beginning of the tree, its root, would be some couple on the African savannah (assuming you believe that theory). The tree would then branch out with each generation. See also *directory tree*.

Trojan Horse   A destructive program that is disguised as a useful program, such as a word processing program or a game. When you run the program, it appears to run as any other program, but in the background it proceeds to erase the files on your hard disk or perform some other feat of vandalism. Unlike a computer virus, a Trojan Horse does not replicate and infect other files and disks; it's found only on computers that run the Trojan Horse program.

troubleshooting An attempt to find the cause of a problem. Say you turn on your monitor and it doesn't work. You might check to see if the monitor is plugged in, if it is securely connected to the computer, and if the power switch is on. You trace the problem back to its cause.

truncate To lop off part of an entry that does not fit in the designated space. If you have a long name and you get a lot of junk mail, look at the mailing labels. Many times, a long last name doesn't fit in the space allotted for the name, so the program drops the last few letters.

The word PRODUCT is truncated.

Spreadsheet programs often truncate entries that are too wide for a column. The program may allow you to type the full entry, but will shorten the entry when displaying or printing it. If you widen the column later, the program will display the complete entry. Other programs will chop off any extra characters in the entry. With numbers, most programs will not truncate the entries, because this could cause you to misjudge a value. Instead, the paragraph displays a series of asterisks or some other symbol to show that the value is too wide for the cell. You have to widen the cell to see the entire value.

TSR   See *memory resident.*

tutorial   A lesson on disk or in a book that teaches you how to use a program by leading you through a series of hands-on examples. For example, a tutorial for a desktop publishing program may lead you through the process of creating a newsletter. You learn the features of the program by using them to perform a practical task.

type ahead buffer   A small waiting room between the keyboard and RAM. When you type faster than the computer can input the characters, this buffer stores them temporarily until they can be processed. Also called a *keyboard buffer.*

typeface   A set of characters that share a unique design, such as Helvetica, Times Roman, or Courier. See also *font.*

Typeover mode   See *Overtype mode.*

typesetting   Typesetting ain't what it used to be. Back in the old days, a typesetter took a manuscript and actually set blocks of text to form a printing plate.

Nowadays, you set the type on-screen, and you can change the style of type for a whole document by pressing a key. In most word processing and desktop publishing programs, you initially type text in a generic format, such as 10-point Courier. You can then go back and set text in different typefaces and sizes. For example, you may want to make chapter headings slightly larger.

type style   Changing the appearance of a font (a set of characters of the same design and size) by adding bold, italic, or underlining attributes. With type styles, the font stays the same, but one aspect of the font is changed.

➤

The U's read like the computer personals: Looking for an upwardly compatible, user-friendly computer to undelete my emotional state.

undelete   Restoring deleted text or deleted files. Many programs offer a feature that temporarily stores the item you most recently deleted. If you delete a section of text by mistake, you can then enter an undelete command to have the text restored. However, in most software, if you delete more than one item, the second item replaces the first item in the temporary storage area; the first item is then lost. So if you want to undelete, you should do it immediately after deleting the item.

Undelete is also used to describe restoring deleted files on disk. How? When you delete a file, the operating system doesn't delete file contents. It simply alters the file's name so it won't appear in any lists, and marks the area used by the file's contents as *free*, so other files can be stored there. As long as you don't save any files to disk or move files, the contents of the deleted file remain on disk. You can use a utility program, such as PC Tools or the Undelete utility in DOS 5, to get the file back.

underline   When you want to underline text at the computer, you don't use the old typewriter method of backing up and running the Shift key plus the dash key under the desired text. Instead, underlining is a formatting choice you can turn on when you plan to type something you want underlined, or you can apply to a block of text you've already typed. If you've already typed the text you want to underline, you have to select it first and then open the appropriate menu to choose underline.

undo   A feature offered by many programs that lets you change your mind. For example, if you move a section of text in a document and then decide that you liked it better where it was, you can enter an Undo command to cancel the move.

unformat   When you accidentally format a disk that was already formatted and had files on it, you can use a utility program with an unformat feature, which often can undo the recent format to get the files back.

uninterruptible power supply (UPS)   A battery-operated unit that supplies power to the computer in the event of a power failure. Why use a UPS? Keep in mind that if you turn off the juice to your computer, it forgets any changes you've entered since the last time you saved your work. A UPS keeps the juice flowing.

UNIX   Sounds like EWE-nicks. An operating system and file manager in one. It was originally developed for minicomputers but is now used on mainframes, minis, and personal computers. Because it easily supports multiple users and is designed for smooth multitasking, this operating system is especially popular in computer networks. The original interface is not very friendly, so there are many shells, including XWindows, Open Look, and XMotif, that create a graphical user interface (just as Microsoft Windows provides a friendly face for DOS). Given its popularity in networked computing, it's ironic that the name is based on UN (standing for single user) MULTICS (the multi-user operating system UNIX was based on, which did not support single user configuration).

unjustified text   Text that's not aligned to the left, right, or center, but simply is left as it appears when typed on the screen. By default, you have an even left margin, but the right margin is ragged due to the uneven line lengths. See *justification*.

unprotected software   Software from which you can make fully running copies. Most software you buy is unprotected because you're encouraged to make a copy, install the copy, and save the originals for an emergency. That doesn't mean, however, you should feel free to lend the unprotected disks to your friends. See *piracy*.

update   To revise the contents of a file so that the information it contains is current. Also used to describe a more recent release of a program.

upgrade   The computer industry's way of keeping up with the Joneses. To purchase and install the latest, greatest version of a program (software upgrade), or to improve your computer system (hardware upgrade). Typical hardware upgrades include installing additional memory chips, a hard disk, or an improved monitor. Users often upgrade their hardware so they can upgrade their software. It's a vicious circle.

upload   To copy files from your computer to another computer, as opposed to *downloading*, or copying files from another computer to your computer.

UPS   See *uninterruptible power supply*.

upward compatibility   Software that is designed to take advantage of the advanced powers and features of computer systems to come.

user-defined   A part of the program that is customized according to the desires of the person using the program. For instance, many programs allow the user to select the colors used in the program or to reassign commands to different function keys.

user-friendly   This term is used to describe anything that is specially designed to be easy to learn and use. But easy to learn and use is a relative term. Some user-friendly programs are easy to learn and use only if you know what you're doing in the first place and you know what keys to press.

user group   A group of people who meet regularly and try to help each other learn more about a specific computer or program. User groups can be local organizations, or the users can meet via modem using an information service. Many user groups provide feedback to software companies about features that they would like to see included in the program.

user interface   A collection of items that make it possible for people to interact with computers. These items include the screen display, the menus, the keyboard and mouse, and the commands assigned to the keyboard. Because the interface is so critical in the communication between person and machine, it is considered one of the most important features of a program.

utility program   A program that helps you manage your files, get information about your computer, diagnose and repair common problems, and keep your system operating efficiently. Two popular utility programs are PC Tools and The Norton Utilities, whose features include the following:

PC Tools shows a list of recently deleted files and their condition.

File and directory maintenance. You can move, copy, and delete files and directories on disk. This allows you to keep your disk organized.

File undelete. If you delete a file accidentally, a utility program will help you get the file back. However, you should use the utility program before copying or moving any files to the disk that contains the deleted files.

Virus protection. This feature checks your computer for viruses or for the effects of viruses and lets you know if your system has been infected. (With most utility programs, you have to purchase this utility separately.)

System information. Provides information about your computer, including how much memory it has and how the memory is being used, how fast the hard disk is, the type of monitor that's connected to the computer, the speed of the central processing unit, and more.

Disk fixing. If a disk is unreadable or if a file on disk gets damaged or lost, the utility program will try to help you find and correct the problem.

Disk performance. As you store files on your hard disk, parts of a file may be stored in different locations on the disk. This makes it more difficult for the disk drive to read the file. Utility programs let you reorganize the files on disk so each file is stored in a single location.

File protection. Most utility programs let you protect your files with passwords to prevent unauthorized people from viewing or changing the files.

If you worry that your computer might catch a virus, the V's will tell you how to get it vaccinated. Of course, it probably already has a VDT, which is good for you.

vaccine   A program designed to prevent computer viruses from attacking your system and damaging your files. There are three types of vaccines: those that *prevent* viruses from attacking your system, those that *detect* viruses after they've entered your system (and hopefully before they've done any damage), and those that help you *remove* the virus.

> *Prevention programs* let you mark files so they cannot be modified. If anything or anybody, including a virus or you, tries to change the file, a warning message appears.

> *Detection programs* focus on the virus or its effects. To detect known viruses, the program keeps a list of *signatures* (a string of characters or codes) for common viruses. Each time you run a program or open a file, the program scans the file for these signatures. To detect unknown viruses, the detection program keeps track of the size of each marked file and warns you if the file size changes (meaning a virus is attacking the file).

> *Removal programs* let you remove the virus from your system once the virus is detected.

value   A numeric entry in a spreadsheet. Values in-clude quantities, dollar amounts, and percentages. See also *numeric format* and *spreadsheet*.

value-added reseller   A company or individual who buys hardware from the original manufacturer and then increases its value with added benefits (such as software installation, free training, improved docu-mentation, a service contract, or some other service that might conceivably make it worth the extra price you pay for it). Commonly called a VAR.

vaporware   A sarcastic term often used in computer industry trade rags, meaning a program or upgrade that's long been promised by the developer, but is not yet on the market. In other words, it disappears into vapor when you try to get your hands on it.

VDT   Short for Video Display Terminal. Also known as *monitor, display,* and *screen.* A television-like screen that lets the computer display information. Many early home computers actually used television screens as their monitors.

vector graphics   See *object-oriented graphics.*

verify   To check whether an operation has been com-pleted correctly or whether a result is correct. In DOS, you can use the VERIFY ON command to tell DOS to check a file whenever it is saved to disk in order to make sure the file has been saved correctly.

version number   The number assigned to a program when it is released. When a software company per-forms a major overhaul of one of its programs, it changes the number to the left of the decimal point. For example, when WordPerfect Corporation cre-ated a major revision of WordPerfect 4.2, it released WordPerfect 5.0. When a software company per-forms a minor revision, it changes the number to the right of the decimal point. See also *release number.*

VGA   Short for Video Graphics Array. A video adapter for the IBM/PC that displays graphics with a resolution of 640 by 480 pixels in up to 256 colors. Compare with CGA, which can display only four colors at the same time with a resolution of 200 by 320 pixels; EGA (Enhanced Graphics Adapter), which can display 16 colors with a resolution of 350 by 640 pixels; and Super VGA, which can display 256 colors with a resolution of 1,024 by 768 pixels.

An added advantage of VGA over EGA is that VGA displays objects in their proper dimensions. EGA sometimes distorts objects to fit them on-screen.

video adapter   A plastic or fiberglass card with electronic components that plugs into a computer and allows a monitor to be connected to the computer. If you have a computer that has a black-and-white screen, you can't just go out and buy a Super VGA monitor and plug it in. You need the proper video adapter to communicate with that monitor. See also *CGA*, *EGA*, *VGA*, and *SVGA*.

Video Graphics Array   See *VGA*.

video standard   A standard for a monitor display. It dictates the minimums for mode (text or graphics), resolution, and simultaneous color display which a monitor must display in order to be sold under a certain classification, such as CGA or EGA. An SVGA monitor, for example, must adhere to one of two sets of requirements: a 16-color SVGA must be graphics-capable with a resolution of 800 x 600 and the capability to display 16 colors simultaneously, and a 256-color SVGA must be graphics-quality with a resolution of 1,024 x 768 and the capability to display 256 colors simultaneously. See also, *CGA*, *EGA*, and *VGA*.

view   To look at the contents of a file without changing it. With databases, the term *view* means to look at only a portion of the database. See also *query*.

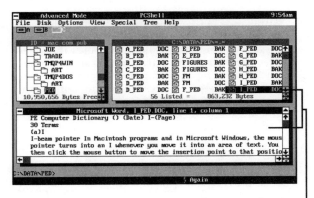

In PC Tools, you can view the contents of the selected file.

virtual memory   Creating the illusion that your computer has more memory that it actually has by making disk space act as memory. A program that uses virtual memory swaps data back and forth between the disk and RAM as needed. However, it takes a lot longer to get data off disk than to get it out of RAM, so virtual memory is slower than extended or expanded memory.

virtual reality   A system that simulates real life. Virtual reality is making great strides in the world of computer games. Equipped with a power glove, a set of special goggles, and a sound board with powerful speakers, Junior will soon be able to see what it's really like to fly a fighter jet—without getting hurt.

virus   A computer program designed to vandalize your
system. The virus enters your system through an
infected floppy disk or through a file that you copy
off another computer using a modem. It infects an
existing program file and then carries out a series of
commands not initiated by the user. For example,
the virus may erase data files, reformat your hard
disk (so you lose all your files), or destroy the system
files your computer needs to get up and running.

The virus replicates and infects any floppy disk
you use. If that floppy disk is then used in another
computer, the virus spreads to that computer. Viruses can also spread via modem by programs you
copy from another system and run. Some viruses
wait for a certain condition to occur, such as April 1
or Friday the 13th. Until that condition occurs, the
virus keeps infecting files. When the day of doom
arrives, the virus attacks.

The best way to stop viruses from destroying files
is to prevent viruses from infecting your system.
Here are some suggestions:

Isolate your system. Don't let anyone insert a
floppy disk in your computer without your
knowledge or copy any files from a non-
reputable source. By the way, isolation is
not very effective or practical.

Write-protect program disks. Before you install
a commercial program, write-protect the
disks you purchased. If your hard disk is
infected with a virus, the write-protection
will at least prevent your new program from
getting infected.

Back up your data files separately. Although
viruses can wipe out data files, they rarely
infect them.

Install an anti-virus program and keep it up-to-date. Antivirus programs prevent viruses from infecting your system and warn you of incoming viruses.

voice/data switch   A switch you use if you have a modem and only one telephone line. When you want to use the phone to talk, you set the switch to voice, which will make the phone line function normally. When you want to use your modem, you set it to data, so that it can be used for transmitting from your computer, rather than your voice.

voice mail   When offices are automated, they sometimes adopt a communications system that digitizes voice messages for storage on your computer network. You can log onto your system anytime and just maybe you'll find a message waiting for you.

voice recognition   The capability of a computer to understand spoken commands and to accept human speech as input. Voice recognition has a long way to go. Most voice-recognition systems can understand a wide range of commands from only one person or only a few commands from several people. Speech patterns vary so much between individuals that it's tough to develop a standard system of converting speech into signals that the computer can understand.

However, many computer users still insist on talking to their computers (often with raised voices), whenever the system is acting up.

voice synthesis   See *speech synthesis*.

volume label   An optional name you can give a disk when formatting it (preparing it to store data). The volume label helps identify the disk and what is stored on it. For example, if you use a disk to store tax information, you might label the disks 91TAXES, 92TAXES, and so on.

➤

No, no, wizzy-wig is not a hair piece, a widow is not a woman whose husband has died, and word wrap is not something that Hammer does for a living.

wait state   A small period of time during which the microprocessor in the computer idles. Wait states are intentionally built into the computer in order to prevent the microprocessor from running ahead of memory like the proverbial chicken with its head cut off. Although you won't notice a wait state because the wait is so brief, wait states can add up and slow down the computer.

　　The need for wait states can be eliminated in computers by adding fast memory and fast memory caches. Such computers are commonly described as *zero-wait-state machines*.

warm boot   See *reboot*.

weight   The relative thickness or thinness of font. It's described in terms of lightness and heaviness. The examples below show a heavy font and a light font, which is comparatively thin and delicate looking.

> ***HEAVY***   LIGHT

what-if analysis   Using a spreadsheet to see what would happen if you changed your mind. For example, you could create a spreadsheet that determines how much money you would spend for your house and how much your monthly house payment would be if you took out a 30-year mortgage on a

$100,000 loan at 9%. (You'd pay $289,664.10 with monthly payments of $804.62.)

Loan Sheet	Enter	Calculated	
Description	Values	Values	
Principal of Loan:	$100,000.00		
Interest Rate:	9		⟵ *Interest rate*
Periodic Interest Rate:	0.750000%		
Years:	30		⟵ *Loan term*
Number of Periods:	360		
Payment Amount:		($804.62)	
Total Cost:	($289,664.14)		*Monthly house*
Date of Loan:	02/20/92		*payment*
Future Value:	0		
Beginning or End (B/E):	B		

Total you will pay for the house

But then somebody at work mentions that they saved bushels of money by going with a 15-year mortgage. So you want to check it out. You simply change the 30 (30-year entry) to 15 and enter the command to recalculate the spreadsheet. One or two seconds later, you get the answer: you'd pay $182,568 with monthly payments of $1014.27. In other words, if you can manage to pay an extra $210 a month, you pay off your mortgage in half the time and save a little over $100,000! Isn't what-if analysis wonderful?

Loan Sheet	Enter	Calculated	
Description	Values	Values	
Principal of Loan:	$100,000.00		
Interest Rate:	9		
Periodic Interest Rate:	0.750000%		
Years:	15		⟵ *Change the*
Number of Periods:	180		*term, and*
Payment Amount:		($1,014.27)	*save a cool*
Total Cost:	($182,567.99)		*$100,000.*
Date of Loan:	02/20/92		
Future Value:	0		
Beginning or End (B/E):	B		

what-you-see-is-what-you-get (WYSIWYG) Pronounced wizzy-wig. A way of displaying your work on-screen so that it resembles the work as it will appear in print. WYSIWYG is not perfect; it has two major drawbacks. First, because the computer must work much harder to display text as it will appear in print, WYSIWYG slows down the program that's using it.

Second, what you see is not always what you get. Most programs that feature WYSIWYG have two types of fonts (type designs): printer fonts and screen fonts. The printer fonts control the way the text appears in print. Screen fonts control the way text appears on-screen. Some programs have printer fonts that have no corresponding screen font. So the program displays what it thinks is the font that most closely resembles the printer font. Sometimes the match is close; other times, it's not.

wide area network (WAN) Rhymes with van. A community of computers that can be miles apart and are linked through the phone lines or via satellite. This distinguishes them from LANs (local area networks), which are often located in a corporation or on a campus.

widow In word processing and desktop publishing programs, the last line of a paragraph that appears alone at the top of the next page. If the first line of the paragraph gets stranded at the bottom of a page, it is called an orphan. Old time printers would distinguish between these terms by noting that an orphan is alone at the beginning, and a widow is alone at the end. See *orphan*. The term widow is also used to describe a line break that leaves only one or two words at the end of a paragraph, especially when the paragraph is at the bottom of a column or page.

Many programs offer a widow/orphan prevention feature that moves one line from the paragraph on the previous page to the next page, so at least two lines appear at the top of the page.

wild card   A special symbol that stands in for other characters. If you've ever played poker, you know what a wild card is—a card that you can use as any card in the deck. So if jacks are wild and you have two kings, two aces, and a jack, you can use the jack as an ace to create a full house.

In the same way, you can use wild-card characters to stand in for any character in a word or name. For example, if you want to search for the name Smith, but you can't remember whether it is spelled Smith or Smyth, you could enter Sm?th to find either Smith or Smyth.

Most programs use two types of wild cards: a wild card for single characters and a wild card for multiple characters. A question mark (?) is commonly used to stand in for single characters, whereas an asterisk (*) or ellipsis (...) is used for a group of characters. Wild cards are commonly used to search for a range of entries or files. Table W.1 shows some examples of wild cards used in searches.

Table W.1   Wild-card Searches.

Wild-Card Entry	Finds	Does Not Find
?age	page, sage	mortgage
?ook	book, took	shook
?ook?	books, looks	bookend
*ith	Smith, with	Dithers
book*	bookend, bookish	Junglebook

window   A rectangular portion of the screen that displays a separate program or document. Windowing environments, such as Microsoft Windows and

GeoWorks, let you run two or more programs at the same time in separate windows. Some programs also allow you to open two or more *document windows*. Each window can contain a different file or display a different part of the same file. You can then copy information from one file to the other simply by cutting and pasting portions of text from one window to the other.

windowing environment   A screen design that treats your display screen as a desktop. You can open one or more windows at a time on the screen just as you can have one or more files open on your desktop. You can bring the window you want to work with to the front, or set the windows side-by-side (tiled), or overlap the windows (cascade). You can quickly switch from one window to the other to work on different projects.

In a windowing environment, you can run various applications in separate windows.

Windows   See *Microsoft Windows*.

word count   An automatic total of the number of words in a document. Many word processing programs contain a *word count* command. Others, like WordPerfect, will even automatically display a word count after performing a spell check. This is a handy feature if you do a lot of writing for minimum or maximum word lengths. It's not always exact, since the program usually calculates based on the number of times you hit the Spacebar, but if your document doesn't contain a lot of numbers or other nonword elements, it's very dependable.

word processing   A program that allows you to use your computer to type letters, create résumés, keep lists, address envelopes, and perform other tasks that you would perform using a typewriter. Is that all? Well, not really. Most word-processing programs can do a lot more. The following list shows several features commonly offered by sophisticated word processing programs:

> *Spell-checker.* The spell-checker compares each word in your document with a word in its dictionary. If it finds a word in your document that does not match a word in the dictionary, the spell-checker lets you know.

> *Thesaurus.* If you can't think of just the right word, the thesaurus may be able to help. You type the word you can think of and then look the word up in the thesaurus to view a list of synonyms (words that have the same meaning).

> *Search and replace.* Say you write a training manual that explains how to make a widget. At the last minute, the company decides to

call the part a gadget instead of a widget. You can use the search and replace feature to replace all occurrences of widget with gadget.

Graphics. A program that supports graphics allows you to place a picture and/or lines on a page. Most word-processing programs do not allow you to create the picture; you must create the picture using a graphics program and then bring it into your document.

Wrap-around text. If a program supports graphics, it may also allow you to wrap text around the picture. You set the picture where you want it, and the program wraps the text around the picture, just like in a magazine.

Cut and paste. With word-processing programs, you can cut text and paste it somewhere else in the document, and you don't even need a pair of scissors. Simply select the text you want to move, cut it, and paste it somewhere else. Most programs let you cut and paste between two or more documents.

Multiple windows. With multiple windows, you can divide your screen into two or more windows and open a different document in each window. You can then switch between windows or cut and paste text from one window to the other.

Mail merge. Have you ever gotten a letter from Ed McMahon, personally addressed to you? Well, Ed personalizes those form letters by using mail merge. He merges a form letter with a list of names and addresses to create a series of letters all saying the same thing to different people.

Macros. A macro is a series of keystrokes you can record and play back. For example, say that whenever you need to print a file, you have to press Shift+F7, select Document, and select Yes. You can record those keystrokes in a macro and assign the macro to a certain keystroke—say Ctrl+P. Whenever you need to print a document, you simply press Ctrl+P.

WYSIWYG or page preview. WYSIWYG stands for What-You-See-Is-What-You-Get. This feature shows text on-screen approximately the way it will appear in print.

word wrap   A feature offered by most word processing and desktop publishing programs that automatically moves words from one line to the next as you type. You press the Enter key (equivalent to the carriage return) only to start a new paragraph or to end a short line. If you later add text within the paragraph, the program automatically rewraps the text for you. See also *soft return*.

WordPerfect   The market leader among DOS word processing programs, which is also not doing too badly in the Windows and Macintosh arenas. The DOS program has won a loyal following for its lightning speed, huge number of features, editable formatting codes, and great technical support from WordPerfect Corporation. WordPerfect for Windows and WordPerfect are often condemned for being too DOS-like, but recent upgrades have made them graphical enough to satisfy the GUI-est user.

WordPerfect Corporation A software publisher founded in 1980 to market WordPerfect. Based on the remarkable success of this product, the company expanded its product line to include WordPerfect Office, DrawPerfect, and related business applications, but it has found the greatest success with its flagship product.

workgroup A group of employees who work on a single project. Workgroups are common in companies that use local area networks. A single file can be kept on a central computer, so all members of the workgroup can keep the file up-to-date.

worksheet See *spreadsheet*.

workstation In a local area network, a desktop computer that is connected to the central computer. Many times, a workstation contains very little computing power of its own—perhaps it has only a display terminal and a keyboard. The keyboard allows the user to talk to the main computer, and the display lets the computer talk to the user.

The term workstation also refers to a high-powered desktop computer that's configured for use in one activity, usually graphics editing, computer-aided design, or computer-aided engineering.

wrap-around type In word processing and desktop publishing programs, a feature that shifts text so it appears around an object on the same page. To get an idea of wrap-around text, look in a newspaper or magazine. You'll see pictures that have been plopped down in the middle of a field of text. The text is shifted to fit around the picture.

write To copy data that's stored in memory to disk, as opposed to *reading* data from disk into memory.

write-protect To prevent data from being written to a disk. 5.25" floppy disks have a write-protect notch that you can cover with a small piece of tape to prevent the disk from being changed in any way. With the write-protect notch covered, no files can be erased from the disk or written to the disk. Likewise, 3.5" disks have a write-protect tab that you can slide open to write-protect the disk. With the tab slid back so that you can see through the window, the disk is protected.

It's a good idea to write-protect any disks that come with a program you purchased. That way, you prevent the disk from being damaged during use or installation. Some program disks come write-protected from the manufacturer.

Write-protect sticker

Window

Write-protect notch   *Write-protect tab*

WYSIWYG   See *what-you-see-is-what-you-get*.

If you think that an x-axis is a former axis, that x-height is how tall you used to be, or that XMODEM is a comic book super hero, these definitions will set you straight.

Why ask Y?

Z words are fun. You get to zoom in and zap things with that great comic book super hero, ZMODEM.

x-axis The horizontal line on a graph that runs from right to left. The x-axis is usually used to display the categories of values being graphed.

x-height The height of a lowercase x in a given font (type design). Type is commonly measured from the bottom of a descending character, such as the g, to the top of an ascending character, such as f. Some type designs, however, have g's that dip down lower than normal and f's that reach up higher than normal. By measuring the height of a lowercase x, you get a better indication of the relative size of two fonts.

x-y plotter   A special type of output device that prints point by point, following x-y coordinates set within a software program. It uses a mechanical arm that can change colored pens as needed to create a multicolored drawing. Plotters are used to print engineering blueprints, CAD drawings, and in other situations where absolute preciseness is needed.

XMODEM   A method of transferring files (a protocol) that checks to make sure the data sent arrives in good condition. XMODEM sends the file in 128-kilobyte chunks. It then waits for the other computer/modem to acknowledge that it received the chunk. If the amount of data sent does not match the amount received, the sending computer sends the same chunk of data again.

y-axis   The line that runs up and down (vertical) in a graph. It is usually used to display the values being graphed.

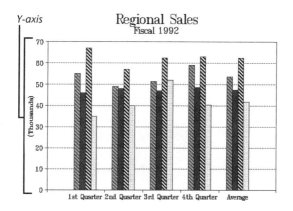

YMODEM   A method of transferring files (a *protocol*) that checks to make sure the data sent arrives in good condition. YMODEM sends data in 1,024-kilobyte packets. It then waits for the other computer/modem to acknowledge that it received the packet. If the amount of data sent does not match the amount received, the sending computer sends the same packet of data again.

YMODEM protocol offers two advantages over XMODEM. First, it sends data in 1,024-kilobyte packets instead of 128 kilobytes, so it sends roughly 10 times the amount of data in each packet. YMODEM also lets you send several files in a batch, a function not offered by XMODEM.

zap   Erase, delete, destroy, vanquish, obliterate. Commonly used to describe the process of blowing up a spaceship full of Klingons (or deleting a file).

z-axis   In a three-dimensional graph, the third dimension. To understand the z-axis, draw a cross on a piece of paper. The horizontal or flat line is the x-axis. The vertical or upright line is the y-axis. Now, take a pencil and poke it through the page where the x- and y-axes cross. The pencil is the z-axis.

ZMODEM   A method of transferring files (a *protocol*) that checks to make sure the data sent arrives in good condition. ZMODEM is an improved version of XMODEM that allows you to transfer data in larger chunks with fewer errors. In addition, if ZMODEM discovers an error during transmission, it resumes transmission at the point where the error occurred rather than starting over.

zoom   To enlarge a portion of a document or to enlarge a window so it takes up the entire screen. In most programs, you will zoom in on a portion of a document or picture in order to view it better or to modify its fine details.

zoom box   In graphical user interfaces, a small on-screen box located in the corner of a window. By clicking on it when a screen is less than full-size, you can maximize the window so that it fills the screen. By clicking on the zoom box again, you can shrink or minimize the window back down.

➤